# Scoundrels

# Scoundrels

## Political Scandals
## in American History

J. Michael Martinez

ROWMAN & LITTLEFIELD
Lanham • Boulder • New York • London

Published by Rowman & Littlefield
An imprint of The Rowman & Littlefield Publishing Group, Inc.
4501 Forbes Boulevard, Suite 200, Lanham, Maryland 20706
www.rowman.com

86-90 Paul Street, London EC2A 4NE

British Library Cataloguing in Publication Information Available

**Library of Congress Cataloging-in-Publication Data**

Names: Martinez, J. Michael (James Michael) author.
Title: Scoundrels : political scandals in American history / J. Michael Martinez.
Description: Lanham, Maryland : Rowman & Littlefield, 2023. | Includes bibliographical references and index. | Summary: "Political scandals have become an indelible feature of the American political system since the creation of the republic more than two centuries ago. This book surveys both the most infamous scandals as well as more obscure episodes in an effort to understand how these incidents have altered the course of American political history"— Provided by publisher.
Identifiers: LCCN 2022054476 (print) | LCCN 2022054477 (ebook) | ISBN 9781538130797 (cloth) | ISBN 9781538130803 (epub)
Subjects: LCSH: Political corruption—United States—History. | Scandals—United States—History.
Classification: LCC JK2249 .M377 2023 (print) | LCC JK2249 (ebook) | DDC 364.1/323—dc23/eng/20230105
LC record available at https://lccn.loc.gov/2022054476
LC ebook record available at https://lccn.loc.gov/2022054477

This book is for my lifelong friend Keith Warren Smith,
who taught me that honest men still exist in the world

CORRUPT, *adj.* In politics, holding an office of trust or profit.

—Ambrose Bierce, *The Devil's Dictionary*

# Contents

# Introduction and Acknowledgments

"Scandal," defined as an action or event causing public outrage and regarded as morally or legally reprehensible by the standards and mores of the time, has been a part of the US political landscape since the founding of the republic. Americans prefer to think that their public officials' misbehavior is the exception rather than the rule, but the record of political corruption and cover-ups, spanning across the entire history of the United States, is too lengthy to suggest that these actions are uncommon occurrences, merely freakish outliers to be discounted as "black swan" events. Politics at its core is about human nature, and human nature, if *The Federalist Papers* serves as our guide, is about acquisitiveness. Human beings seek to acquire things—power, influence, fame, and money, among other goals. Assuming this view of human nature is accurate, it is little wonder that elected officials engage in scandalous behavior. Their acquisitive zeal can lead them to cut corners and seek advantages unavailable to the masses. Add to that a political leader's elite status and his or her superior access to information and resources, and the temptation to risk a scandal is almost irresistible.

Strongly associated with the concept of scandal is a "scoundrel," defined as a dishonest or disreputable person. According to this definition, a scoundrel is someone who engages in dishonest behavior, eventually leading to the loss of a good reputation. Many (if not most) public officials seek the approbation of their fellow citizens. They long for a good reputation. The scoundrel engages in scandalous behavior in hopes of avoiding detection and evading punishment. Sometimes scoundrels succeed, and sometimes they do not.

*Scoundrels: Political Scandals in American History* is about scoundrels who were caught in scandals—specifically, political scandals. Often the original behavior was outrageous, but the subsequent cover-up was worse. The 1972 Watergate break-in, for example, may have been a "third-rate burglary"—although

1

that point is debatable—but the Nixon administration's attempted cover-up led to impeachment proceedings and the president's resignation.

The scandalous behavior of elected officials and public figures initially seems to be an odd topic for serious scholarly inquiry. Indeed, for individuals who bemoan the death of reasoned political discourse and the *People* magazine–style nature of current events, such a book appears to be part of the problem, not the solution. Why dwell on the shortcomings and misdeeds of public figures when such a project initially seems only to titillate the masses and feed into the public cynicism and hysteria that coarsens political rhetoric and further erodes trust in government?

If examining the misdeeds of public figures were merely an exercise in scandal-mongering, the point would be well taken. Wallowing in tales of political corruption for no other purpose than the "entertainment" value of such endeavors is unproductive, at least as a topic of serious inquiry. Yet political scandals have been (and continue to be) commonplace in American political life. They must be examined as part of the political process because, quite simply, they are crucial components of public policy. Scandals take away from the time that could be spent tackling large, systemic problems such as national defense, fiscal responsibility, health care, crime, racism, immigration, and poverty, among many other issues. Yet scandals are part of the fabric of the American experience; they go to the heart of politics.

Americans like to mythologize their government (or at least government in its formative years) as a beacon of liberty, the proverbial shining city on a hill. While the American republic has had its share of virtuous actors, the vices of elected officials cannot be ignored. Not surprisingly, the causes of political scandals reveal political figures to be all too human. A burning desire for power, money, fame, adulation, or simply the thrill of taking a risk leads a public figure to act in ways he or she would deem anathema under ordinary circumstances.

*Scoundrels: Political Scandals in American History* examines thirteen of the most famous (or infamous) and not-so-famous scandals in American history. It is designed as a "between" book, which means that it strives to appeal to scholars and yet remain accessible to a popular audience. It is not an encyclopedia of all political scandals in American history. Some episodes are well known, while others are obscure.

Readers might well question why some scandals were included and others omitted. Choices always must be made in a book that does not purport to be an exhaustive treatment of its subject. Some scandals were obvious choices—Teapot Dome, the Watergate break-in and cover-up, the Iran-Contra affair, and the 2016 Russian election interference, for example—while others required a judgment call. Suffice it to say that the cases discussed in this book arguably are representative of the range of situations featuring public officials behaving badly.

A few cases (including President Donald J. Trump's two impeachments and the January 6, 2021, insurrection resulting from Trump's false claim that he won the 2020 presidential election) merit inclusion, but they are so recent as of this writing that all the facts have yet to surface. Other authors will have to explore these cases in subsequent works.

In examining these thirteen cases, it is difficult to generalize about the motives of political figures who engage in mischief. From the outside looking in, the exalted position of public figures apparently contributes to the event. Consider a president of the United States. Anyone who believes he can raise sufficient campaign funds, capture his party's nomination, and win the general election is an audacious risk-taker. The rules that apply to most people do not apply to a successful presidential candidate. That person has accomplished feats that few people will ever accomplish. For someone who possesses the strong ego and desire for public adulation necessary to succeed in high political office, risky behavior is a sine qua non of that person's life. For some opportunistic politicians already accustomed to risky behavior, using dirty tricks (or accepting bribes) is not a bridge too far.

This observation is not to suggest, of course, that every prominent public figure is an amoral, greedy miscreant. Rather, most figures are flesh-and-blood human beings who surrender to temptation because the sources of temptation are so readily available. It is safe to conclude that some of the figures portrayed in *Scoundrels* would never have engaged in the offending behavior had they not been involved in a public career. Think about the Abscam scandal. Federal Bureau of Investigation (FBI) agents did not approach average citizens because the Abscam sting was designed to entice elected officials into accepting bribes.

Political corruption almost always stems from calculations of self-interest before, during, and after the fact. The calculations may be legally and ethically misguided, factually inaccurate, and/or blind to political realities, but nonetheless they are almost always deliberate and premeditated. Political corruption can involve lone individuals acting on their own accord, or they can implicate systemic corruption with a large group, sometimes within a presidential administration. Examples of the former include the actions of Aaron Burr, Preston Brooks, "Wild Bill" Langer, Spiro Agnew, and Jack Abramoff. Critics might argue that the actions of these men were emblematic of the widespread corruption practiced by other similarly situated individuals, but their transgressions nonetheless were based on the choices they made as individuals. By contrast, the Grant administration scandals, Teapot Dome, Watergate, the savings and loan crises, the Iran-Contra affair, and Russian interference with the 2016 presidential election involved corruption by multiple individuals acting as part of a group, following through on a conspiracy, or working inside a presidential administration.

Here, then, are thirteen quintessential cases of political corruption. The book opens with a prime example of systemic corruption: the Yazoo land fraud case. In 1795, a large group of Georgia state legislators accepted bribes from private land companies to enact a law allowing the sale of land from the state's western boundaries at scandalously attractive prices. When they learned of the malfeasance, angry citizens voted out the venal legislators in the 1796 election. Their replacements sought to rescind the sale by invalidating the previous law. Therein lay the problem. Much of the land had been conveyed to third parties who bought the land in good faith before the recission was enacted. Faced with economic ruin, innocent purchasers argued that they were bona fide owners who relied on the clear title conveyed by the previous owners. The issue wound up in the courts, resulting in a major United States Supreme Court case on the sanctity of contracts. The Yazoo land fraud example demonstrates the extensive damage that can be caused when elected officials, acting collectively, place their own self-interest ahead of the public good.

Chapter 2 discusses a murky situation involving a former vice president of the United States. Aaron Burr had killed the former treasury secretary, Alexander Hamilton, in a duel in 1804. Although he was never charged with a crime, Burr had tarnished his name and reputation, which were already suspect. Finding himself a pariah within the corridors of power, he fled out west, to an area where many a would-be reprobate sought sanctuary. There he met General James Wilkinson, a Machiavellian character who may or may not have been a Spanish agent even as he claimed allegiance to the US government. Burr's participation with Wilkinson in a scheme either to aid the Spanish or to establish a newly independent republic was never clear. What was clear was Burr's frenetic attempt to recruit privateers for God-knows-what purpose. When US authorities became alarmed at this activity, Wilkinson repudiated Burr's plan and turned against his former partner.

Arrested for treason, Burr found himself on trial, the ultimate indignity for a man who had served as vice president and had harbored realistic presidential ambitions. President Thomas Jefferson, still incensed that Burr had tried to steal the presidency from him in the 1800 election, urged the authorities to prosecute Burr using all the might and majesty of the United States government. Yet Burr was acquitted of the charges because the nature and extent of the conspiracy were not understood. Burr's fall from grace was unsatisfactory for everyone. The Jefferson administration did not secure a conviction, while Burr's reputation (such as it was) was obliterated, and historians were left to ponder what really happened on the western frontier in 1805 and 1806.

Fifty years later, one of the most spectacular cases of political corruption—in this instance, an extraordinary act of violence—occurred on the eve of an American civil war. As discussed in chapter 3, Preston Brooks, a South Carolina congressman, charged into the United States Senate and viciously clubbed Senator Charles Sumner of Massachusetts with a cane. Senator Sumner had previously delivered an incendiary speech blasting South Carolina as well as the state's senior senator, Andrew Butler, who was Brooks's cousin. Brooks attacked Sumner in retaliation for the insults.

If representatives and senators from all parts of the country had united in condemning Brooks's attack, the incident might have been dismissed as the insane act of a lone nut hell-bent on violence and destruction. Sectional tensions were at a fever pitch, however; it was too late for unity. When Southern partisans overwhelmingly applauded Brooks's actions—they sent him new canes to replace the one he broke when he walloped the Massachusetts senator—it was obvious that Brooks represented a level of political corruption that spread across an entire region of the country. The North and South were too divided. Civil war erupted less than five years later, and the Brooks-Sumner incident sometimes is cited as one of many causes of the conflagration.

Ulysses S. Grant emerged as a hero of that war. He had risen through the ranks from unremarkable beginnings to become the greatest general officer in the Northern army during the 1860s. As a reward for his stellar service, voters sent him to the Executive Mansion in the 1868 election. His campaign motto— "let us have peace"—was a welcome pledge to a war-weary populace.

Yet President Grant could not compete with General Grant as a leader, as explained in chapter 4. The Grant administration was riddled with corruption, although the president remained personally unsullied by the multiple scandals. Examples of corruption included the "salary grab," which became an issue after Grant signed a law doubling the president's annual salary to $50,000 a year and raising congressional salaries from $5,000 to $7,500 a year. In the "Whiskey Ring," whiskey distillers bribed treasury department officials to neglect tax collections in exchange for kickbacks. Treasury Secretary Benjamin Bristow eventually broke up the ring, but two of Grant's private secretaries, Orville E. Babcock and Horace Porter, were implicated.

Crédit Mobilier was at the center of the best known of the Grant administration–era scandals. The Union Pacific Railroad created a company, Crédit Mobilier, in 1864 to oversee construction of the transcontinental railroad. From its inception, Crédit Mobilier was a fraudulent entity, established so it appeared that the Union Pacific board of directors and principal officers had selected an independent construction management firm to build the railroad. Instead, Crédit Mobilier was a shell company that allowed Union Pacific officers to contract with the supposedly independent firm. Crédit Mobilier officials used checks issued by Union Pacific to purchase stocks and bonds in the Union Pacific project at par value, driving up stock prices. Crédit Mobilier officers then sold the stocks and bonds on the open market at inflated prices.

The Grant administration scandals were case studies of how not to operate government programs. Lacking public transparency and accountability—and relying on an inept president and an inattentive Congress to ignore their numerous transgressions—corrupt public officials took advantage of a political system with few oversight mechanisms. When progressives pushed for government reforms late in the nineteenth century, they cited the Grant scandals as evidence of the misdeeds that can occur when public servants are not effectively regulated.

Chapter 5 is devoted to an infamous case of political corruption in the administration of Warren G. Harding during the 1920s. Of all the stories of political corruption before the Watergate break-in and cover-up in the 1970s—even eclipsing malfeasance in the Grant administration—Teapot Dome stands out as a classic story of greed and a betrayal of the public trust. As the scandal illustrated, President Harding was a weak administrator and a terrible judge of character. "In this job, I'm not worried about my enemies," he groused. "It's my friends, my Goddamned friends, who are keeping me awake nights."[1] Preoccupied with other matters, including his numerous sexual trysts, the president allowed his cabinet members to handle issues as they saw fit, which they did—to Harding's (and the country's) everlasting detriment.

Teapot Dome occurred after Harding allowed the transfer of oil-reserve lands from the United States Navy to the Department of the Interior. Following the transfer, the secretary of the interior, Albert Fall, leased oil deposits at various locations, including Teapot Dome, Wyoming, to petroleum companies in exchange for bribes. When the US Senate investigated the leases, they learned that Fall and his family members had enriched themselves at the public's expense. A more extensive investigation revealed that private-sector oilmen also had benefited from the oil leases with the interior department.

Albert Fall and his confederates endured multiple trials for conspiracy and bribery. Following his conviction, Fall spent a year in prison, earning the dubious distinction of becoming the first cabinet official in American history to serve a prison term owing to misdeeds that occurred while he was in office. His actions ensured that Harding's administration would be remembered chiefly for the scandal. Harding, however, knew nothing of his tarnished legacy, although he recognized that all was not well inside his administration. The sordid details of the Teapot Dome scandal did not emerge until after the president's unexpected death in August 1923.

Chapter 6 follows the case of William "Wild Bill" Langer, a colorful, larger-than-life character who was something of a charming rogue. As governor of North Dakota in the 1930s, Langer required all state employees to donate a portion of their annual salaries to the Nonpartisan League (NPL), a third party that supported his programs. Langer did not see his actions as corrupt. In his view, he was practicing the hardball politics of his predecessors. He might have avoided state law violations in favoring the NPL. After all, he was the governor, and he had many friends in high places to defend his actions. Unfortunately for Langer, he violated federal law when he required highway department employees to contribute funds to the group, as those employees were paid through federal relief programs. He was charged with engaging in a criminal conspiracy to defraud the United States government.

Langer endured a slew of trials and appeals, eventually winning his case. Later in his career, however, the charges came back to haunt him. After he was elected to the United States Senate in 1940, he traveled to Washington, DC, and found that his colleagues would not seat him owing to his original felony conviction. Seated conditionally while a Senate committee investigated, Langer served with a cloud of suspicion looming over his head. Although the committee recommended that he not be seated permanently, the full Senate declined to follow the recommendations. Langer served in the Senate from 1941 until his death in 1959.

The Langer case shows that an elected official charged with corruption can survive a scandal, especially if his constituents believe that he is the right man for the job. In the case of the populist Langer, voters loved the public figure *because* he faced corruption charges. Many voters believed that he was singled out for his work on behalf of the people. Others supported him to defy his detractors without any regard for the truth or falsity of the charges leveled against him. If a large plurality of the public believes that a "man of the people" has been persecuted by elites, his political career can be enhanced by a whiff of scandal, as the Langer case illustrates.

Another populist, Spiro Agnew, the subject of chapter 7, enjoyed his share of political support in the face of corruption charges. Unlike Langer, however, Agnew did not escape the legal consequences of his actions. Allegations that Agnew accepted numerous bribes eventually became too burdensome and well documented for Agnew to survive in high office, but in his heyday the Maryland governor and vice president of the United States was a prominent public figure, equally beloved and reviled.

Agnew's boss, President Richard M. Nixon, enjoyed a long (albeit controversial) political career as a congressman, senator, and vice president before he captured the top prize. Nixon was never afraid to use "dirty tricks" to maximize his political power. Although he had not known about his subordinates' specific plans for breaking into the Democratic National Committee headquarters in the Watergate building ahead of the June 1972 burglary, Nixon generally approved of campaign espionage, as chapter 8 makes clear. He saw politics as a blood sport in which participants either win or lose, but no one is morally virtuous. Naive concepts such as ethics and virtue have no place in the rough-and-tumble world of electoral politics.

As the old saying goes, it is the cover-up, not the crime, that creates maximum legal jeopardy. Nixon illustrated the veracity of this adage when he learned of the break-in by the men staffing his administration. Rather than denouncing their lawlessness and cleaning house, Nixon fully participated in a criminal conspiracy to cover up the episode.

The "third-rate burglary" might have been forgotten quickly but for the existence of tape recordings with Nixon's own words convicting him of impeachable offenses. In retrospect, observers can ask why the president would tape-record himself discussing illegal acts. On its face, such an action appears to be the height of folly and arrogance, if not downright stupid. Nixon was not the first president to tape-record his conversations to preserve them for posterity, but he was the first chief executive to provide a handy prosecutorial tool for his innumerable detractors to use against him.

Watergate occurred during the early to mid-1970s. Fast-forward to the end of the decade. Chapter 9 discusses a mostly forgotten episode in American political history: the Abscam scandal of the late 1970s. The FBI undertook an undercover sting operation to determine whether elected officials would accept money in exchange for private legislation benefiting fictional Arab sheiks. A disturbingly large number of public servants accepted the bribes.

When the scandal came to light, citizens were appalled at the behavior of their elected representatives, but they also expressed distaste for the FBI's tactics. Luring a person to a hotel room and pushing him to provide favors for cash is entrapment, a crime-fighting technique dependent on investigators initiating the criminal behavior. Save for a small number of officials who refused to accept the money, no one emerged from the Abscam investigation with his reputation intact or his hands clean.

Abscam illustrated the quest for money that drives some ambitious individuals, but it also highlighted the powerful, corrosive effect of money in American politics. Many cases in this book illustrate the slippery slope that public figures face. House Speaker Jim Wright and the Keating Five senators profiled in chapter 10 presumably did not set out to violate the law. They each considered Charles H. Keating Jr., chairman of the Lincoln Savings and Loan Association, a constituent—and a large campaign contributor as well—who asked for their assistance. In a political system in which elected officials desperately need campaign donations, the incentive for elected officials to walk a fine line between assisting a constituent and engaging in improper influence peddling always exists. Stepping on the wrong side of the line can destroy a person's reputation and career. Reforming federal campaign laws could be an effective means of removing such incentives.

Moving into the 1980s, chapter 11 addresses the Iran-Contra scandal that occurred during Ronald Reagan's second term as president. The facts were convoluted, but the episode involved a presidential administration that circumvented the law as well as the will of Congress. Reagan sought to assist a ragtag group of rebels (the Contras) in their struggle against a Marxist regime (the Sandinistas) in Nicaragua. Congress limited the amount of funds that the administration could use for such purposes. In response, the president's National Security Council developed an elaborate scheme to raise money by selling American arms to Iran and using the proceeds from the sale to finance the Contras as well as fund the release of Americans held hostage in Lebanon.

The most troubling aspect of the Iran-Contra affair was the administration's willingness to bypass the constitutional checks and balances enshrined in the United States Constitution. Reagan's men justified their actions as necessary to achieve the president's policy goals, effectively endorsing the Machiavellian principle of the ends justifying the means. Although the scandal sullied Reagan's reputation and some participants were convicted of crimes, presidential pardons and numerous legal appeals (most of which were successful) ensured that a full and fair accounting of the episode was elusive. Some figures, most notably Lieutenant Colonel Oliver North, even emerged from the scandal with an enhanced reputation. Iran-Contra demonstrates that not all scandals are equal. Sometimes realpolitik trumps constitutional principle, and a scoundrel can prosper in the face of scandal.

Chapter 12 discusses Jack Abramoff, a lawyer-lobbyist who became infamous for bribing members of Congress. Abramoff reinforced stereotypes about the corrupting role of lobbyists in American politics. The reality, of course, is far different. The typical lobbyist does not provide fistfuls of cash to greedy politicians in hopes of buying a vote or producing a bill to help private parties. Lobbyists often educate elected officials on important topics and testify at public hearings about complex public policy issues. Without the expertise of former lawmakers, businesspeople, community leaders, and acknowledged subject matter experts, the American political system would be hamstrung by the lack of credible third-party information and data.

The Abscam scandal and Jack Abramoff's malfeasance demonstrate the dark side of politics when elected leaders place their own self-interest ahead of the public good. These cases should not lead to the cynical conclusion that all lobbyists offer bribes and all elected officials accept them. Instead, they should be the exceptions that prove the rule. Political figures occasionally are corrupt, but they need not be so.

The final chapter of *Scoundrels: Political Scandals in American History* covers one of the most recent examples of political corruption in American politics (as of this writing). Intelligence officials have long known that the Russian Federation seeks to interfere in the elections of Western democracies. During the 2016 election cycle, incontrovertible evidence indicated that the Russians had interfered in American elections through computer hacking and the use of bots to sow confusion and mistrust via social media, among other things.

One of the most confounding developments from the 2016 election interference case was President Donald J. Trump's refusal to acknowledge Russia's role in the affair. As both a candidate and later president of the United States, Trump demonstrated an inexplicable affinity for Russia's strongman leader, Vladimir Putin. Perhaps Trump admired Putin's authoritarian control over the Russian people, his ability to operate with little regard for institutional controls, and/or his disdain for political dissent inside his own country. Perhaps Putin and his oligarchs possessed compromising information on Trump—many critics of the president surmised that this was the case, although no one knew for sure—or perhaps Trump simply worried that acknowledging Russian interference would delegitimize his own unexpected electoral victory. Whatever the reason, Trump and his confederates labored mightily to shut down any serious inquiry into Russian involvement in the 2016 elections. Despite Trump's dismissal of the issue, Russian interference in American elections is the most worrisome scandal in this book. If Americans cannot count on the integrity of their elections, and if some or all their elected leaders refuse to accept evidence of foreign meddling, the political system established in the United States Constitution may not last in perpetuity.

The objective in writing about these political scandals across the broad expanse of American history has been to enlighten and inform the reader about instances where the actions of public figures have fallen short of the aspirational goals established by the Founders. It is easy to adopt a cynical attitude— "everybody cheats, so nothing matters"—but that attitude should not be the takeaway from this book. Instead, the conscientious reader should conclude that sometimes people cheat. Accordingly, we must remain eternally vigilant so that we can recognize instances when human behavior falls short of the ideal, assign punishment when it is appropriate, and constantly strive to live up to the American creed. Perfection is impossible, but striving for a better life and a stronger, healthier republic is essential.

As I have learned throughout my writing career, no one produces a book alone. All errors and omissions are my responsibility, of course, but I had help in my research and writing. It was gratifying to see how many people cared about the project.

First and foremost, I must thank Jon Sisk, vice president and senior executive editor at Rowman & Littlefield. Jon and I worked together on several previous books, and, as always, he was integral to the success of this endeavor. Thanks also to Katherine Berlatsky, assistant acquisitions editor at Rowman & Littlefield, as well as Patricia Stevenson, assistant managing editor.

Breanne Hewitt, archivist at the Georgia Historical Society, assisted in locating the "Burning of the Yazoo Act" image. Curt Hanson, head of the Elwyn B. Robinson Department of Special Collections, Chester Fritz Library, at the

University of North Dakota, graciously provided the image of Governor William Langer (figure 6.1). Sarah M. Walker, head of Reference Services, North Dakota State Archives, pointed me in the right direction on my research about Governor Langer. Evan Sapio, Charlotte Jackson, and Princess Pratt at Alamy provided invaluable assistance in searching for the photographs included in chapters 9 and 11.

As always, I appreciated assistance from the staff of the Horace W. Sturgis Library at Kennesaw State University (KSU), who provided guidance with the interlibrary loan process. KSU has been my academic home since 1998.

Family, friends, and colleagues provided support and assistance, especially Dr. William D. Richardson, a distinguished professor emeritus at the University of South Dakota. Dr. Richardson has been an invaluable mentor, teacher, scholar, colleague, and friend throughout my academic career. The late Dr. Jeffrey L. Brudney, formerly the Betty and Dan Cameron Family Distinguished Professor of Innovation in the Nonprofit Sector at the University of North Carolina Wilmington, was a treasured resource. Dr. Brudney helped me get back on track as I searched for a full-time, permanent academic position in 2019 and 2020. His sudden, unexpected death in April 2021 left a void in my life, as well as in the lives of his family, friends, colleagues, and former students. Dr. Bradley Wright, a professor of public administration in the Department of Public Administration and Policy within the School of Public and International Affairs at the University of Georgia, provided encouragement and moral support during the research and writing process. A longtime friend and confidant, Dr. Thomas Rotnem, a professor in the School of Government and International Affairs at Kennesaw State University, helped me through many a rough patch during my research and writing. Another longtime friend, W. Clifton Wilkinson, a senior lecturer in political science and public administration at Georgia College & State University, also provided moral support.

I deeply appreciated the support and encouragement of my longtime friend Keith Warren Smith. He and I met on the first day of law school at Emory University in August 1984, and we have remained close. This book is dedicated to Keith.

I met Chuck Redmon in 1992, and he has supported me at every step on my journeys through the worlds of academe and publishing. Thanks also to Shirley Hardrick, housekeeper and babysitter extraordinaire, and Gabriel Botet, part-time babysitter and full-time creative spirit.

Finally, I express my appreciation for family members who are fellow writers: Walter Russell Mead (cousin), Christopher A. Mead (cousin), Robert Sidney Mellette (cousin), William W. Mellette (uncle), and Jim Wise (cousin). They have inspired and continue to inspire me.

J. Michael Martinez
Monroe, Georgia
July 2021

# CHAPTER 1

# "The Day Will Come, When Another & a More Pure & Virtuous Legislature, Will Make Null & Void This Sale of Birthright."

## THE YAZOO LAND FRAUD

The case that became known as the Yazoo land fraud arguably was the worst example of financial malfeasance in American history. In 1795, a group of Georgia state legislators accepted bribes from four private land companies to enact a law that allowed the sale of land from the state's western boundaries at prices far below market value. When the public learned of the fraudulent sales, angry citizens expressed their sense of outrage by turning out most of the legislature in the 1796 election. Seeking to rectify the damage, the new legislature attempted to rescind the sale by enacting a law invalidating the previous law. Unfortunately, most of the land already had been conveyed to third parties, who argued they were bona fide purchasers who had acquired the property in good faith.

The claims between the state of Georgia and the land companies continued well into the next decade. A case eventually made its way to the United States Supreme Court. Robert Fletcher bought a tract of the disputed land from speculator John Peck in 1795. Unable to use or convey his property free and clear of encumbrances, Fletcher sued Peck in 1803, charging that Peck had sold him land without clear title. In a landmark United States Supreme Court case, *Fletcher v. Peck*, Chief Justice John Marshall wrote an opinion finding that the Contract Clause of the United States Constitution did not allow a state to void contracts for the transfer of land, even though the land was secured through illegal bribery. It was one of the most important Supreme Court cases on the sanctity of contracts in the court's history.[1]

No one knew, of course, that Georgia territorial claims would lead to a groundbreaking case in American history, although the court probably would have weighed in eventually to settle the numerous conflicting land disputes in the territories. Speculators had been trading in land since early in the eighteenth century. As people flooded into the area in search of arable land, speculators snatched up parcels as quickly as they could, intent on reselling the land for higher prices. Because land titles often were not free and clear of encumbrances, speculation carried huge risks. An unlucky speculator might be left holding the bag if he failed to flip the purchase before a defect in the chain of ownership were found or if state legislators imposed regulations on land sales. For the crafty speculator, buying cheap land and quickly reselling it for a handsome profit could be lucrative if the timing worked in his favor.

Despite their reputation as avaricious and opportunistic, speculators insisted that they were not villains. They came into an unsettled area and bought up land at great personal risk. Their willingness to be trailblazers ensured the spread of "civilization," which they defined as clearing land for farming and allowing families to relocate farther west. It was, they said, a laudable goal. As proponents of free markets would later argue, an entrepreneur who accepted big risks was entitled to earn big rewards. It became a fundamental principle of what later was called the capitalist system.

Ownership of Georgia's western lands in the 1780s was murky and ripe for exploitation by unscrupulous adventurers. Aware of the confusion, state legislators sought to determine the state's boundaries after the Revolutionary War ended. New residents flocking into the area were desperate to develop tracts of land, but they needed assurances that their purchases were legitimate and legally enforceable. Georgia had claimed a swath of land westward to the Mississippi River, which included an area comprising the later states of Alabama and Mississippi. The claim was complicated because Native American tribes living in those areas believed that the land belonged to them. Spain also had staked out claims.

Aside from the possibility of abuse by private speculators, elected officials recognized that easy profits from land sales could be had by legislative fiat. Mired in debt from expenditures during the Revolutionary War, states could earn ready cash by selling off large parcels. As subsequent events would illustrate, it was a situation rife with potential conflicts of interest.[2]

During the 1780s, Georgia's western lands were not seen as desirable. They were heavily wooded, with few roads, and populated by Native American tribes, including the Creeks in present-day Alabama, the Cherokee in a small portion of northern Alabama, the Choctaw in southern Mississippi, and the Chickasaw in northern Mississippi. Spain claimed part of the northern boundary of its West Florida territory.[3]

Although much of the land was uninhabitable in its current state, one area that seemed suitable for settlement was the land around present-day Vicksburg, Mississippi, where the Yazoo River flows into the Mississippi River. Over time, the name "Yazoo lands" or the "Yazoo line" became a shorthand reference to all of Georgia's western lands.[4]

For Georgia, a sparsely populated state, to insist that it owned all lands extending from the city of Savannah on the Atlantic coast to the Mississippi River was audacious in the 1780s. Surrounded by Native American tribes to the east and west, and facing Spanish claims down south in Florida, Georgia state government barely functioned. Enforcing its land claims was virtually impossible. No one who understood the situation believed that the state would or could do anything to retaliate against an entity that interfered with the alleged western boundary.

The state legislature encouraged new residents to settle down in Georgia, and, as an inducement, land was cheap. As larger numbers of white settlers arrived, the number of able-bodied men to serve in the state militia increased. The militia was necessary to keep the tribes in line and provide a disincentive for industrious Spanish troops to wander up from South Georgia in search of an easy land grab. The law originally limited the available acreage to one thousand acres per individual settler, but speculators easily circumvented that figure, especially in the western lands.[5]

In 1784 and 1785, the state of Georgia attempted to establish counties in what later became Alabama and Mississippi, but those efforts came to naught. By the mid-1780s, the state legislature became increasingly concerned about the Yazoo lands. Fearful that their claims would dissolve owing to the state's inability to enforce the boundary, legislators resolved to accept the first reasonable offer that came along. When the Confederation Congress showed no interest in acquiring the land because it was too remote to be useful, the only viable option was to allow private land speculators to submit proposals and sell out to a commercial enterprise.

Private land companies submitted proposals to the state legislature in November 1789. Among the competitors, the South Carolina Yazoo Company, headed by Thomas Washington (who also used the alias Walsh), was a notorious land speculation venture with a reputation for predatory business practices. Alexander Moultrie, the attorney general of South Carolina, partnered with the company. Patrick Henry and seven other partners formed the Virginia Yazoo Company and submitted a proposal, as did the Tennessee Yazoo Company.[6]

Using their considerable political connections, the land companies pushed a bill through the state legislature approving their proposals. Georgia governor George Walton signed the bill into law on December 21, 1789. Under the terms of the agreement, the South Carolina Yazoo Company received ten million acres of land stretching between the Mississippi River and the Tombigbee River for just under $67,000. The Virginia Yazoo Company captured eleven million acres north of the South Carolina Yazoo Company's claim in return for $94,000. The Tennessee Yazoo Company procured four million acres around Muscle Shoals for $47,000.[7]

The sales provoked howls of outrage. Some Georgia legislators objected on the grounds that selling large parcels of land to out-of-state speculators cheated

Georgia citizens out of a chance to own the land themselves. A Georgia company had tried and failed to procure large acreage—and it had offered the state a better deal—suggesting that the other companies had engaged in behind-the-scenes lobbying that lacked even a semblance of accountability.[8]

The Congress under the Articles of Confederation had not been interested in acquiring the lands, but by 1789 a new government was in place, established by the new United States Constitution. The Washington administration was worried that the land sales threatened to create problems with the Native American tribes that would be displaced as new settlers flooded into the area and bought up land from the speculators. Anxious to preserve the peace with the Cherokee, Chickasaw, and Choctaw nations, President George Washington issued a proclamation in August 1790 warning any citizen seeking to settle in the Yazoo lands that they must not violate federal treaties signed with the Native Americans.[9]

As if the federal objections were not enough to vitiate the sales contracts, the land companies became mired in a bitter dispute about payment. In June 1790, the Georgia state legislature adopted a resolution directing the state treasurer to accept only gold or silver as payment for debts owed to the state. The original contracts had specified the amounts, but they were silent on the manner of payment. Company representatives argued that, because their contracts predated the resolution, it should not apply to them. Instead, they should be able to tender payment using Georgia currency or audited certificates of the state's Revolutionary War debt. Georgia currency and certificates of war debt did not hold their value as well as gold and silver, which meant that purchasers received a better deal if they could avoid trading in precious metals.[10]

The companies had a two-year deadline to pay for their land purchases, but the dispute dragged on so long that they did not receive their land grants. In the meantime, the South Carolina Yazoo Company was mired in its own controversy. Alexander Moultrie was impeached as the South Carolina attorney general in 1792 and convicted of embezzling state funds, which he probably did to raise enough money to pay for the Yazoo real estate. His partner, the unsavory Thomas Washington, was hanged in 1791 for counterfeiting South Carolina debt certificates. Moultrie later sued the state of Georgia after a new set of land speculating companies offered proposals, but the case was dismissed because the Eleventh Amendment, ratified in 1795, restricted the ability of individuals to bring lawsuits against states in federal court.[11]

Chastened Georgia state legislators realized that their plan to sell the western lands had been ill fated from its inception. They should have known that any sale of so large an area—the Yazoo lands were twice the size of Georgia's settled boundary—would be controversial. They also had erred in dealing with patently unscrupulous speculators. If state legislators hoped to sell the land (and a majority still did), the deal would have to be worked out with greater precision.

For the next five years, the original problems with the western lands remained. Georgia lacked a stable government; therefore, the state legislature had no way to enforce laws or decrees. Native American unrest occasionally led to armed clashes, and the legislature was desperately short of funds. A desire to engineer a sale remained strong, but the challenges were daunting.[12]

Enter James Gunn. The proverbial poor-boy-made-good, he had a large personality and an even larger desire to brawl and duel with his opponents. Gunn served in the Continental army during the Revolutionary War and eventually became a lawyer in Savannah before winning election to the United States Senate representing Georgia in the first Congress. A Federalist, Gunn supported a robust federal government that would promote elite interests. As soon as the state legislature reelected him to the United States Senate in January 1795—state legislators selected United States senators until 1913—he aggressively promoted a new scheme to sell off the Yazoo lands. Recognizing that the enterprise was politically perilous, Gunn was willing to take the risk because the rewards promised to be astronomical. He vowed to avoid the same type of brouhaha that had ensued in 1789.

He was nothing if not bold, and he had been planning for the purchase ahead of his Senate reelection. In November 1794, Gunn and two partners created the Georgia Company and joined with another group, the Georgia Mississippi Company, headed by a speculator named Thomas Glascock. Gunn's group planned to purchase a landmass equal to approximately half of the present-day states of Alabama and Mississippi while Glascock's organization would purchase land below Gunn's claim, an area encompassing the old South Carolina Yazoo grant. Together, the two companies would pay $400,000, with $80,000 of that sum provided as a down payment.

Gunn likewise negotiated with John B. Scott of the Virginia Yazoo Company, who sought to revive his 1789 claim. Zachariah Cox of the Tennessee Yazoo Company soon engaged in talks as well. His company also wanted to resurrect its original proposal. Gunn's goal was to present a single, unified package to the legislature. He knew that Georgia's leaders were anxious to resolve the issue, and his plan would enjoy a greater likelihood of success if he could simplify the transaction.[13]

To that end, all the land companies agreed to the same stipulations. They would pay 2.33 cents per acre for forty million acres, with 20 percent due up front and the balance due on November 1, 1795, the last day of the legislative session. Gunn fervently hoped that a new legislature in 1796 would not modify the sale, especially if the contracts were signed and the money in hand by year's end. To ensure that the deal would not become embroiled in controversy about the manner of payment, which had doomed the 1795 venture, the contracts specified that the companies would remit payment in United States bank bills.[14]

The deal initially went according to plan. On December 8, 1794, a legislative joint committee reported favorably on the package, although the committee allowed for the possibility that other companies could submit late proposals. They would be considered if they provided terms favorable to the state. To ensure that other companies would not snatch all or part of the deal away from the four land companies, Gunn promised to reserve a million acres of land for sale to Georgia citizens.[15]

The state legislature gathered the four companies' proposals into a single bill for consideration. Following the second reading, the deal appeared to be completed when, suddenly, a rival group of speculators emerged. This new group, the Georgia Union Company, pledged to pay $500,000 for the lands identified in Gunn's and Glascock's proposals—$100,000 more than their offer. Plus, the company would set aside five million acres for Georgians to purchase land. This generous proposal threatened to derail Gunn's carefully laid plans. He was saved when the Georgia Union Company failed to produce the required down payment by the deadline. It had been an uncomfortably close call.[16]

On December 20, 1794, the bill, having passed both legislative chambers, landed on the desk of Georgia governor George Mathews. Much to Gunn's consternation, the governor vetoed the bill on December 29. As Mathews explained in his veto message, the price was "inadequate to the value of the lands." Moreover, the acreage reserved for Georgians was too small. He also objected to the lack of public notice for the sale. In Mathews's opinion, notice probably would have brought out additional rivals, which would have driven up the price for the entire parcel.[17]

Gunn scrambled to work his legislative contacts. The Georgia House of Representatives appointed a committee of five to approach the governor to determine whether they could assuage his concerns. After two conferences, the legislators produced a modified bill, which was joined with a measure to allow state troops to be paid with part of the land. It was styled as a supplementary state troops act, presumably to disguise the sale and provide political cover. Who could object to a patriotic bill to reward state troops for their service in policing state boundaries?

Governor Mathews certainly did not object. He was in an awkward position with the new bill. If he vetoed the measure because of concerns about the land deal, he would cut off funding for the troops who were tasked with defending the state's borders. No doubt he was not completely satisfied with the legislation, but on balance he thought it worth signing. On January 7, 1795, he did exactly that, allowing thirty-five million acres of western lands to be sold to private companies in the Yazoo Act.[18]

The Virginia Yazoo Company withdrew its offer before the law went into effect, and its agents formed a new concern, the Upper Mississippi Company, which submitted a proposal under the supplementary act. Of the total purchase price of $500,000, the Georgia Company paid $250,000; the Georgia Mississippi Company, $155,000; the Upper Mississippi Company, $35,000; and the Tennessee Company, $60,000. Altogether, they put up a $98,000 down payment. The Georgia Union Company again offered a counterproposal on more favorable terms, but, again, the consortium failed to provide a sufficient down payment. The legislature rejected the proposal, and the deal with the four land companies moved ahead.[19]

From the outset, critics argued that the deal was rife with corruption and self-dealing. It soon became clear that James Gunn and his associates had circulated throughout the bars, taverns, and hallways where legislators met in Augusta, the temporary state capital. When a legislator waffled in his support, Gunn or his agent offered a sweetened deal. The waffler could have a share of the land at a favorable price. An astute recipient might choose to sell his share at a higher price, use the proceeds to pay for the original purchase, and pocket the difference. Numerous legislators became land speculators owing to Gunn's inducements. Because they were trading their support for a land speculation scheme in exchange for a stake in that same scheme, the enterprise became a testament to corruption.[20]

Gunn was not worried that his plan would engender a negative public backlash. As a lawyer, he had faith that legislation, once it was enacted into law, would be a fait accompli and difficult to overturn. Should the public object, it would be too late to abrogate the deal.[21]

Yet as soon as the public learned of the sale, signified by the governor's signature on the Yazoo legislation, an uproar ensued. The Washington administration grumbled about a state selling property, but it was the citizens of Georgia who felt especially betrayed. United States senator James Jackson, a longtime rival of his colleague Senator Gunn, joined with the anti-Yazoo forces to consider nullifying the deal. Jackson had opposed the measure all along, denouncing the bill in January 1795 as "a confiscation Act of the rights of your Children & mine, & unborn Generations, to supply the rapacious graspings of a few sharks." He outlined a strategy for opponents of the Yazoo sale, predicting that "the day will come, when another & a more pure & virtuous Legislature, will make null & void this *Sale of birthright*—for in my opinion the Legislature will constitutionally have a right to do so."[22]

As was the custom of the time, Jackson took to the newspapers to galvanize support. In his "Letters of Sicilius," he argued against the "monstrous grant," couching his reasoning in appeals to ancient political philosophers. He contended that a genuine democracy prevented power from being consolidated in the hands of elites. Georgia's constitution, in his reading of the document, did not authorize the state legislature to grant land monopolies to a few select individuals. Such transactions were not undertaken for "the good of the state"— only for "the good of their own private interests." Jackson had the letters compiled into a pamphlet that was widely circulated throughout the state. It became an intellectual articulation of the general feelings of discontent experienced by the populace.[23]

Jackson became so involved in the anti-Yazoo effort that he resigned from the Senate to devote his time and energies to the cause. Arguing that voters should remove state legislators who voted to sell the Yazoo lands, Jackson offered himself as a candidate for state office. He won. Jackson proved to be an effective speaker in the Georgia House of Representatives. Recognizing that the series of land transactions was too complex for many citizens to understand, Jackson became adept at characterizing the sale in stark, colorful terms. In selling off the lands, Yazooists had succumbed to the "spirit of speculation" that "had invaded our happy land." These corrupt public officials had destroyed the "love of virtue and democracy," allowing "speculation, monopoly, and aristocracy" to become "triumphant." He promised that the first order of business for a newly elected legislature would be to rescind the land sale.[24]

With most state legislators who supported the 1795 sale defeated in the next election, the new legislature convened in January 1796 in Louisville and took up the rescission question. Governor Mathews's term was about to expire, but he nonetheless sent a note to the state legislature cautioning members against rescinding the sale. The outgoing governor doubted "whether a law can be constitutionally made to repeal another that has been so fully carried into effect as the one now in question." His successor, Jared Irwin, had no such qualms about the legality of recission.[25]

A committee established by the new legislature investigated the constitutionality of the original legislation authorizing the land sale. A hint about the committee's proclivities could be found in its chairman. James Jackson, now fully ensconced in the Georgia House of Representatives, took the helm. He presented materials from the May 1795 state constitutional convention as well as grand jury presentments and petitions indicating that the sale should never have occurred. The findings outlined in the committee's final report, published on January 22, were a foregone conclusion.[26]

"It appears to your committee," the report concluded, "that the public good was placed entirely out of view, and the private interest alone consulted; that the rights of the present generation were violated, and the rights of posterity bartered, by the said act; and that by it, the bounds of equal rights were broken down, and the principles of aristocracy established in their stead." Not surprisingly, the report found that "sufficient grounds" existed to declare the Yazoo sale "a nullity in itself, and not binding or obligatory on the people of this State."[27]

The committee sent along a proposed bill to nullify the sale. Yazoo defenders had argued that the appropriate remedy was to be found in a court of law, but the bill insisted that a "notorious" injury that had harmed the general populace must be rectified by the state legislature. In fact, the previous act must be expunged so that all legal documents relating to the sale would be destroyed as though they had never existed.

Jackson and his supporters sought to garner as much political support as possible. To that end, the committee directed that the official 1795 act be burned "in the square, before the State House" with "a line to be formed by the members of both branches" of the legislature attending to bear witness. This public act would demonstrate to the populace that the new state legislature was truly a sentinel of the public good.[28]

The legislature passed the bill overwhelmingly on February 13, 1796—by a vote of 44 to 3 in the state house and 14 to 4 in the state senate. Governor Irwin signed it into law that same day. In accordance with the committee's directive, two days later state legislators gathered in the state house square to burn the Yazoo Act. According to popular legend, the fire was lit not by the hand of man but by the sun's rays passing through a magnifying glass, causing "fire from heaven" to consume the offending law "as by the burning rays of the lidless eye of Justice."[29]

Jackson and his allies in the emerging Republican Party of Thomas Jefferson were firmly in control of state offices—he eventually became governor largely because of his leadership on the anti-Yazoo issue—but they knew the rescission was controversial. Critics charged that the legislature could not legally rescind the original law, especially since subsequent purchasers had relied on the Yazoo companies' legal claims to clear title when they bought tracts of land. During the Georgia constitutional convention of 1798, Jackson had the principles codified into the state constitution to silence detractors who raised the specter of an unconstitutional legislative enactment. It was a wise move, but the effort was too late to prevent Yazoo land purchasers from challenging the 1796 law.[30]

As soon as the four Yazoo companies acquired the land in 1795, they sold parcels to third parties. Not only did they wish to turn a tidy profit as soon as possible, but they also needed to accumulate enough capital to pay off the balance of the purchase price by the November 1795 deadline. The typical transaction involved dividing parcels and selling them. Buyers usually divided the parcels still further. In a short time, the number of bona fide purchasers multiplied.[31]

James Gunn's Georgia Company sold a large part of its grant to a Boston land speculator, James Greenleaf, in August 1795 for $225,000. A month later,

This drawing, *Burning of the Yazoo Act* (1914), by C. H. Warren, depicts a pivotal moment in the Yazoo land fraud scheme. James Jackson is pictured at left, holding the magnifying glass through which the "fire from heaven" consumed the offending law "as by the burning rays of the lidless eye of Justice." *(Georgia Historical Society, MS 1675-01-01-01)*

Greenleaf conveyed 2.8 million acres of his land to two New York merchants, Nathaniel Prime and Samuel Ward Jr., for $180,000. Prime and Ward wasted no time in selling parcels to purchasers throughout New England. One buyer, a Connecticut land speculator named Oliver Phelps, bought an unspecified amount of land in February 1796, the same month that the law rescinding the original sales to the Yazoo companies went into effect. In December 1800, Phelps sold 400,000 acres to John Peck of Newton, Massachusetts, and an associate. Peck, in turn, sold 15,000 acres to Robert Fletcher of Amherst, New Hampshire, in May 1803. A up-and-coming young land speculator, Peck bought many parcels over time, eventually totaling almost 2 million acres, of which he sold approximately 1.5 million acres.[32]

Speculators always hope that they can enjoy a bubble when they purchase land. If the initial demand is high, subsequent purchasers will pay top dollar for parcels. Each successive conveyance grows in price as speculators desperately seek to buy and sell property in hopes of pocketing large profits. Should the bubble burst, however, a purchaser who holds land that is suddenly devalued may find himself bereft, perhaps bankrupt.

As the original Yazoo companies hurriedly sold off tracts before the February 1796 act rescinded the sale, their investors enjoyed the positive effects of the speculation bubble. When news of the rescission reached the northern states, however, prices plummeted. Some purchasers had bought the land on credit, paying a down payment in hopes of paying off the purchase with proceeds collected after they sold their shares. It was not uncommon for a land speculator to buy beyond his means, which, of course, is the idea of speculating in land. It is a form of legalized gambling. In gambling, someone wins—usually only a very few—and someone loses, often the multitudes who can ill afford to cover their losses.[33]

Faced with innumerable debts and essentially useless promissory notes, some subsequent purchasers simply walked away from their investments. The intricate web of complex transactions invariably resulted in a slew of lawsuits as the parties looked to the courts to figure out who owed what to whom. It was one of those cases, *Fletcher v. Peck*, that landed in the United States Supreme Court and became a landmark expression of the sanctity of contracts in American law.[34]

The case originated in May 1803, when Robert Fletcher sued John Peck in the United States circuit court in Boston, claiming that the latter did not supply clear title to the parcels of land that Peck sold. The original complaint alleged four breaches of contract. First, Georgia had no authority to sell the Yazoo lands in 1795. Second, the original 1795 act was illegal because legislators received bribes to curry their favor. Third, John Peck's land title was constitutionally and legally impaired by the 1796 rescinding act. Finally, at the time that Georgia enacted the 1795 act, the United States government, not Georgia, owned the Yazoo lands.

The prayer for relief indicated that Fletcher sought a refund of the $3,000 purchase price. Subsequent legal commentators have characterized *Fletcher v. Peck* as "a mere feigned case," with both parties seeking a United States Supreme Court opinion that would void the Georgia state legislature's 1796 act rescinding the 1795 law. As evidence, critics cite the quick nature of the suit—a writ commanding that John Peck appear in court was issued four days after the purchase—not to mention that the 1796 rescission was well known when the transaction occurred. If Fletcher feared that Peck could not provide clear title, why did he purchase land that he knew or should have known was the subject of a long-standing dispute regarding the legitimacy of the initial conveyance?[35]

The high court has a long aversion to issuing advisory opinions when no genuine case or controversy exists. In fact, Article III of the United States Constitution requires that a case or controversy is necessary before the court can render a judgment. If legal commentators on the origins of the *Fletcher* case are correct, the litigants colluded to use the court for their own purposes.[36]

The questionable character of the litigation was evident at the outset, but the courts accepted the case nonetheless. It was conceptually a simple matter concerning the effect of a state legislative act on a contract between two private parties. In short, could the contract between Fletcher and Peck be invalidated by an act of the Georgia legislature?

Originally filed in May 1803, the case came before the circuit court in the June 1803 term. Both litigants consented to a continuance from term to term until October 1806. Apparently, the litigants as well as the rest of the New England claimants waited to see whether Congress would enact legislation that would provide compensation for the injured landowners. After a lapse of more than three years, it appeared likely that Congress would not act, and the case should move forward.[37]

United States Supreme Court justices "rode the circuit" early in the nineteenth century, which meant that a justice presided over circuit court cases. *Fletcher v. Peck* finally came before Associate Supreme Court Justice William Cushing in the fall of 1806. Acting in his capacity as a circuit court judge, Cushing ruled in Peck's favor, after which Fletcher applied for a writ of error allowing him to appeal the decision. The justice granted the writ on November 11, 1806.[38]

Once again, the litigants and their fellow landowners delayed the case as they waited to see what, if anything, Congress would do. In 1804, Congress had debated a compensation bill for claimants, but the measure had been controversial, and nothing had passed. Members debated it again in 1807 and 1808, but the matter failed again. By the latter year, the litigants recognized that they must seek redress in the courts.[39]

Because the original lawsuit had not been prosecuted, Fletcher had to refile. Justice Cushing again heard the case, ruled in Peck's favor, and allowed a second writ of error. A certified record of the case appeared in the United States Supreme Court in February 1808, with oral arguments scheduled for February 1809.[40]

The high court announced its decision on March 16, 1810. Writing for the court majority, Chief Justice John Marshall established a precedent heralding the importance of contracts in American law. He struck down Georgia's 1796 law rescinding the 1795 sale, finding that the rescission was unconstitutional. Marshall grounded his opinion in a strict interpretation of the Contract Clause of the United States Constitution, Article I, Section 10, Clause 1: "No State shall enter into any Treaty, Alliance, or Confederation; grant Letters of Marque and Reprisal; coin Money; emit Bills of Credit; make any Thing but gold and silver Coin a Tender in Payment of Debts; pass any Bill of Attainder, ex post facto Law, or Law impairing the Obligation of Contracts, or grant any Title of Nobility."[41]

According to Marshall, the Contract Clause prohibited Georgia from voiding contracts for the transfer of land, even if votes for the original legislation were secured through illegal bribery. "That corruption should find its way into the governments of our infant republics and contaminate the very source of legislation, or that impure motives should contribute to the passage of a law or the formation of a legislative contract are circumstances most deeply to be deplored," Marshall wrote.[42]

The problem is that innocent third-party purchasers must have faith that a contract, negotiated in good faith, will be upheld in a court of law. The original fraud was deplorable, but "the rights of third persons who are purchasers without notice, for a valuable consideration, cannot be disregarded." Ruling otherwise, Marshall explained, would undermine American business because a person could never rely on a contract to secure their legal rights. "If there be any concealed defect, arising from the conduct of those who had held the property long before he acquired it, of which he had no notice, that concealed defect cannot be set up against him," Marshall argued. "He has paid his money for a title good at law; he is innocent, whatever may be the guilt of others, and equity will not subject him to the penalties attached to that guilt. All titles would be insecure, and the intercourse between man and man would be very seriously obstructed if this principle be overturned."[43]

*Fletcher v. Peck* is remembered not only because it strictly interpreted the Contract Clause but also because it was the first time that the United States Supreme Court struck down a state law as unconstitutional. (*Marbury v. Madison*, the court's landmark 1803 case, struck down part of a federal law.) The case represented a further expansion of national power.[44]

In the aftermath of the court's opinion, Yazoo claimants continued to clamor for compensation. Congress finally passed an indemnity law to do exactly that. The Senate passed its version of the bill by a 24–8 vote, on February 28, 1814. The House passed the bill by a closer margin, 84–76, on March 26, 1814. President James Madison signed the measure into law on March 31, 1814. The law provided $4.2 million to claimants. In 1815, a group of commissioners began hearing claims and determining how the money would be allocated. This resolution satisfied most claimants, although Native Americans who lived in the disputed lands were excluded from the settlement. Their claims were extinguished through a series of treaties in the 1820s.[45]

Aside from its impact on constitutional law, the Yazoo land fraud episode became one of the most visible cases of widespread malfeasance in American history. For idealists who believe that the United States is a shining city on a hill, a virtuous nation that, while not perfect, can serve as an example for other nations on the efficacy of self-rule, the case is a distressing illustration of avarice in human affairs. As well structured as the American republic may be, a government is only as good as the behavior of its sentinels. If, as in the case of the Georgia state legislature in 1795, corruption is rife and unchecked, the American experiment is threatened not by foreign enemies but by domestic charlatans.[46]

# CHAPTER 2

# "If I Were to Name This, I Would Call It the Will o' Wisp Treason."

## THE AARON BURR CONSPIRACY

Aaron Burr was a member of the revered founding generation of political leaders, but he suffered an ignominious fall from grace and faced treason charges in court. One biographer described him as a "fallen founder." The standard narrative portrays Burr's contemporaries—Benjamin Franklin, George Washington, John Adams, Thomas Jefferson, James Madison, and Alexander Hamilton, among others—as virtuous men, geniuses who forged a mighty nation from the backwater lands of the former British colonies south of Canada. No Founder was perfect—some owned slaves, suffered under massive debt, and engaged in petty partisan politics—but their public virtues far outweighed their private vices, at least according to conventional wisdom. Burr was the exception that proved the rule. His public career held much promise, according to this perspective, but his avaricious nature and villainous conduct transformed him into a pariah, a man whose vices consumed him. He became a Founder without a country, a political leader with little or no constituency.[1]

Burr was always a contrarian, but his major difficulties arose owing to a falling-out with Thomas Jefferson, leader of the Democratic-Republican Party. In the election of 1800, Jefferson stood for president and Burr for vice president. The Jefferson-Burr ticket handily defeated the incumbent president, the prickly and perennially unpopular John Adams, but Burr was not satisfied with the vice presidency. He was expected to discard few electoral votes to ensure that Jefferson was selected as president. When Burr refused to follow the plan, his tie vote with Jefferson forced the election into the United States House of Representatives for resolution, as required by the Constitution. Although Jefferson won the contest and Burr became his second, the episode left both men embittered.[2]

Banished from the halls of power, Burr lashed out at his enemies, one of whom was former treasury secretary Alexander Hamilton. Burr and Hamilton were ambitious men, and both coveted the highest office in the land. They engaged in an ongoing dispute, each side hurling invectives and working against the other. The feud led these proud, impetuous public figures to demand satisfaction on the field of honor. On July 11, 1804, Burr killed Hamilton with a pistol in a duel in Weehawken, New Jersey. Although Burr was not arrested, he faced a possible criminal indictment, an astonishing turn of events for a sitting vice president who might have become president. The duel essentially ended his political career. He finished his term as vice president before heading west in 1805.[3]

Burr had long been fascinated with the undeveloped lands of the Louisiana Purchase. It was an area populated by Native Americans, Spaniards, and a variety of characters of mixed ancestry and questionable character. A man headed west when he was at odds with the settled world of East Coast society. If he played his cards right, he could gamble on future migration and buy up land. Speculators could turn a tidy profit if they invested well.

Because the Spanish empire claimed lands adjacent to the Louisiana Purchase, the possibility of a war between Spain and the United States was ever present. Burr contemplated a risky plan in which he would lead a private army into Spanish territory to grab as much land as he could. Known as "filibustering," the endeavor was fraught with peril. Filibustering was a criminal offense when nations peacefully coexisted because the head of a private army did not enjoy his government's imprimatur. For this plan to work, then, the two nations would have to become belligerents. The prospect of a shooting war was reasonable, but it remained a gamble.[4]

Burr had served in a presidential administration that viewed western expansion as inevitable. America was an "empire of liberty," and the empire required land. President Jefferson was not ready to send armed forces against Spain, but he was willing to turn a blind eye toward private citizens who tried their hand at wresting territory from the Spanish. It was a common belief that Spanish territory, perhaps Florida and even Mexico, could be had without much difficulty.

Burr's plan was not altogether clear. He may have intended to snatch land from Spain or from the United States to form his own private fiefdom. Perhaps he was a garden-variety land speculator and nothing more, or he may have been the traitor that Jefferson came to believe he was. Observers then and now have found it difficult to reach definitive conclusions. With his motives hidden away, the best that can be done is to trace his movements when he headed west.[5]

A crucial factor complicating the question of motive was Burr's association with a shady character, United States Army general James Wilkinson—characterized in one source as "an arch intriguer"—who served as a surreptitious Spanish agent. It is possible that Wilkinson and Burr knew each other in earlier times, but they had not been close associates. After Burr became vice president in 1801, Wilkinson sought him out and expressed his fidelity to Burr as well as

Burr's party, the Jeffersonian Republicans. Wilkinson understood how politics worked, and he played the game with passable skill. A lifelong military officer, he had finagled patronage and commissions while serving under two Federalists, George Washington and John Adams, but he was devoted to his own advancement, not to a party or a cause. It cost him nothing to embrace Burr's party, and it gained him a great deal.[6]

Wilkinson approached Vice President Burr for assistance on several occasions. Fearful that Congress might deprive him of his military commission, the general successfully convinced Burr to intercede on his behalf. The vice president also helped Wilkinson's sons secure positions at the College of New Jersey (later renamed Princeton University).[7]

The general arrived at Burr's New York City house, unbidden, one evening in 1804 seeking accommodations. During that visit, he showed his host a series of twenty-eight maps of the Louisiana and Orleans territories. As usual, Wilkinson had a request: he wanted to be appointed governor of the Louisiana Territory. As Wilkinson had suspected, Burr could—and would—help. The general knew his man well. In due course, Wilkinson won the appointment even as he remained a general officer in the army.[8]

Although he could be a persuasive fellow, Wilkinson was not without his critics. Treasury Secretary Albert Gallatin believed that the general was unscrupulous as well as "extravagant and needy." If so, Wilkinson undoubtedly found a kindred spirit in Aaron Burr. By 1804, the vice president was already mulling over a western adventure.

Even before he killed Hamilton in the July 1804 duel, Burr's prospects in the East had dimmed. He had much to draw him out west. Two relatives, Dr. Joseph Browne, the brother-in-law of Burr's dead wife, and John Bartow Prevost, Burr's stepson, had acquired positions there—Browne as secretary of the Louisiana Territory, and Prevost as a superior court judge in New Orleans. Burr's childhood friend, Jonathan Dayton, a former speaker of the United States House of Representatives and current senator from New Jersey, was interested in western land speculation, and he had connections with Daniel Clark Jr., former consul in New Orleans and General Wilkinson's business partner.[9]

After Hamilton's death, with Burr's term as vice president ending and the likelihood of continuing his political career remote, it was time for a change. Sometime late in the year, he pondered the possibility of a filibuster. During the summer of 1804, Burr sent a proposal to Anthony Merry, Great Britain's United States minister, offering to assist the British in separating western lands from Spain and apparently from the United States as well. The British and the Spanish were jockeying for position in the Americas and beyond, which made the proposal possible. Burr's motives have baffled historians. It was unclear what Burr sought. Was he helping the British in hopes that he would be compensated

for his services? Was this an attempt to procure the money and equipment necessary to carry off a successful filibuster? Did he hope to carve out a swath of land
extending all the way into Mexico, the first step in an ambitious plan to install
himself as an emperor of sorts? Merry notified his government in London that
Burr had offered "to lend his assistance to His Majesty's Government in any
manner in which they may think fit to employ him, particularly in endeavoring
to effect a separation of the Western part of the United States from that which
lies between the Atlantic and the mountains." The British government did not
respond to Burr's offer, and Merry's letter was hidden away for decades.[10]

Rebuffed by the British and restless for adventure, Burr continued planning
for a western sojourn. Spain apparently was plotting to seize territory from the
American Southwest, possibly to reassert the fading empire's stake in North
America. Burr may have agreed to assist the Spanish, or perhaps he sought to
create a newly independent republic and act as its founding father. There was
talk of "revolutionizing Mexico." His intentions were unclear. In any event, Burr
raised a group of private troops and filibustered along the frontier after he left
the vice presidency.[11]

During his journey traveling along the Ohio and Mississippi Rivers, Burr
reveled in the reception afforded by citizens unaccustomed to meeting a former
vice president. He was treated as a dignitary and "received with much hospitality
and kindness," which boosted his morale and encouraged him to continue his
travels. Often, he traveled by barge in a grand style.

Residents sometimes asked Burr to stay with them for several days, and he
was only too happy to oblige. In one encounter, he enjoyed the company of an
Ohio Valley couple, Harman and Margaret Blennerhassett, Irish immigrants
who had fled to America to avoid a scandal. They had erected a sanctuary on an
island fourteen miles from Marietta, Ohio, near modern-day Parkersburg, West
Virginia. The Blennerhassetts were lacking no resources, and it showed. They
built a large, rambling mansion on their 179-acre estate. Fancying themselves
natural scientists, they enjoyed discussing philosophy and gardening. Harman
could often be found gazing through his telescope at the stars.

Residents dismissed the Blennerhassetts as harmless eccentrics, but Burr did
not have the luxury of ignoring potential allies. He brought Harman Blennerhassett into his scheme, to the eventual dismay and detriment of both men.
When they first met, however, each man saw in the other a dreamer with a thirst
for adventure in the untamed lands of the western United States.[12]

After leaving Blennerhassett Island, Burr moved on to Cincinnati before
pursuing a leisurely route through Kentucky. By May 30, 1805, he had found
his way to Nashville, Tennessee, where he stayed with Andrew Jackson. The
military general had not yet become the Old Hickory of legend. The Battle of
New Orleans was almost a decade away, and his presidency was still a quarter

century distant, but the up-and-coming leader recognized in Burr a bold figure to emulate, an audacious man who would not back away from a fight.[13]

To all outward appearances, the Aaron Burr of 1805 was a disgraced politician who was turning his back on established society to lick his wounds and lose himself in the hinterlands. He may have encouraged that perception, but it was not completely accurate. Throughout his travels, Burr spoke to potential allies about a wealth of possibilities—grabbing land, forging an empire, or annexing Mexico. With each new contact he made, Burr sized up his host or interlocutor to determine whether the fellow might be a willing and able confederate.[14]

Late in the year, Burr was back in the nation's capital. He had kept a low profile, but in his absence his political enemies were active. Federalists wondered how long it would be "before we shall hear of *Col. Burr* being at the head of a *revolution* party on the western waters," and it was a prescient inquiry. In the meantime, Thomas Jefferson had never forgotten or forgiven Burr's effort to hijack the 1800 presidential election. He was willing to believe that his former vice president was a man without scruples and that Burr was the head of a conspiracy to promote secession in the western territories. Critics everywhere likened the New Yorker to a would-be "emperor." Even if no one quite knew his intentions, virtually everyone agreed that he could, and probably would, act in bad faith.[15]

Burr sent conflicting signals of his intent. He allowed the rumors to circulate, unabated, even as he worked his contacts about the possibility of reviving his political career. Perhaps he could capture a judgeship. He put out feelers about making amends with his political foes, although the inquiries met with stiff resistance. Burr was nothing if not flexible, and he was open to all avenues and takers if they advanced his interests.[16]

While he was in Washington that season, he learned that a war with Spain was unlikely. President Jefferson had employed bellicose rhetoric on occasion, but they were empty threats. The United States had few military forces to devote to an extended campaign, and the president backed away from a protracted adventure.

This bit of intelligence did not deter Burr from heading west again, but it did require him to modify his plans. Finding a lukewarm reception to his inquiries about reentering New York politics, Burr set his sights on acquiring forty thousand acres of land known as the Bastrop property situated along the Ouachita River in Louisiana. If he could not fight the Spanish government, which claimed the territory, perhaps he could grab enough land to establish a western settlement. From there, he could explore his options, launching a filibuster if favorable conditions prevailed, perhaps setting himself up as a land baron.[17]

In August 1806, Burr set off for his second western journey. At several stops along the way, he courted acquaintances, offering opportunities to join him in his murky western schemes. He reappeared at Blennerhassett Island, meeting with suppliers and arranging for construction of fifteen boats. Around this time, he sent a coded dispatch to General Wilkinson: "I have at length obtained funds and have actually commenced."[18]

What the funds would be used for and what mission had commenced were not clear, but Burr was on his way. While he moved farther west, however, unfavorable news coverage (much of it based on unverified stories, rumor, and innuendo) followed in his wake. Letters also poured into the Executive Mansion about Burr's questionable activities. Always alert to Burr's nefarious schemes, Jefferson convened a cabinet meeting on October 22, 1806, to mull over what should be done. The president believed that Burr intended to separate the western lands from the United States and establish a wholly independent confederacy. Although this conclusion was based on dubious sources, Jefferson insisted that Burr was up to no good.[19]

The president told his cabinet that he would send letters to state governors and attorneys general to keep an eye on Burr and discern, if possible, his plans. Burr, on "committing any overt act unequivocally," must be "arrested and tried for treason, misdemeanor, or whatever other offence the act may amount to." This statement was extraordinary. A sitting United States president was prepared to order the arrest of his former vice president on vague, unsubstantiated, confusing facts, charging the man with treason, a capital offense.[20]

Perhaps Jefferson, driven by his intense hatred for Burr, got ahead of himself. Three days later, he and his cabinet officers resolved to stand down. The president remained wary of Burr's schemes, but he recognized that patience was necessary. He may have been persuaded by some cabinet members, notably Treasury Secretary Gallatin, that any case brought against Burr must be instituted with good cause. If Jefferson played his hand too soon, the wily rascal might escape and enjoy a measure of public sympathy to boot.[21]

Not everyone was willing to wait for a clear picture of Burr's plans. In Kentucky, an anti-Burr district attorney, Joseph Hamilton Daveiss, presented an affidavit before Judge Henry Innes alleging that Burr was hell-bent on invading Mexico. Daveiss was one of the correspondents who had dashed off a letter to Jefferson warning of Burr's dangerous activities. The district attorney claimed to possess convincing evidence of Burr's plot, and he sought an arrest warrant. Alas, his evidence was not as convincing as he had claimed; it was unclear which law Burr supposedly had violated. Moreover, Burr's Kentucky attorney, a brilliant young advocate named Henry Clay, outmaneuvered Daveiss. Clay later went on to an illustrious career as a leading member of Congress for close to half a century; in the meantime, Burr was free to carry on his business, at least in the short run.[22]

While Clay was jousting with a Kentucky district attorney, James Wilkinson was in New Orleans forging a truce with the Spanish. Burr had been counting on hostilities to legitimize his filibuster. Denied such a pretext, his entire western project was at risk.[23]

Worse for Burr, Wilkinson was having second thoughts about joining the hazy quasi-conspiracy. By October, he had received Burr's coded message. Perhaps realizing that the scheme could never succeed, the general abandoned the plot. Writing to President Jefferson, Wilkinson, never a man known for his loyalty, betrayed Burr, warning of a "deep, dark and widespread conspiracy." Wilkinson pledged to restore law and order if the president declared martial law. Demonstrating his audacity, the general arrested Burr's confederates and ruled New Orleans with an iron fist. For his part, Jefferson issued a proclamation urging the citizenry to reject any attempts to foment insurrection, although Burr's name was conspicuously absent.[24]

Jefferson understood that Wilkinson was not an honest broker. The man's reputation preceded him. Moreover, the general's heavy-handed administration of New Orleans suggested that he was looking out for his own interests above all else. Nonetheless, despite his flaws, Wilkinson was telling Jefferson exactly what the president wanted to hear. In a second letter, the general was over the top, describing Burr's imminent assault on New Orleans. Although it was clear that Wilkinson was fond of hyperbole, the message was unavoidable: the former vice president was up to no good, and he must be stopped.[25]

On January 22, 1807, Jefferson sent his evidence to Congress, publicly accusing Burr of heading a conspiracy to separate the western lands from the United States. Although forced to confess that his sources were hardly unimpeachable, the president insisted that Burr was guilty. The precise details of the plot remained elusive, but Jefferson was confident that he knew enough about Burr's scheme to have the man arrested and tried for treason against his country.[26]

Events occurred quickly, or as quickly as they could in the west. At the direction of Jefferson's federal agent, the Ohio militia seized several of Burr's boats in Marietta. In Cincinnati, federal agents procured cannons to use against Burr's soldiers, if necessary. Burr did not have the rumored soldiers under his command, but no matter. It was best to be prepared. Harman Blennerhassett learned that the Wood County militia of Virginia was on its way. He fled Blennerhassett Island ahead of the militia, which plundered his estate and acted as a mob rather than soldiers preventing civil unrest.[27]

Owing to the dearth of wilderness communications, Burr had not known of Wilkinson's treachery. He had spent the fall of 1806 recruiting men to join his operation. It was only in January that he recognized the full extent of his former partner's duplicity. The filibuster would not happen, and any efforts to raise money and train men to serve under his command would fail. If he were not careful, he would be arrested. Only two years after leaving the vice presidency, Aaron Burr was a fugitive from justice.[28]

When he saw that he could not escape, Burr resolved to negotiate his surrender. He negotiated with the acting governor of Mississippi, Cowles Mead, preferring to deal with a civil authority rather than place himself at the mercy of James Wilkinson's martial law. A grand jury refused to indict him, but he was not free to leave the state. Living in legal limbo, Burr worried that Wilkinson's men would snatch him off the street and whisk him down to New Orleans. Before that could happen, he fled.[29]

His escape was short-lived. On February 18, 1807, a federal land registrar, Nicholas Perkins, spotted Burr near Wakefield, a small village in the Alabama Territory. It was late at night and Burr was on horseback, accompanied by another rider. Traveling at night on a dark, dangerous path, the duo appeared strange to Perkins, who alerted the local military authority, Lieutenant Edward Gaines. When Gaines found Burr, he asked questions, and the former vice president did not conceal his identity. Gaines promptly arrested him.[30]

It took some three weeks to transport the prisoner back to Washington, DC, for trial. During the arduous journey, Burr did not attempt to flee. He was a model prisoner. Newspapers reported on his progress, including unflattering portrayals of Burr's dress and condition. He had been known as a dapper gentleman, always adorned in expensive, expertly tailored clothes. His appearance after months in the wilderness was far different from what it had been when he was a man about town. Now he wore homespun, shabby rags, outwardly demonstrating how far he had fallen from his lofty perch as the second-in-command of the federal executive branch.

The trial of a leading public figure on charges of treason was unprecedented, and it generated intense public interest. Unrepentant and unbowed, the defendant appeared before Chief Justice John Marshall in Richmond, Virginia, on March 30, 1807. In that era, Supreme Court justices not only heard appellate cases but also served as trial judges in their designated circuit courts. Thus, Marshall appeared in his capacity as a trial judge.

The question before the court was whether Burr should be bound over for trial. The prosecutors in *United States v. Aaron Burr* were required to prove an overt act of war to sustain a treason charge. They claimed that Burr intended to assemble a private army on Blennerhassett Island, apparently recruiting soldiers from many ranks, including foreigners.[31]

Wisely leaving nothing to chance, Burr retained powerful advocates on his behalf. Edmund Randolph, a well-known statesman, had served as governor of Virginia and George Washington's first attorney general and second secretary of state, and he had enjoyed a prominent career as a private lawyer. John Wickham was widely regarded as a brilliant member of the Virginia bar, a man who knew how to construct a devastating legal argument as well as appeal to a jury. Burr eventually added Luther Martin, a leading anti-Federalist at the Constitutional Convention, and Benjamin Botts, a prominent Virginia attorney. The defense attorneys knew they must attack the central weakness in the prosecution's case—namely, the lack of an overt act required to prove treason.[32]

It was a difficult prosecution. Burr's intentions were unclear, and his efforts to recruit men for the journey had been largely unsuccessful. Whatever happened at Blennerhassett Island immediately before the militia raid could be only tenuously linked to Burr. He was not on the scene when key events in the alleged conspiracy occurred. The government's case rested predominantly on three crucial pieces of evidence: a so-called cipher letter that Wilkinson claimed Burr had written explaining his plot, an affidavit that Wilkinson had provided detailing Burr's guilt, and an affidavit sworn by General William Eaton demonstrating Burr's elaborate plans for the western lands.[33]

Randolph and Wickham immediately attacked the character of Burr's accusers. Eaton, it seems, had exaggerated his relationship with Burr and inflated the conversations they had had about the western enterprise. Even worse for the prosecution, the attorneys attacked Wilkinson's character and his series of clandestine activities. A well-known lawyer himself, Burr also participated as an advocate in his own defense, outlining how Wilkinson had manufactured evidence and tried to imply guilt without providing corroborating evidence.[34]

The initial proceedings ended quickly. On April 1, 1807, Chief Justice Marshall announced his decision. He supported the prosecution's contention that circumstantial evidence indicated that Burr probably had organized a military expedition against Spain's territory. Filibustering, Marshall insisted, was inappropriate under these circumstances.[35]

Yet Burr's activities, as ill advised as they were, did not amount to treason against the United States. The chief justice strictly interpreted Article III, Section 3, of the United States Constitution, which states, "Treason against the United States, shall consist only in levying war against them, or in adhering to their enemies, giving them aid and comfort. No person shall be convicted of treason unless on the testimony of two witnesses to the same overt act, or on confession in open court." The prosecution had not proved that an overt act existed. Both Wilkinson and Eaton had stated claims that Burr might have had a treasonable intent, but his activities had to have "ripened into the crime itself by actually levying war." The only arguably overt act was the activity at Blennerhassett Island, which was far from clear, and Burr had not been present. Marshall left open the possibility that the prosecution could rehabilitate its case, but he allowed Burr to be released on bail pending a second court appearance on May 22.[36]

James Wilkinson appeared in court when the session reconvened and swore that Burr had committed the overt act necessary to sustain a treason charge. Wilkinson was not the most credible witness, but obtaining a criminal indictment is not as difficult as proving guilt beyond a reasonable doubt. On June 24, 1807, the Virginia federal circuit court indicted Burr, charging him with one count of treason and one count of high misdemeanor for "unlawfully, falsely, maliciously, and traitorously . . . intending to raise and levy war" against the United States.[37]

Now that he had been indicted, Burr stayed behind bars until his trial commenced. No bail was provided for a man accused of treason. Fortunately, he did not have to wait for long. On August 3, 1807, the trial opened in Richmond. A crowd of spectators flooded the House of Delegates to watch the proceedings. It was the event of the season.

**This image of Aaron Burr dates from the early 1800s. (*Library of Congress*)**

Prosecutors argued that Burr was guilty of constructive treason. Even if he had been absent from Blennerhassett Island when preparations for war were undertaken, he had set events in motion. He was the ringleader, the sine qua non of the conspiracy. Burr, his opponents charged, was a man without scruples who cared for nothing but himself and his cause. That his motives were mysterious and not altogether clear did nothing to obviate his guilt.[38]

General Wilkinson was the make-or-break witness. He had produced the cipher letter showing Burr's plans. Faced with the letter, Burr vehemently denied he had written it. On closer examination, the letter was not in Burr's hand, leading to the conclusion that it was forged. Coupled with successful attacks on Wilkinson's veracity, the case against Burr could not stand. Defense attorney Luther Martin ridiculed the supposed crime. "If I were to name this, I would call it the Will o' wisp treason," Martin argued in his summation. "For though it is said to be here and there and everywhere, *yet it is nowhere*." Not a single credible witness or piece of evidence tied Burr to a demonstrable crime. The overt act of treason "only exists in the newspapers and in the mouths of the enemies of the gentleman for whom I appear."[39]

Chief Justice Marshall agreed, dismissing the indictment because the prosecution had failed to prove the overt act necessary to sustain a treason charge. Nonetheless, the jury was left to render a verdict, which it did on September 1, 1807: not guilty of treason. Eight days later, Burr faced a new trial on the misdemeanor charge. The jury in that case also found him not guilty.[40]

Aaron Burr left the courthouse a free man, but his reputation was in tatters. He lived for almost three decades after his acquittals, but he never again held high office. Recognizing that he was a persona non grata, the former vice president eventually decamped for Europe. Later, he returned to New York and practiced law. He became something of a cult figure in his dotage, as a new generation found his roguish reputation charming. He remained an intriguing, somewhat mysterious figure—the proverbial "bad boy" of the founding period—until the end of his days.[41]

Historians have long debated exactly what Burr was doing in the western lands in 1805 and 1806. He told conflicting stories, as did the figures around him. Perhaps he was merely a land speculator who sought to amass a large tract. He might have been plotting against Spain, Mexico, or the United States. His plans likely changed over time. No one knew what he was up to, then or now. Whatever else that can be said about Aaron Burr and his plans, he remains one of the few prominent Americans—and the only vice president of the United States—to be tried for treason.[42]

# "Mr. Sumner, I Have Read Your Speech Twice Over Carefully. It Is a Libel on South Carolina, and Mr. Butler, Who Is a Relative of Mine."

## THE CANING OF CHARLES SUMNER

He was an arrogant, aloof, erudite senator representing the state of Massachusetts. To all who knew him, he was a fascinating public figure. Northerners saw him as a fierce, uncompromising opponent of slavery while Southerners feared him as a threat to their way of life owing to his repeated calls for abolition of the peculiar institution. Love him or hate him, Charles Sumner was not a man to be ignored. He was unusually tall—standing six feet, four inches—with a commanding presence. A well-educated lawyer and proud of his intellect, he delighted in speech-making, and no wonder. He was an exceptional orator. Flowery phrases and ferocious rhetoric, dripping with classical allusions and witty wordplay, flew from his lips, apparently effortlessly. His voice was booming, its tone smooth and mellifluous. He was not a man who believed in temperate language, and he paid a steep price for his lack of moderation.[1]

During a two-day period, May 19 and 20, 1856, Sumner stood in the well of the United States Senate and excoriated a fellow senator, Andrew P. Butler of South Carolina. Like so many Southern legislators, Butler defended slavery as a necessary feature of American life. Angry that Southerners constantly threatened to rend the Union if their demands to protect slavery were not honored, the Massachusetts man ripped into Butler for supporting the odious Fugitive Slave Act, which required free state citizens to return escaped slaves to their Southern masters. Demonstrating his superior education and verbal prowess, Sumner peppered his speech with sexual innuendo, portraying slavery as a harlot and Butler as her customer.

It was more than Congressman Preston Brooks of South Carolina could stand. Andrew Butler was his cousin, and Brooks was incensed that his relative had been maligned. On May 22, 1856, the enraged congressman marched into the Senate and brutally assaulted Sumner with a cane, almost killing him. Southerners hailed Brooks as a hero while horrified Northerners cited the attack as an example of the brutality of the slaveholding class. Many historians credit this incident as one of the causes of the American Civil War.

In retrospect, Sumner's political prominence seemed almost preordained. Born in Boston, Massachusetts, on January 6, 1811, he hailed from an accomplished family. His father, Charles Pinckney Sumner, was a free-thinking abolitionist and integrationist, a self-made man who became a lawyer, clerk of the Massachusetts House of Representatives, and a county sheriff. The Sumners never enjoyed a family fortune, but they emphasized the value of education and diligent work as a means of ensuring upward mobility.[2]

His family gave young Charles every opportunity to succeed, first by enrolling him in the prestigious Boston Latin School, the oldest public school in the United States. He later graduated from Harvard University and Harvard Law School. While in law school, Sumner was a protégé of Joseph Story, a renowned associate justice of the United States Supreme Court.[3]

Sumner entered private law practice in Boston before heading off to Europe for three years. While he was there, he was stunned to discover how little race and skin color mattered in other countries. It was ironic that most European countries, known for their stodgy ways and rigid class systems, had abolished slavery while the United States, famously committed to allowing its people to enjoy "life, liberty and the pursuit of happiness," in the words of the Declaration of Independence, continued to protect human bondage as a legal institution. It was a lesson he never forgot.[4]

Returning to the United States, Sumner spent the 1840s honing his craft as a lawyer. He was not a run-of-the-mill lawyer, though. He became a leading advocate with wide-ranging, eclectic tastes. He published essays in law journals, lectured at Harvard Law School, and hobnobbed with poets, writers, and artists. He also became an increasingly strident voice against slavery. At the end of the 1840s, he helped organize a short-lived antislavery political party, the Free Soil Party. The party's slogan was "free soil, free speech, free labor, and free men."[5]

Free Soil Party members and Democrats seized control of the Massachusetts legislature in 1851, the same year that the state needed to select a United States senator. A majority of the legislators chose Sumner for the seat. Northern Democrats dissented, fearing that the choice would inflame passions in the South. Three months of infighting ensued before Sumner won the post in April 1851 by one vote in the state legislature. He was forty years old.[6]

Sumner arrived in Washington, DC, and took his seat quietly. It was an uncharacteristic position for a verbose partisan, and it did not last. After he learned his way around, the newly minted senator was primed to make his first major speech on August 26, 1852. It was titled "Freedom National; Slavery Sectional." Relying on his customary deep research, scorching rhetoric, and searing wit, the senator attacked the 1850 Fugitive Slave Act in a masterful performance.

Tracing the long, tortuous history of slavery, he highlighted the inconsistencies between the Founders' actions at the constitutional convention and the actions of congressional representatives who enacted the Fugitive Slave Act. "Repeal this enactment," he urged his congressional colleagues. "Let its terrors no longer rage through the land. Mindful of the lowly whom it pursues; mindful of the good men perplexed by its requirements; in the name of charity, in the name of the Constitution, repeal this enactment, totally and without delay. Be inspired by the example of Washington. Be admonished by those words of Oriental piety— 'Beware of the groans of the wounded souls. Oppress not to the utmost a single heart; for a solitary sigh has power to overset a whole world.'"[7]

Abolitionists took heart, for here was a man to take up their cause. Daniel Webster, the legendary Massachusetts senator, had disappointed them with his support of the Compromise of 1850, but Sumner was a worthy successor to the young Webster. For too long New England congressional representatives had gingerly worried that their actions would upset Southerners, who always griped about their mistreatment in the halls of power. Charles Sumner was not interested in placating the South. He would not mince words.[8]

In the ensuing years, Sumner buttressed his reputation as an unrelenting opponent of slavery. His oratorical skills, already fully developed, improved with each passing year. When spectators and members of Congress heard that the Senate's learned man was slated to deliver a speech, they packed into the chamber to listen. The master showman did not disappoint. Standing erect, facing his audience, pacing the room, he spoke in a sonorous voice about the evils of human bondage. Each speech became a performance as one of the nation's great speakers held onlookers spellbound. He was compared favorably to the Senate's past oratorical giants, notably Daniel Webster and Henry Clay.[9]

Sumner had taken up the mantle as the nation's leading antislavery voice in Congress. His addresses invariably invited spirited rebuttals from Southerners, most of whom denounced Sumner as an irresponsible firebrand inching the nation ever closer to civil war with his incendiary words. To Southern men, the Massachusetts senator was a frightening symbol of the abolitionist movement that seemed to be sweeping through the North.

Sumner's most famous speech was a blistering denunciation of slavery and slaveholders. Like many Americans, he was upset by events in "Bleeding Kansas," a territory where armed confrontations between abolitionists and slaveholders became commonplace. Beginning on May 19, 1856, Sumner rose to his feet and delivered a five-hour oration that spilled into the next day. He called his speech "A Crime against Kansas."

The senator reminded his listeners that Kansas was "a soil of unsurpassed richness, and a fascinating, undulating beauty of surface, with a health-giving climate, calculated to nurture a powerful and generous people, worthy to be a central pivot of American Institutions." Yet all was not well in this promised land. "Against this Territory, thus fortunate in position and population, a crime has been committed, which is without example in the records of the Past." The crime, he charged, was unparalleled in history, for "the wickedness which I now begin to expose is immeasurably aggravated by the motive which prompted it. Not in any common lust for power did this uncommon tragedy have its origin. It is the rape of a virgin Territory, compelling it to the hateful embrace of Slavery; and it may be clearly traced to a depraved longing for a new slave State, the hideous offspring of such a crime, in the hope of adding to the power of slavery in the National Government."

Had he continued in this manner, the speech likely would have been a powerful tour de force against the peculiar institution, but it would have been but another in a series of forceful Sumner harangues. On this occasion, however, Sumner made the attack personal:

> I must say something of a general character, particularly in response to what has fallen from Senators who have raised themselves to eminence on this floor in championship of human wrongs; I mean the Senator from South Carolina [Mr. Butler], and the Senator from Illinois [Mr. Douglas], who, though unlike as Don Quixote and Sancho Panza, yet, like this couple, sally forth together in the same cause. The Senator from South Carolina has read many books of chivalry, and believes himself a chivalrous knight, with sentiments of honor and courage. Of course he has chosen a mistress to whom he has made his vows, and who, though ugly to others, is always lovely to him; though polluted in the sight of the world, is chaste in his sight—I mean the harlot, Slavery. For her, his tongue is always profuse in words. Let her be impeached in character, or any proposition made to shut her out from the extension of her wantonness, and no extravagance of manner or hardihood of assertion is then too great for this Senator.[10]

This attack was especially vitriolic to a Southern man who often spoke of honor and chivalry. Comparing Butler's defense of slavery to a wanton, fallen fellow cavorting with a prostitute was too much for a Southern gentleman to take. Yet the attack grew worse. Butler was known to have a speech impediment, and Sumner, who talked with enviable clarity and precision, mocked his fellow senator. He noted that Butler spoke "with incoherent phrases, discharged the loose expectoration of his speech." Sumner dryly observed that Butler "cannot open his mouth, but out there flies a blunder."[11]

Senator Butler was not present in the chamber when Sumner delivered his speech. Nonetheless, Sumner must have known that Butler or his allies would respond. They simply could not allow such a vicious verbal assault to go unanswered. In fact, anyone who heard the speech would have concluded that Sumner was inviting an angry response.

If he hoped to stir Southern anger at the address, Sumner's wish was fulfilled. Two days after the Massachusetts senator concluded his speech, Congressman Preston Brooks of South Carolina, Senator Butler's cousin, marched into the Senate. Finding Sumner seated at his desk, Brooks angrily confronted the man. "Mr. Sumner," he said, "I have read your speech twice over carefully. It is a libel on South Carolina, and Mr. Butler, who is a relative of mine."[12]

Satisfaction might be found on the dueling ground, but the South Carolinian was far too angry to engage in the back-and-forth negotiations necessary to arrange a duel, assuming Sumner would have agreed to it in the first place. Moreover, the congressman was not prepared to engage in verbal jousting with Sumner, who was known for his debating prowess. Physical violence was Brooks's preferred method of resolving their dispute. Without preamble or warning, he swung a gold-handled cane down onto Sumner's head, repeatedly smacking the startled senator.

Recognizing the danger at the last minute, Sumner tried to stand, but the first blow forced him back into his seat. Before Sumner could react, Brooks raised his weapon and struck the man again and again. Now bloodied and in

SOUTHERN CHIVALRY — ARGUMENT versus CLUB'S.

*The Caning of Charles Sumner* is depicted in this 1856 lithograph. The caption sarcastically reads, "Southern Chivalry—Argument versus Club's." Sumner holds a copy of his speech, "A Crime against Kansas," in his left hand and a quill pen in his right hand. (*John L. Magee, 1856*)

pain, Sumner tried to stand a second time, but the desk was bolted to the floor and the blows prevented him from moving.

Eyewitness accounts differed on the sequence of events. Some onlookers recalled that Sumner eventually pulled the desk from the floor and got to his feet before he stumbled across the aisle and collapsed. Others insisted that Sumner lay prostrate on the desk, unconscious. Everyone agreed that Brooks continued striking the supine figure even after Sumner had lost consciousness. Brooks's cane broke into pieces.

After recovering from a momentary shock, bystanders tried to intervene, but South Carolina congressman Laurence M. Keitt prevented their intervention. Accounts vary. Keitt may have brandished a pistol as he screamed, "Let them be!" A few senators said Keitt waved his own cane, but he did not have a pistol.[13]

It was an astonishing, audacious act of violence, but it was not unprecedented. There had been a few instances of violence in congressional history, notably on the floor of the United States House of Representatives in 1798 when Vermont congressman Matthew Lyon, wielding a pair of tongs, tussled with Connecticut congressman Roger Griswold, who armed himself with a club. During a debate on the Senate floor concerning the Compromise of 1850, Mississippi senator Henry S. Foote allegedly pointed a pistol at Missouri senator Thomas Hart Benton, who thrust out his chest and dramatically declared, "I have no pistol! I disdain to carry arms! Let him fire! Let the assassin fire!" Foote either laid down his gun or was disarmed.[14]

Preston Brooks's attack on Charles Sumner was in an altogether different class than the previous episodes. The viciousness of the attack and the fact that Brooks did not allow Sumner an opportunity to defend himself shocked Northern men. They were galvanized by the South Carolina congressman's brutality. To critics of the South, the incident proved that the façade of the genteel Southern gentleman, a fellow obsessed with honor and reputation, was a carefully constructed myth. Lurking beneath the surface was a beast who was as barbaric toward his colleagues as he was toward his slaves. The notion that Northerners could compromise with a bestial group of hellions was unthinkable following the Sumner attack. Many an observer living north of the Mason–Dixon line recognized that civil war was a strong possibility after 1856.

Southerners viewed the matter quite differently. They were proud that Preston Brooks had defended his cousin's honor. Charles Sumner was a self-righteous, arrogant, dangerously unstable man who had demeaned the South and its traditions in general, and Senator Butler in particular. Such attacks could not go unanswered. Learning that Brooks had broken his cane during the assault, admirers sent him replacements by the score. The Massachusetts senator had gotten what was coming to him.[15]

THE CANING OF CHARLES SUMNER     45

Charles Sumner almost died that day, but he somehow managed to survive. Yet his recovery was long, slow, and painful. He probably suffered from what later generations called post-traumatic stress disorder. It would be three years before he returned to the Senate. Massachusetts kept his seat vacant until he could resume his duties. As he inched his way back to good health, Sumner could take solace in the realization that he had become a larger-than-life figure, a symbol of the antislavery sentiments of the abolitionist North.[16]

When Sumner finally returned to Washington, DC, the nation was closer to civil war than it had ever been. Representatives from North and South constantly traded vile epithets and apocalyptic warnings of impending bloodshed. The senator might have been cowed by his experience, fearful of launching into his usual fire-and-brimstone speeches of yesteryear, but he was not. Preston Brooks had unexpectedly died of croup early in 1857, but other extremists, dubbed the "fire eaters," championed the Southern cause. No shortage of would-be assailants existed in the South, but Sumner shrugged off all suggestions that he temper his remarks. He was not intimidated.

Sumner delivered his speeches with the same vim and vigor as he had before the 1856 attack. "This is no time for soft words or excuses. All such are out of place," he thundered in a speech delivered on June 4, 1860. He called the address "The Barbarism of Slavery." Some Northern critics of slavery, Abraham Lincoln among them, distinguished between the monstrous institution of slavery and the men who supported the institution. Moderates suggested that most Southerners were good people at their core but misguided about the evils of slavery. They simply did not understand how the institution both destroyed the lives of slaves and reflected poorly on slaveowners. This view allowed Southerners to escape the moral blame for supporting human bondage because they were, in essence, victims of their own ignorance.

Charles Sumner disagreed. Anyone who supported slavery was guilty of crimes against humanity. It was incumbent on people of good will to assail the institution. "In undertaking now to expose the Barbarism of Slavery, the whole broad field is open before me. There is nothing in its character, its manifold wrong, its wretched results, and especially in its influence on the class who claim to be 'ennobled' by it, that will not fall naturally under consideration." He said that he would accept no excuses: "Say, sir, in your madness, that you own the sun, the stars, the moon; but do not say that you own a man, endowed with a soul that shall live immortal, when sun and moon and stars have passed away."[17]

As the 1860s dawned and the nation faced a bloody civil war, Sumner joined a group of congressional leaders known as the Radical Republicans. Devoted to eradicating legal slavery in the United States, the Radicals emerged as critics of the newly elected Republican president, Abraham Lincoln. Lincoln came into the presidency in March 1861 convinced that he could mollify Southerners without engaging in a war. In his view, pro-Union citizens had been eclipsed by hotheaded secessionists, but they would come to their senses if given enough time. The Radicals, including Sumner, believed that Lincoln had naively misjudged the deteriorating situation in the South. The time for avoiding conflict had long passed. Lincoln soon understood their point. The firing on Fort Sumter in Charleston Harbor in April 1861 demonstrated the Radicals' prescience.[18]

Charles Sumner knew as well as anyone—better than most—the savagery that existed in the South. He literally had the scars to prove it. Like most Americans, he had hoped that war would not erupt, but once it had, he believed that the time was right to remake the South. If Southerners wanted war, they would have it. Afterward, they would be at the mercy of a self-righteous government that would not allow them to reenter the Union without abolishing slavery.[19]

Sumner enjoyed an illustrious Senate career until his death in 1874. He reached the pinnacle of power the day after Lincoln's inauguration when he became chairman of the Senate Foreign Relations Committee, a position he held for a decade. As a committee chair, he was one of the most powerful men in the United States. From this lofty perch, he cajoled the president to emancipate the slaves. Although Lincoln was not ready to take that momentous step at the outset, he eventually moved in that direction due in no small part to Sumner's pressure. Later, after the war, Sumner was involved in postwar Reconstruction, including the impeachment of Lincoln's successor, Andrew Johnson. As one of the final acts of his life, Sumner helped enact what became the Civil Rights Act of 1875, which passed into law after his death. The law aimed to guarantee that every American would be provided with equal treatment in "public accommodations" such as inns, public conveyances on land or water, theaters, and places of public amusement regardless of race, color, or previous condition of servitude. It was the last major civil rights statute enacted by the United States Congress until 1957. Unfortunately, the 1875 law was honored more in breach than in practice.[20]

On March 11, 1874, Sumner suffered a fatal heart attack at his home in Washington, DC. He was sixty-three years old. As the accolades poured in, he was celebrated for his many accomplishments during more than two decades in public life. The Preston Brooks affair, one of the events that precipitated the Civil War, was remembered as a major scandal as well as a turning point on the march toward a fundamental change in American life.[21]

## CHAPTER 4

# "Have Those Men Dismissed by 3 O'Clock This Afternoon or Shut Down the Bureau."

## GRANT ADMINISTRATION SCANDALS OF THE 1870S

The United States suffered through a series of political scandals during the Grant administration in the 1870s. President Ulysses S. Grant was not a career politician, and he proved to be unprepared for the complex, nuanced political issues facing his administration after he entered office in March 1869. He had been trained in military affairs at the United States Academy at West Point. Rather than skillfully navigating through political and economic problems with a sense of possibilities and options, Grant operated his presidential administration in the same manner that he had managed his army campaigns during the Civil War. He installed a handful of trusted aides in positions of authority and relied on them to implement his directives with minimal direction or oversight. Largely ignored, his cabinet officials were not actively involved in many administration decisions, which freed them to act as rogue operators or advance their own interests. In the meantime, Grant's close friends and allies engaged in malfeasance on an unprecedented scale. The president was an honest man, but he depended too much on his friends for his own good.[1]

The first major administration scandal occurred the same year that Grant became president. It began on Black Friday, September 24, 1869, when financiers Jay Gould and Jim Fisk—joined by a small-time speculator, Abel Corbin, who had married Grant's sister-in-law—attempted to corner the gold market. Master manipulators who sought every advantage, fair or unfair, in the marketplace, Gould and Fisk had persuaded Corbin to introduce them to the new president. Hoping to glean insider information about government policy, the financiers believed they could corner the market and multiply their riches. As the president's brother-in-law, Corbin used his connections with Grant to aid the enterprise. It worked initially, and the market manipulation undermined Grant's public reputation. Only the administration's decision to release more government gold into the marketplace prevented a larger panic. Nonetheless, the collapse of gold prices ruined many speculators and underscored weaknesses in the economy. It was not an auspicious beginning to a new presidential administration.[2]

The 1870s proved to be an era of economic turmoil for many Americans. Following the Black Friday debacle of 1869, a cataclysmic fire that destroyed much of Chicago in 1871, an equine influenza outbreak that swept the nation in 1872, and the Grant administration's scandals, it was an uncertain epoch in the United States. Americans longed for a time of quiet prosperity after the Civil War, but the decade of the 1870s was anything but quiet.[3]

The administration's scandals stretched across the decade. In 1871, the New York Custom House was the leading collector of imports in the country. Charges of corruption among customs collectors led to congressional investigations as well as an investigation by the Treasury Department. Officials discovered that two Grant appointees, collectors Moses H. Grinnell and Thomas Murphy, provided warehouse space to private merchants without requiring the goods to be listed—a clear violation of the law. Grinnell and Murphy charged lucrative fees for this service. Grant's friend George K. Leet and his two secretaries, Horace Porter and Orville E. Babcock, received kickbacks from this scheme as well. After learning of the scam, Treasury Secretary George S. Boutwell recommended better record-keeping and insisted that imports be stored on company docks. A successor in the customhouse, future president Chester A. Arthur, implemented the recommendations.[4]

Postal route contracts were also sources of corruption in the 1870s. It had long been official United States government policy that citizens should enjoy the right to mail service. In areas of the South and along the Pacific coast, government officials awarded postal delivery contracts to third parties to handle mail deliveries. Star routes, as they were called, usually involved long stretches of road in rural areas with few inhabitants. A contractor could earn exorbitant fees by agreeing to handle the star routes and subsequently providing shoddy service. With minimal or no oversight and few complaints lodged by rural mail recipients, a private contractor could promise much and deliver little. To make matters worse, contractors often offered bribes to federal postal employees, who would select a favored contractor's bid even though it was not the lowest price among the competition. In some cases, there were no bids at all—simply a preordained selection. In 1876, Democratic investigators closed the "ring" of corrupt star route contractors, although a new ring arose until another round of prosecutions closed it permanently in 1882.[5]

One of the worst financial scandals of the era involved a company known as Crédit Mobilier. The Grant administration was tarnished by the scandal, but most of the events occurred during the administration of President Andrew Johnson. Unfortunately for President Grant, the facts did not become public until September 1872, shortly before his reelection bid. That month, Congressman Oakes Ames of Massachusetts, a member of the House Committee on Railroads and a leader in constructing the transcontinental railroad, was implicated in the Crédit Mobilier bribery scheme.

The Union Pacific Railroad originally created Crédit Mobilier in 1864 to oversee construction of the transcontinental railroad. The United States government as well as railroad companies had sought to build tracks from coast to coast as a means of connecting one end of the continent with the other. In time, the transcontinental railroad became a symbol of a unified nation.

Despite public pressure to complete the project as quickly as possible, it was a monumental, seemingly impossible demand. Crossing innumerable rivers, plains, and mountains to lay track was an unprecedented engineering feat, and it would require a Herculean effort to complete the task. Crédit Mobilier was supposed to be a company dedicated to solving the myriad problems associated with designing and building the transcontinental railroad, but instead it was a fraudulent entity. Through an elaborate series of contrived conveyances, Union Pacific drove up the price of its own stock by funneling money through a dummy company controlled by the railroad's management, guaranteeing a huge profit even if the project was never completed. The ruse initially succeeded because the company appeared to be an independent construction management firm. Behind the façade, however, it was a shell company to allow Union Pacific's board of directors and principal officers to execute contracts with their cronies. Dummy individuals also signed contracts with Union Pacific, and the railroad assigned the contracts to Crédit Mobilier. Crédit Mobilier officers used Union Pacific checks to purchase stocks and bonds in the Union Pacific project for par value and sell them on the open market for inflated prices. The company, working with other partners, eventually completed the transcontinental railroad, but the cost overruns were enormous.

Congressman Ames served as the Crédit Mobilier chairman while he also served in the United States House of Representatives—dual careers for members of Congress were fairly common in the nineteenth century—and he took it on himself to advance the scheme by whatever means he could. He bribed influential members of Congress, offering them cash as well as discounted prices for Crédit Mobilier shares. After he was exposed, the congressman opened his records to public scrutiny. His records implicated many high-ranking officials, including Vice President Schuyler Colfax. Facing reelection, President Grant allowed Colfax to be dropped from the ticket in favor of Massachusetts senator Henry Wilson. Wilson was implicated as well, but he was exonerated by the House committee investigating the scandal.

Coupled with other stories of administration scandals, Crédit Mobilier became a symbol of Grant's ineptitude as a leader. Why wasn't the project better managed? At the very least, the administration was embarrassed, even if Grant was not personally involved. It was the totality of malfeasance that staggered the imagination; it seemed that every few months a new scheme was exposed.[6]

Despite his challenges, Grant won a second term as president. He soon found that his problems only proliferated. The day before he was sworn in, Congress passed a law—the Legislative, Executive, and Judicial Expenses Appropriation Act—to double the salary of the president from $25,000, where it had stood since George Washington's time, in addition to doubling the salary for United States Supreme Court justices. The act also provided members of Congress with a retroactive pay increase amounting to a 50 percent raise. The law made the congressional pay raise retroactive for two years, which meant that members of Congress would receive a lump sum payment equal to $4,000 for "services rendered." Grant signed the measure on March 3, 1873, the last day of the 42nd Congress.

The intent of the law was not unreasonable. Elected officials had not received pay raises in many decades; naturally, the purchasing power of their salaries had declined. In fact, members of Congress had last enjoyed a pay raise in 1852, more than two decades earlier. Because the president and legislators were expected to pay their own expenses, inadequate salaries sometimes drove scrupulous men of modest means from government office and unscrupulous men of great wealth into office, where their priority was enacting laws to assist them and their business colleagues with little or no regard for the public interest.

The genuine need for a pay increase was lost in the ensuing brouhaha. As soon as news of the new law became public, critics across the country expressed their outrage at the "salary steal" (or "salary grab"). The $4,000 lump sum was far beyond the typical yearly wage of most Americans in 1873. Moreover, the seemingly underhanded way that Congress enacted the legislation—on the last day of the session, with little public notice—suggested that the measure was corrupt.

Unable to explain the need for more money to an increasingly incensed public, elected officials scrambled to distance themselves from the unpopular law. Coming as it did after numerous high-profile instances of corruption, the salary grab illustrated to many citizens that government could not be trusted to act in the public interest. The episode contributed to the widespread perception of the Grant administration as fundamentally dishonest. The "salary grab" so rankled the public that Congress subsequently rescinded the act.[7]

Many Americans believed that Ulysses S. Grant was a nice enough man, but his administration was another matter. His associates were a collection of rogues and rascals, and his secretaries seemed especially lacking in morality. As an example, in 1874, the "Sanborn Incident" occurred. Grant's treasury secretary, William A. Richardson, hired a private citizen, John D. Sanborn, to collect back

THAT SALARY GRAB.
" You took it."

This drawing appeared in *Frank Leslie's Illustrated Newspaper* on December 27, 1873. It shows members of Congress deflecting blame for supporting legislation to increase salaries for high-ranking government officials. The caption reads, "That salary grab—'you took it.'" Congressman Benjamin Butler of Massachusetts (in the front row, second from the left) was a leading force in moving the legislation through the House of Representatives. (*Library of Congress*) taxes owed to the federal treasury. The process of using private parties to collect taxes based on commission was known as moiety, and it was a common practice in that era. As an incentive to collect as much money as possible, Richardson agreed that Sanborn could retain half of the funds he collected. Sanborn went to work, eventually collecting $213,000, with $156,000 earmarked for his assistants, including Richardson himself. The Republican Party campaign committee received funds as well. Reacting to public criticism, President Grant signed an anti-moiety law to guard against future abuses.[8]

Probably the most damning of the administration's abuses involved criminal enterprises labeled "rings." The Whiskey Ring involved whiskey distillers who bribed Treasury Department officials to evade taxes, reportedly as much as $2 million a year. Corrupt government officials quietly refused to collect required taxes. Instead, they shared the funds that should have been paid into the United States Treasury with the distillers. Treasury Secretary Benjamin Bristow broke up the ring, but several Grant advisers were implicated in the criminal enterprise, including two of the president's private secretaries, Orville E. Babcock and Horace Porter.[9]

Babcock was caught up in another scandal. On April 15, 1876, just fifty-one days after Babcock was acquitted in the Whiskey Ring scandal, prosecutors indicted him again. This time, he was charged with complicity in the so-called Safe Burglary Conspiracy. The strange case began in 1874, when an assistant district attorney for Washington, DC, Richard Harrington, decided to plant false evidence against a well-known reformer, Columbus Alexander. Alexander had prosecuted a ring of corrupt building contractors. At Harrington's direction, dishonest Secret Service agents broke into the safe of another assistant district attorney using explosives. The plot required the agents to stage the break-in, take materials from the safe, and transport the materials to Alexander. Afterward, authorities would arrest Alexander for accepting stolen documents.

The scheme fell apart when Alexander refused to answer his door or accept any materials from the corrupt agents. In a fruitless effort to rehabilitate the criminal enterprise, the Secret Service agents arrested two other men and persuaded them to sign false affidavits swearing that they had stolen the contents of the safe at Alexander's behest. The supposed thieves later turned state's evidence, leading to Alexander's exoneration in court.

During an investigation into the affair, Babcock's name surfaced as a conspirator in the theft. Although he was acquitted at trial, Babcock's reputation, already poor, suffered. Evidence suggested that the jury had been tampered with, which further suggested that Babcock could not be trusted with public business. Although he was one of Grant's oldest and closest advisers, Babcock had become a political liability. The president dismissed him from the White House, although he appointed Babcock to a lower-profile post. In his new position as chief lighthouse inspector, Babcock drowned at sea while on duty.[10]

If Babcock had been the only unsavory character in the administration, his absence might have solved Grant's problems. Unfortunately for the president, news of criminal rings in the administration seemed endless. The Trading Post Ring involved Secretary of War William Belknap, who accepted bribes to allow a trading post agent to remain on duty at Fort Sill, Oklahoma. In another episode, a House investigative committee discovered that the navy secretary, George M. Robeson, had purchased eighteen home lots in Washington, DC, with $15 million in naval construction appropriations in a crime known as the Naval Ring. In yet another case, Interior Secretary Columbus Delano resigned in disgrace when he was charged with accepting bribes to allow fraudulent land grants.[11]

President Grant knew he had multiple problems that required major reforms. He appointed a former United States senator from Michigan, Zachariah Chandler, to succeed Delano at the Interior Department. Chandler unearthed numerous instances of malfeasance. The department was staffed with fictitious clerks who supposedly earned salaries that unscrupulous administration officials pocketed. Even when real clerks held positions, they often performed little or no work. Chandler discovered similar abuses in the Department of Indian Affairs.

Recognizing the damage that Delano had caused for the administration, Grant had reached the end of his tether. Referring to the employees who had been Delano's supporters, the president believed it was time to clean house. "Have those men dismissed before 3 o'clock this afternoon or shut down the bureau," he instructed Chandler. The new secretary did as he was told. It was a constructive move. A group of "Indian attorneys" had collected fees to represent Native Americans in Washington, DC, but they had performed few services. Chandler banned these agents from appearing before the Department of Indian Affairs.[12]

In the Justice Department, Attorney General George H. Williams had carried out his duties in a reputedly lackadaisical manner. In fact, he was so lax that some critics charged that Williams had accepted bribes to forgo prosecuting pending criminal cases. In one high-profile case involving a merchant house, Pratt & Boyd, that had allowed fraudulent customhouse entries, Williams refused to prosecute the case. Investigating the matter, the Senate Judiciary Committee discovered that the attorney general's wife had received $30,000 from Pratt & Boyd. To add insult to injury, the Williamses had commingled funds, using Justice Department money to pay their household expenses. Mrs. Williams enjoyed the use of an expensive carriage as well as a liveried coachman and a footman. When these facts came to light in 1875, Grant insisted on Williams's resignation.[13]

Aside from the political corruption that overwhelmed the administration, the Panic of 1873 occurred just after the start of Grant's second term. The panic was not Grant's fault, of course, but his mismanagement only heightened the public perception that his administration was not equal to the crises of the time. The panic could be traced to frenetic railroad construction expansion that began as soon as the Civil War ended in 1865. Railroads laid more than thirty-five thousand miles of track between 1866 and 1873. Both the Johnson and the Grant administrations provided generous grants and subsidies to spur economic development. Railroads were good for American business and for citizens, who enjoyed transportation benefits unknown to earlier generations.[14]

Rapid investment in railroad companies created a colossal employer, the largest in the nation outside of the agricultural sector. It seemed that the good times would last forever. Large infrastructure projects can be risky, but virtually everyone believed that the expansion would not end in the foreseeable future. Outside of the railroad industry, ancillary businesses enjoyed benefits as well—docks, factories, steel mills, lumber companies, and suppliers of farm animals, among others. As the years passed, stock prices in railroad companies and attendant businesses rose beyond the underlying value of the companies, creating an artificial bubble.[15]

The bubble created problems for small farmers, who found that banks possessed few funds to lend outside of the railroad industry. Before railroads claimed the available private capital, farmers had used bank loans to purchase seed, equipment, livestock, and day-to-day necessities to finance their operations until their crops were harvested. With a lack of capital, cash-starved small businessmen were squeezed out of the marketplace.[16]

Anxious to move beyond the horrors of the Civil War and promote a robust economy, the federal government accommodated the postwar bonanza by passing a series of laws to create the modern banking system. The first laws required each bank designated as part of the national system to accept each other's notes as legal tender for all public and private debts. Citizens were pleased that the national public policy was geared to something apart from the war and Reconstruction. Policies championing a larger, more robust economy were enormously popular. If the new system triggered inflation, hurt small farmers, or interfered with treaties signed with Native Americans as tribal lands were gobbled up, many Americans were not bothered by the costs of progress. Grant and his advisers were only too happy to tout economic expansion to counterbalance innumerable tales of administration corruption.[17]

Financial concerns dominated the decade. In 1873, Congress passed (and President Grant signed) the Coinage Act, which decreed that the national currency would not be backed with silver and gold. Gold would become the standard. The new law caused a depression in silver prices. Although silver miners and producers made up for their losses by investing abroad, the downturn roiled financial markets and created enormous anxiety.[18]

Administration officials finally turned their attention to the problem of inflation following the unprecedented economic growth of the late 1860s and early 1870s. The administration resolved to contract the money supply. Regrettably, investment capital devoted almost exclusively to infrastructure projects coupled with fewer government notes in circulation left many a company strapped for funding. Jay Cooke & Company, a large investor in railroads, did not accept the possibility that the railroad expansion bubble would burst sooner or later. Cooke had gambled that a second transcontinental railroad would mirror the success of the initial enterprise. He was mistaken. Ignoring warning signs of an impending economic slowdown, Cooke and his investors developed plans to support a new railroad line after ground was broken near Duluth, Minnesota, in 1870. Yet Cooke could not obtain an expected $300 million government loan, and he did not have cash on hand to fund his operations. To the shock and dismay of many market observers, Jay Cooke & Company declared bankruptcy on September 18, 1873.[19]

The collapse of Cooke's company triggered a chain reaction of bank failures throughout the nation's industrial centers. To halt widespread panic, the New York Stock Exchange closed for ten days beginning on September 20, but the damage was done. The United States slipped into a depression as industrial demand declined, and factories laid off workers in droves. The national unemployment rate ticked up to 14 percent. From 1873 until 1875—the period when so many of the Grant administration's failures came to light—89 of the country's 364 railroads declared bankruptcy and eighteen thousand business concerns folded permanently.[20]

Ulysses S. Grant had won the presidency in 1868 because he was a Republican, and Republicans, having successfully put down the rebellion and prosecuted the war, supposedly were virtuous. Grant had never been politically active, nor did he prove to be politically astute. The multiple scandals during his years in office demonstrated his naivete when it came to controlling his subordinates and allies. He simply could not or would not believe that the men he had befriended could be so callous and greedy that they would abuse the public trust. As for the financial meltdown that occurred during the 1870s, it demonstrated how inept Grant was in producing effective policies to lessen the effects of a national economic crisis.

Incredibly, the public understood that Ulysses S. Grant the man was far more trustworthy than his administration. He had generated a vast reservoir of goodwill as the commanding general of Union armed forces in the Civil War. That goodwill allowed him to win a second term and even contemplate running for a third term. Despite the scandals and the depression, Grant enjoyed an enviable level of personal popularity during his heyday. Even after he had been absent from the presidency for a term, Republicans in 1880 debated whether he should be returned to office.[21]

History has not been as forgiving to Grant as his contemporaries were. Despite occasional reappraisals, his reputation has suffered from the scandals and economic problems of the 1870s. Historians generally have ranked him in the bottom quartile of American presidents. Whether any rankings of presidents are valuable assessment tools remains a debatable point, but the hapless Grant probably will be forever tarnished by the corruption and failures that characterized his time in office.[22]

CHAPTER 5

# "Do You Believe This Man Is a Crook? If He Is a Crook, Convict Him."

## THE TEAPOT DOME SCANDAL

The most infamous example of government corruption before the Watergate era was a scandal that occurred during the presidency of Warren G. Harding in the 1920s. Harding had transferred supervision of oil-reserve lands from the United States Navy to the United States Department of the Interior. After the transfer, the president's unscrupulous secretary of the interior, Albert Bacon Fall, leased oil deposits at Elk Hills, California, and Teapot Dome, Wyoming, to petroleum companies in exchange for kickbacks. When the United States Senate investigated the leases, they learned that Fall had received a suspicious loan, among other considerations, from oilmen, including a longtime friend, Edward L. Doheny.[1]

Oil had become a precious commodity early in the twentieth century. The oil industry had grown quickly, eventually supplanting agriculture, railroad, and steel as the engine of American commerce. As with the other industries, oil barons sought any market advantage they could acquire by any available means. It was common in that era to contribute large sums to political candidates in hopes of ensuring that elected officials remembered where the financing had originated when the time came to develop public policy.

Oil was important to commerce because the internal combustion engine ran on the material. The United States Navy, upgraded in the last years of the nineteenth century, was an especially large consumer. By 1912, the navy had converted almost all vessels from coal-burning to oil-burning ships. Consequently, national security depended in large measure on the ability to secure plentiful oil supplies.

Public officials worried that oil supplies were subject to wild price swings and potential shortages. To ensure the availability of necessary supplies, in September 1909, President William Howard Taft issued an executive order withdrawing public lands to use as oil reserves for the United States Navy. In

1912, Taft issued an executive order establishing the Naval Petroleum Reserves. Naval Petroleum Reserve No. 1 at Elk Hills, Kern County, California, consisted of 38,969 acres. Naval Petroleum Reserve No. 2 at Buena Vista Hills, Kern County, California, consisted of 29,341 acres. In 1915, President Wilson created Naval Petroleum Reserve No. 3, consisting of 9,481 acres, at Teapot Dome, Natrona County, Wyoming.[2]

As soon as he came into office during the Wilson administration in 1913, Navy Secretary Josephus Daniels found himself besieged by aggressive oil executives desperate to lease the naval reserves. To handle the requests, Daniels created the Naval Fuel Oil Board in 1916, with Commander H. A. Stuart installed as its head. Daniels and Stuart found the pressure unrelenting as oil lobbyists argued that valuable oil was draining into adjacent field and was being wasted. Oilmen promoted legislation to allow private leases of the public oil fields.[3]

Daniels resisted the pressure thanks to full support from President Woodrow Wilson, but he worried that future administrations might be less resilient. He recalled watching Congress debate the issue, "fearing that some act might be passed that would turn over these invaluable oil reserves to parties who laid claim to them without even decent shadow of title." His fears were justified, as subsequent events demonstrated.[4]

In the 1920 election, many oilmen threw their support behind the Republican nominee, Senator Warren G. Harding of Ohio. On the surface, Harding was an attractive candidate—handsome and barrel chested with a deep, baritone voice and a full head of silver hair. He looked "presidential." His career in the United States Senate had been undistinguished, but he promised a return to "normalcy" at a time when many Americans longed for an end to the upheaval and grim news flowing in from European battlefields during the Great War of 1917 and 1918. Best of all for petroleum producers, Harding was a nonentity, an empty vessel so easygoing and compliant that he could be used for all sorts of purposes.[5]

When Harding won the presidency and stepped into office in March 1921, oil prices were the highest they had been in two decades. Competition among oil producers was fierce—and ruthless. The problem was that capital costs were high, and no guarantees existed that an oil well would produce sufficient yields. Finding the right land, drilling wells, striking oil, tapping the well, and bringing the oil to market were enormous gambles. Fortunes could be earned quickly, but they could be lost just as swiftly. Oil speculators desperately sought a "sure thing" to maximize their return on investment.[6]

Enter Albert Bacon Fall, who soon became Harding's secretary of the interior. Born in Frankfort, Kentucky, on November 26, 1861, Fall received little formal education. As he grew to adulthood, he engaged in a wide range of activities, including cowboy, farmhand, prospector, and miner. He studied law on his own in his spare time. As a young man, Fall headed to the Southwest. He became a member of the New Mexico bar in 1889.[7]

Three years before he joined the bar, Fall met a young man, Edward L. Doheny, in Kingston, New Mexico. Fall's senior by five years, Doheny hailed from Fond du Lac, Wisconsin. Doheny, like Fall, came from a poor family and had tried numerous means of earning a living. He was a fruit picker, mule driver, and waiter. He decided early on that he would set out to make a living searching for precious metals and minerals underground, a quest that led him to Arizona and New Mexico.[8]

The friends parted as Doheny headed off to Los Angeles, California, while Fall settled down in New Mexico, eventually pursuing a political career. During the waning years of the nineteenth century, Fall was a self-professed Democrat, a strong supporter of President Grover Cleveland. Fall's support paid off when Cleveland appointed the self-made lawyer to the Supreme Court of the New Mexico Territory.[9]

Even in those early days, Fall cared little for legal niceties. He was a judge, ostensibly a symbol of law and order as well as a defender of the rule of law, but Fall nonetheless led an extralegal posse to capture a bandit. As word of the episode filtered up to Washington, DC, Cleveland removed him from the judgeship. Despite this episode, he remained a Democrat.[10]

The Spanish-American War erupted in 1898. At the age of thirty-six, Fall was a bit long in the tooth to join the military, but he recognized the political value of military service. He enlisted and became an infantry captain.[11]

When he returned from the war, Fall saw that his political fortunes would improve if he joined the Republican Party. Always willing to set aside principle or ideology in service of self-interest, Fall declared himself an admirer of the Grand Old Party. It was a shrewd move given the conservatism of the territory. When New Mexico became a state, Albert Fall won election to the United States Senate representing his adopted state.[12]

He was a distinctive figure as he prowled the halls of the Senate. He typically dressed in black and sported a large hat. His ever-present cigar jutted from between his teeth. One observer commented, "With a long drooping mustache, he looks like a stage sheriff of the Far West in the movies. His voice is always loud and angry. He has the frontiersman's impatience. From his kind lynch law springs."[13]

Senator Fall was a zealot on matters of law and order. New Mexico shared a border with Mexico, and a revolution south of the border ensured that bandits struck at Americans on occasion. Fall urged President Woodrow Wilson to take an aggressive stance toward Mexicans, even if that meant engaging in armed intervention across the border. The senator had another reason for urging military intervention in Mexico: he had acquired ranch property and was interested in mineral rights, especially oil reserves. Fall saw the value of tapping Mexico's vast petroleum reserves.[14]

Fall detested Woodrow Wilson, and he was relieved that the approaching 1920 election would lead to a new man, ideally a Republican, in the White House. He had a more immediate concern, however. By early 1920, Fall's finances were, to put it mildly, in disarray. He seriously considered resigning from the United States Senate to pursue private sources of capital. He worried that he could not even pay the taxes on ranch land that he owned.[15]

When Fall's friend and fellow senator Warren G. Harding became the Republican presidential nominee and went on to win the general election, the calculation changed. Perhaps Fall could use his contacts to his advantage. Harding wanted Fall in his administration, first considering him as secretary of state. They finally settled on secretary of the interior. Harding initially thought that Fall would be disappointed. Interior was a cabinet position, but it was not as prestigious as the State Department. The incoming president need not have worried. Fall recognized the possibilities inherent in the position.

Secretary Fall decided that he would stay in office for a year. If he could position himself well, he might secure a lucrative position in an oil company based on his track record as a lax interior secretary. Aside from his personal needs, Fall had been outraged by the conservation policies of the Roosevelt, Taft, and Wilson administrations, which sometimes acted to protect public lands. From Fall's perspective, lands were valuable only insofar as they could serve human needs. Removing federal property from private exploitation was a waste of resources and an abuse of political power.[16]

So anxious was he to bring those resources under his control that he lobbied the new navy secretary, Edwin C. Denby, to transfer control of the Naval Petroleum Reserves to the Department of the Interior. Many navy officers were dismayed by the prospect of losing control of the reserves, but President Harding approved the initiative. He believed that centralization of control over all federal lands under the Interior Department was astute management. The president eventually issued an executive order transferring Teapot Dome in Wyoming as well as the Elk Hills and Buena Vista oil fields in California to the Department of the Interior.[17]

Secretary Fall contacted his longtime friend Edward L. Doheny as well as oilmen Jake Hamon; Colonel Robert W. Stewart, chairman of Standard Oil Company of Indiana; and Harry Ford Sinclair, president of the Sinclair Consolidated Oil Corporation. These men were desperate to lease the government's oil fields, and Fall was desperate to accommodate them. The secretary lost no time in negotiating leases with them.[18]

Within six weeks of Harding's executive order, Fall awarded the first lease to Doheny. In an amazing display of chutzpah, Doheny complained that he had paid too much for the lease. To placate his friend, Fall offered him preferential leases on other oil fields. Doheny ended up with leases on the California fields while Harry Sinclair won access to Teapot Dome. Fall assisted his friends in acquiring leases on other federal lands outside of the oil reserves. He even designated portions of Navajo reservation acreage as public lands so that oil companies could drill there as well. Always compliant, President Harding agreed to allow his interior secretary to open public lands in Alaska for development.[19]

Fall was not satisfied with waiting for his rewards after he left government service. He pocketed money for the Teapot Dome contract from Doheny and Sinclair. Considering his dire financial straits, the money saved his ranch and allowed him to improve the property. Back taxes had been strangling Fall, but suddenly he settled with the government for the full amount, which dated back to 1912. Not content to increase his own property values, he bought an adjacent ranch for $100,000, a princely sum for a man who until recently had been a step away from bankruptcy. He also bought a $35,000 hydroelectric plant, a racehorse, and fine cattle. With no source of revenue save his government position, Fall could not account for the large sums of money he was spending. It was a clear case of selling his high office for personal gain.[20]

Fall had hoped to keep the transactions secret, but his suddenly opulent lifestyle raised public questions about the origins of his newfound wealth. Clinton W. Anderson, a New Mexico newspaperman and later a United States senator, learned of Fall's extravagant purchases and inquired of his fellow reporters whether they knew anything about Fall's finances. Anderson worked for the *Albuquerque Journal*, and he brought his suspicions to the owner, Carl Magee. Intrigued, Magee published stories about the suspicious transactions as well as the Teapot Dome lease.[21]

Incensed that his secrets were spilling into a public arena, Albert Fall, who once had co-owned the *Albuquerque Journal*, charged into the newsroom one day. "Who is the son of a bitch who is writing these lies about me?" he bellowed. A tall, imposing man, Anderson rose and confronted the senator.

"I'm the son of a bitch," he said, "and I don't write lies." Fall wisely scampered out of the office.[22]

April 1922 proved to be a turning point. That month, independent oil operators in Wyoming, acting through their trade association, Rocky Mountain Oil and Gas Products, telegraphed their United States senator, John B. Kendrick, complaining about the lease to Sinclair without competitive bids. Kendrick contacted the Department of the Interior, but he could not get answers to his questions. On April 15, the senator introduced a resolution in the Senate requesting that the secretary of the interior and the secretary of the navy address the issue. Specifically, the secretaries were required to disclose the nature of the Teapot Dome contract, the terms and conditions of any and all agreements, and whether competitive bids had been entertained. In the wake of this resolution, which passed the Senate, other members of Congress intervened.[23]

Wisconsin's progressive champion, Robert M. La Follette Sr., was arguably the most effective of the senators who took an interest in Teapot Dome. "Fighting Bob" had established a reputation as a feisty, politically liberal reformer, a man who relished a legislative fight without flinching. As soon as he learned of the lease, La Follette introduced a resolution of his own. Standing on the floor of the Senate, he argued that his fellow senators must pass the resolution, or they would be complicit in the scheme. According to La Follette, the Department of the Interior was the "sluice-way for ninety percent of the corruption in government." Under Fall's leadership, the department was "befouled with corruption." Even in his dotage, as he was in the 1920s, La Follette retained a modicum of his legendary oratorical prowess. He convinced the Senate to pass his resolution unanimously on April 29, 1922.[24]

The Committee on Public Lands and Surveys was tasked with leading the investigation. Despite the initial outrage over the sweetheart leases for Fall's favored oilmen, Republican senators feared what a detailed investigation might reveal. Chairman Reed Smoot of Utah dragged his feet. The committee did not begin its investigation in earnest until October 1923, seven months after Fall had resigned from office and two months after President Harding's unexpected death in August.[25]

If Smoot hoped to launch a perfunctory investigation with little due diligence, he was sorely disappointed. Montana's Democratic senator, Thomas J. Walsh, hated Albert B. Fall, and he was determined that the interior secretary would not escape justice. A true believer in elected officials as sentinels of the public trust, Walsh had spent much of his career combating corruption. He viewed the Teapot Dome shenanigans as unprecedented malfeasance on a grand scale.[26]

In response to La Follette's resolution, the Interior Department sent over a mountain of documents. The page count was daunting. If Fall and his cronies hoped to overwhelm their opponents with reams of paperwork, they had misjudged Walsh. An indefatigable worker, the Montana senator spent the summer of 1923 sifting through voluminous documents for evidence. He believed he had found what he needed to prosecute Fall and his confederates.[27]

Public hearings commenced on Monday, October 23, 1923. Fall was the first witness, followed by Navy Secretary Denby, Harry Sinclair, and Edward Doheny. The former interior secretary took the stand in a cavernous caucus room in the Senate Office Building. Anticipating the possibility of lively, acrimonious testimony, reporters crowded into the room to observe Senator Walsh spar with the first witness. By this time, details of the Teapot Dome transactions were filtering into the press, and it seemed likely that Fall and his associates would be bludgeoned by the weight of the evidence.[28]

Albert Fall was not as healthy and robust as he had been during his tenure at the Interior Department, but old age had not softened him. He appeared at the hearing with his characteristic arrogance and superior attitude wholly intact. Anyone who thought he might be chastened by his recent bad press would have been surprised to see how acerbically he responded to Walsh's patient, persistent questioning.

Fall insisted that he had never broken the law. He was a conscientious administrator doing his best to implement President Harding's policies, and he resented any suggestion that he had enriched himself at the public expense. At times evasive, loquacious, and audacious, he stared at Walsh with his piercing blue eyes as though examining an inferior creature and finding it seriously deficient.

Walsh pressed the former secretary on why he had leased the Teapot Dome oil fields without calling for competitive bids. Fall defended the practice, arguing that Sinclair's bid was the best offer the government could have received. Relying on his own superior business acumen, Fall resolved to do business with Sinclair because it was in the best interests of the public.[29]

In Fall's view, the murky world of oil leases and the government's business had not been sufficiently regulated by Congress. Accordingly, a cabinet secretary was justified in stepping into the breach and using his own judgment. "The Congress of the United States has very little to do with this whole proposition," Fall asserted. "We took the responsibility, and I am very proud of the contract."[30]

Throughout his testimony, Fall cloaked his behavior in patriotism. He acted in secrecy without competitive bidding and without alerting Congress because he valued military security above all else. To hear him tell it, Secretary Fall was above reproach, and the congressional hearings were a sham. Try as he might, Walsh could not dissuade the witness from advancing his fanciful narrative. Observers who hoped to glimpse even a modicum of remorse from Albert Fall came away from his performance with little to show for their faith.[31]

A large, balding man, Secretary Denby demonstrated none of Albert Fall's unbridled arrogance or preening overconfidence. He took the stand on October 25, and it was immediately obvious that Denby was, at best, inattentive or, at worst, criminally negligent in performing his duties. Unlike his predecessor, Josephus Daniels, Secretary Denby possessed neither the character nor the intestinal fortitude to withstand Secretary Fall's relentless push to transfer the Naval Petroleum Reserves from navy to interior. When pressed, Denby said he had never met Harry Sinclair and knew little or nothing of the details surrounding the Teapot Dome lease. He left the impression that he was naive and in over his head, but he was not guilty of deliberate criminal conduct. Edwin Denby, despite his imposing physical stature, left the stand with a public reputation as an irrepressibly small man.[32]

Harry Sinclair appeared on October 29, but he shed little light on events at Teapot Dome. He said that he had entertained Harding cabinet members at social functions and had contributed money to Republican Party coffers but denied any wrongdoing. He also had friends in the Democratic Party, he said.[33]

When geologists and other experts testified in subsequent days, the crowds disappeared. For a time, Teapot Dome dropped from the headlines, especially after the committee recessed for a month. Proceedings recommenced on November 30, 1923.[34]

Sixty-seven-year-old Edward Doheny testified on December 3. He and Thomas Walsh were longtime friends, and they had been close in earlier years. Nonetheless, Walsh served notice that he had a job to do, and he would not allow personal considerations to intrude.

Doheny told committee members that oil had been lost in the naval reserves owing to drainage, and his deal benefited the government because it helped recoup those losses. The oilmen, according to this perspective, had saved the public $1 million. They were generous patriots doing their duty to assist the United States government in solving a seemingly intractable problem. According to Doheny, the oil barons deserved approbation, not opprobrium. Senator Smoot had been aggravated by Walsh's questions about Harry Sinclair's campaign contributions to the Republican Party. Smoot intervened to ask whether Doheny, a well-known Democrat, had contributed money to his favored group. Yes, Doheny had contributed money, perhaps as much as $75,000 to assist the Democrats in bridging their 1920 campaign deficit. To level the playing field, he had given $25,000 to Republicans as well.

Walsh was having none of this obvious chicanery. He attacked the witness without restraint. During an especially heated exchange, an exasperated Doheny erupted. "I do not want you to ask me to assume anything that is against my interest, and your questions are not going to make me do it," he exclaimed. "I claim my lease was made in the interest of the United States government, of which you are a senator and I am a citizen. You cannot get me to admit that it is a bad lease, because I certainly do not think it is."[35]

Walsh would not stop his relentless, pointed examination. He pressed the witness and eventually coaxed out important details. Doheny had received preferential treatment. Doheny repeatedly insisted that he had aided the navy by drilling wells to capture oil that was draining away, but Walsh showed that the damage could have been mitigated if Doheny had alerted the navy to the drainage problem. The witness had said nothing to naval officers because it was to his advantage to stay quiet.

Committee members understandably posed numerous questions about Doheny's relationship with Secretary Fall. Doheny admitted that the two men had known each other since 1886, but Doheny had never employed his friend except as an unpaid adviser. Upset about the damage to his friend's reputation, Doheny said that Fall was an honorable man. Although he had never employed Albert Fall, "I want to say right here, though, that I would be very glad to take Mr. Fall in my employ if he ever wanted to come to us."[36]

During a second interrogation before the committee on January 24, 1924, Doheny pledged to be more forthcoming than he had been in December. Thomas Walsh and the committee had heard testimony from minor figures in the scandal about the details of the oil leases, and the facts had undermined the principals' credibility. Reading a prepared statement, Doheny confessed regret at not having been completely transparent in December. Nonetheless, he insisted that Secretary Fall had not directly or indirectly profited from the leases. As for a $100,000 "loan" to help Fall improve his ranch and other properties in New Mexico, that transaction did not amount to an illegal quid pro quo related to the oil leases.

Walsh knew his man, and he went to work on Doheny. It was curious that Doheny delivered this supposedly aboveboard "loan" in a black satchel with his son, Edward L. Doheny Jr., as the messenger. The witness acted as if this was standard operating procedure, observing that he had transacted business in this manner on numerous occasions during the past five years. That statement did not enhance Doheny's credibility.

His answers continually strained credulity. Doheny insisted that the $100,000 delivered to the interior secretary at a time when the man was desperate for money and was also deciding whether to lease oil reserves to private businessmen had no effect on his choice. According to the oil magnate, "Senator Fall, in my opinion, was not influenced in any way by this loan, because the negotiations were carried on by men who were not under his control." All defendants in the Teapot Dome cases eventually used this defense—namely, the negotiators did not directly report to Secretary Fall—but it was not persuasive owing to the clear pattern of widespread corruption.[37]

During a third appearance on the stand, Doheny produced what he said was a copy of the promissory note guaranteeing that Fall would repay the loan. The signature line had been torn from the page. The slippery witness explained that he could find no record of the note in his books. Perhaps the loan had come from Doheny's son's bank account. In short, the entire transaction was suspect, leading committee members to conclude that the "loan" was a bribe. Doheny also revealed that he had conducted business with influential members of both parties. Although those transactions did not involve bribery, any public association with Edward Doheny was now a serious detriment to an elected official's political career.[38]

When Albert Fall returned to testify on February 2, 1924, he looked ill, leaning heavily on a cane. In fact, he had tried to avoid testifying altogether, citing his poor health. Unimpressed with his excuse, the committee issued a subpoena. Fall began by reading a statement prepared by his lawyer declining to answer questions because the committee did not have the authority to investigate his actions. Fall contended that the Senate had discharged the committee after committee members recommended to the president that he cancel the oil leases. Fall also "pled the Fifth," stating that he would not answer questions because litigation was pending, and his responses "may tend to incriminate me."[39]

After Fall left the room, committee members debated whether he should be held in contempt of Congress. No one believed that the committee lacked jurisdiction. Nonetheless, the Fifth Amendment claim complicated matters. Members wondered whether he might be impeached retroactively as interior secretary. He had already resigned his office, but his departure might be modified to clarify that he had not left on his own volition. Eventually, the committee chose to allow the courts to determine Fall's fate.[40]

Litigation involving the oil leases stretched across the 1920s. As the facts emerged, it was clear that Fall had spent a total of $140,000 improving his New Mexico property at a time when he earned approximately $12,000 a year. His accounts held $230,500 in Liberty Bonds that bore the serial numbers of bonds earlier provided to Harry Sinclair as well as to Colonel Robert W. Stewart, chairman of Standard Oil Company of Indiana.[41]

Government lawyers initiated civil suits to cancel the leases with Doheny and Sinclair. They won the suit against Doheny but lost against Sinclair. On appeal, Doheny persuaded the appellate court to overturn the lower court judgment.[42]

The criminal cases against Fall and Doheny for conspiracy to defraud the government contained much drama. In the first set of proceedings in November 1926, the prosecution and the defense presented competing narratives, as frequently occurs in criminal cases. Prosecutors argued that the $100,000 "loan" Doheny had given to Fall was a payment for services rendered—leasing the oil reserves to Doheny—and was not intended to be a bribe. The prosecution narrative suggested that the naive and careless navy secretary, Edwin Denby, was unwittingly duped by the insidious villains of the set piece, Albert Fall and Edward Doheny.[43]

Doheny had hired a prominent lawyer, Frank J. Hogan, cofounder of the celebrated Hogan & Hartson law firm, to represent his interests. A consummate courtroom advocate, Hogan once quipped that "the best client is a rich man who is scared." He had exactly that type of client in this case.[44]

As Doheny well knew, Hogan was an inspired choice. The lawyer excelled at the histrionic style of oratory that was in style at the time. Standing before the jury, Hogan painted a portrait of Edward Doheny as a rugged, self-made man, an individualist who was above reproach and who would never consciously disobey the law. During his five-hour summation before the jury, Hogan thundered, "Do you think that a man who left his home at the age of sixteen and followed the trails of the pioneer West, who dug in mother earth for the minerals hidden therein, who with pick and shovel sunk wells that he might bring out the gold and the liquid that today mean safety for the world, would, even if he himself could, stoop so low as to bribe an official of his government, the friend of his youth and his former days, would, if he could, stoop so low as to bribe a Cabinet officer of the United States of America in order that he might swindle and cheat the land that had given him plenty?"[45]

The answer might have been "yes, he would stoop that low," but Hogan was determined to rehabilitate his client's good name. His narrative would allow for no criticism of the upstanding oilman Edward Doheny. While he was at it, he compared Doheny's crucifixion to Christ's crucifixion. He also defended the late, great Warren G. Harding "as fine-hearted a President as we have ever had, or ever will have." Hogan confessed, "how I wish I had the strength to break in twain the traducers of Harding's name! While I live I will defend him, despite all the character assassins that attempt to invade the sanctity of his tomb and tear the shroud from his dead body."[46]

He had good reason to build up Harding's reputation. Summoning Harding's spirit from "his sacred tomb in Marion, Ohio," he produced a letter written by the late president indicating that he approved of the oil leases: "I stand his splendid figure before twelve of his fellow men, and from his resting place I quote his words." Hogan read the letter, which he said completely exonerated his client because the dead president "stands here today as the best silent witness in this case."[47]

The next day it was Albert Fall's turn. His lawyer, Mark Thompson of New Mexico, launched into a paean to womanhood, describing Fall's wife as a "daughter of the matrons of Sparta and Rome" as well as a "mother of the West, who in the sunset of life had taken her place by the side of her husband and refused to believe he was or could be guilty of the great crime the government alleges he committed." As for Albert Fall, he was a fine man of sterling character. The money that Doheny had given to Fall was "the cleanest money that ever passed from the hands of one man to another."[48]

Thompson admitted that Fall originally lied about the source of the money, but his motives were hardly as nefarious as the prosecutors had charged. As a loyal friend, the secretary sought to protect Doheny from extreme embarrassment because Doheny could not find the note with the signatures attached.

"Lie?" Thompson asked. "Of course, he lied, and every red-blooded man in New Mexico is proud of him for it." In any case, the transaction was merely a private matter between two friends and wholly unrelated to government business. Consequently, the Senate committee investigating the oil leases had no right or jurisdiction to question either man on the matter.[49]

The next day, the jury acquitted both men. The lawyers had done their jobs. It was a joyous occasion for the defendants, but the travails had not ended. In March 1927, after a one-day trial, a jury convicted Harry Sinclair of contempt of the Senate for refusing to answer ten questions related to Sinclair's transactions involving the oil fields. Relying on the grounds that the committee had no jurisdiction over him, Sinclair and his lawyers argued that the case should be dismissed. The judges disagreed. After they denied Sinclair's challenge to the Senate's jurisdiction, it was a simple case. Prosecutors only had to demonstrate that the Senate committee had summoned Sinclair, he had appeared, and he had refused to answer the senators' questions.[50]

The jury deliberated for eight hours. After the jurors convicted Sinclair, the judge sentenced him to serve three months in jail and pay a $500 fine. It was the first Senate contempt trial since Elverton R. Chapman, a New York broker, was jailed for a month and fined $100 in 1895. Sinclair appealed to the United States Supreme Court but eventually lost. Having avoided his sentence for as long as possible, he reported to the Washington Asylum and Jail on May 6, 1929.[51]

Next came a trial for defrauding the government in the Teapot Dome lease. Albert Fall and Harry Sinclair were the defendants in this proceeding. Anxious to avoid another conviction, Sinclair hired detectives from the William J. Burns agency to follow members of the jury. One juror bragged that he could earn between $150,000 and $200,000 to deadlock the jury. When Judge Frederick L. Siddons learned of the tampering, he declared a mistrial. Incensed, he placed Sinclair, his export official Henry Mason, William J. Burns, and Sherman Burns on trial for criminal contempt. Each man was convicted. Although the United States Supreme Court later reversed William J. Burns's conviction, the other defendants lost their appeals.[52]

Harry Sinclair eventually served seven and a half months for his two convictions. He left prison on November 21, 1929. Far from repentant, he told reporters that "I was railroaded to jail in violation of common sense and common fairness." Remarking on his lack of contrition, Sinclair was defiant: "I cannot be contrite for sins which I know I have never committed, nor can I pretend to be ashamed of conduct which I know to have been upright. The precedents set in my case are against the interest of the American people. If politics can railroad me to jail, it can railroad others."[53]

Despite his bitterness over the two trials where he was convicted, Sinclair enjoyed good news in other proceedings. In a fourth trial for fraud, which took place in April 1928, Albert Fall was excused owing to illness. He was said to be at death's door. Harry Sinclair's trial for fraud was brief. After deliberating for an hour and fifty-six minutes, the jury acquitted Sinclair, to widespread astonishment. Nebraska's Progressive United States senator, Republican George W. Norris, spoke for many outraged legislators. "Why, everybody in the United States and even the Supreme Court knows he is guilty. The whole transaction has been held to be fraudulent and it could not have been fraudulent except for Sinclair." The senator, disgusted, lapsed into sarcasm: "He has too much money to be convicted. We ought to pass a law now to the effect that no man worth a hundred million dollars should ever be tried for any crime. That would make us at least consistent."[54]

In May 1928, Colonel Robert W. Stewart stood trial for contempt of the Senate. He had lied to the committee previously, but he insisted that he was an honest man. The jury rewarded him with an acquittal. Because Stewart had perjured himself, prosecutors brought another case against him. Jurors acquitted him on those charges as well.[55]

The final legal proceedings of the Teapot Dome era occurred late in 1929 and early in 1930. First up was Albert Fall's trial for accepting a bribe from Edward Doheny. Fall was in poor shape by this time. Frail and sickly, he walked, when he walked at all, with the aid of a cane but spent much of his time nestled in a wheelchair. Earlier in the year, a sheriff's sale of his seven-hundred-thousand-acre ranch in New Mexico fetched $168,250 from none other than Doheny.[56]

Fall had hired Doheny's attorney, Frank J. Hogan, to join his original attorney, Mark P. Thompson, in his defense. Part of their strategy was to portray Fall as too sick to spend time in prison. As if to illustrate this thesis, Fall collapsed during Hogan's opening statement. Despite the prosecutors' suggestions that the proceedings be postponed, Fall dramatically insisted that the trial must continue. In Hogan's words, Fall felt that he deserved "vindication before he passes to the Great Beyond."[57]

Wallowing in pathos, the defense made a great show of Fall's deteriorating health. To ensure that the jury would not be overly influenced by the sight of this broken man shuffling into court each day, prosecutors asked (and the judge agreed) that Fall's entrances and exits be timed so the jury was never present. Nonetheless, defense attorneys arranged it so that Fall was covered with a blanket as he sat in either his wheelchair or another chair brought in especially for his comfort. Members of his family solicitously attended to the old man. On the day that Hogan stood to deliver his summation, Fall's adoring granddaughter looked on from the comforting arms of her grandmother. The scene was courtroom theater at its finest.

**Pictured from left to right, former secretary of the interior Albert B. Fall and oil magnate Edward Doheny, accompanied by lawyers Frank J. Hogan and Mark B. Thompson, arrive at the courthouse for the defendants' arraignment on October 2, 1929. (*Library of Congress*)**

It was the standard tale, by now familiar to anyone who had followed the legal proceedings. The prosecution carefully, methodically presented the case. Fall had accepted a bribe in exchange for oil leases of government land. Special counsel Owen J. Roberts, later appointed to the United States Supreme Court, argued that although the details were labyrinthine, the case was conceptually simple. "There are four things of a controlling nature for you to remember," he told the jurors. "One is that Doheny wanted the lease of Elk Hills. The second is, Fall wanted money. The third is, Doheny got the lease, and the fourth is, Fall got the money." As for the claim that oil had been lost in the naval reserves because of excessive drainage, Roberts rejected the idea. "The only drainage in this case was from Doheny's to Fall's pocket," he said.[58]

Fall's lawyers knew they could not argue the facts. Their only recourse was to offer an emotional appeal. Hogan and Thompson took to the task with gusto, frequently mentioning patriotism and pathos. To hear them tell it, Albert Fall was a great American hero who should never have been tried for his courageous actions as secretary of the interior. Edward Doheny was an upstanding business-man who would never break the law or compromise his friend's position inside the government. Mark Thompson tried to paint a portrait of two dear friends—Fall and Doheny—who met "on the deserts of the Southwest" when one "was a red-haired young man, the other a black-haired young fellow from Kentucky."[59]

The jury deliberated for more than eleven hours before calling it a night. The next day, the jurors announced a guilty verdict. Fall slumped in his chair while his wife and daughter broke into sobs. His lawyer Mark Thompson fainted and had to be revived with a heart stimulant. "That damned court," Edward Doheny muttered.[60]

Judge William Hitz sentenced Fall to serve a year in jail and pay a $100,000 fine. The judge said he would have sentenced the defendant to the maximum sentence allowed by law—three years of confinement and a $300,000 fine—but for Fall's frail physical condition.[61]

In a public statement, Fall insisted that he was innocent. "My borrowing the money may have been unethical," he conceded. "I certainly did not realize it at the time, and my employing a falsehood to prevent a volcano of political abuse pouring upon the administration that had honored me deserves condemnation; but neither one nor the other justified the charge that I was disloyal or dishonest as Secretary of the Interior and as a member of President Harding's Cabinet."[62]

On March 12, 1930, Edward Doheny went on trial for bribing Albert Fall in the same court that had handled Fall's case the previous October. Doheny's attorney, Frank Hogan, also pursued the same strategy of eliciting an emotional plea for leniency from the jurors. Doheny's wife took the stand, as did Doheny himself. At seventy-three years of age, bent, stooped over, and white haired, Doheny did not appear to be the demon the prosecutors had said he was. He told the story of his life, including one new tale. He recalled the time when he fell down a mine shaft and broke both legs. His friend Albert Fall loaned Doheny lawbooks so that Doheny could study for the bar examination while he recuperated. The anecdote proved nothing, but it may have been a subtle way of saying that when a fellow lends you his books in 1886, you can legitimately provide him with $100,000 in cash thirty-five years later.[63]

Hogan led his client through the ups and downs of the man's life. Doheny choked up when he mentioned his son, Edward L. Doheny Jr., who had been shot and killed by his own secretary in February 1929. After a five-minute recess to collect his thoughts, Doheny held forth on the importance of the storage tanks for the United States Navy. He portrayed himself as a patriot for his will-ingness to help finance and build the storage tanks.[64]

Special counsel Owen J. Roberts lost no time in laying out the prosecution's case in his closing statement. Yes, Roberts admitted, Doheny had helped build the storage tanks, but he did it with the expectation that he would receive profitable oil leases. He did not act because he was a patriot. He acted to maximize his own self-interest. The $100,000 transaction was a bribe, and nothing more. "The crime in this case strikes at the very heart of government," Roberts told the jury.[65]

Hogan was at his melodramatic best in delivering his summation. "Do you believe this man is a crook?" he asked. "If he is a crook, convict him. But can you believe that his mind was so corrupt that he conceived bribery and that he had fallen so low that he selected his own son, whom a few years before he had given to the Navy, as the instrument of his bribery?" According to Hogan, "It isn't human to believe it!"[66]

The jury deliberated for an hour before announcing that Doheny was not guilty. It was ironic, of course, that Albert Fall was convicted of accepting a bribe while Edward Doheny was acquitted of providing it. Such were the vagaries of the justice system. Facing the press after the verdict, Doheny noted the strange result: "I am only sorry that the same verdict might not have gone to my friend, Mr. Fall, who deserved it as much as I do."[67]

Fall repeatedly appealed his conviction, but to no avail. Several petitions for clemency went to Herbert Hoover, but the president refused to intercede. Having exhausted his options, Albert Fall climbed into an ambulance on July 18, 1931, and rode to his temporary prison home in Santa Fe, New Mexico. He became the first, but by no means the last, cabinet official in American history to serve a prison term owing to misdeeds that occurred while he was in office. He sought parole, unsuccessfully, in November 1931, but he was released the following May. His $100,000 fine was never paid. He died twelve years after his release, on November 30, 1944, at the age of eighty-three.[68]

Edward L. Doheny spent his twilight years battling stockholders' suits and civil suits initiated by the United States government. After he died at the age of seventy-nine on September 8, 1935, twelve hundred people crowded into St. Vincent's Cathedral in Los Angeles, which he had built for the Roman Catholic Church, to bid him farewell. He died a rich man, with assets in the range of $100 million (or $1.45 billion in 2019).[69]

With the cancellation of the Teapot Dome lease, the United States Navy recovered $12 million from Harry Sinclair. The Doheny lease also was canceled, bringing back $35 million into the government's coffers. The Teapot Dome oil field was left idle for almost a half century before production recommenced in 1976. The United States Department of Energy sold the oil field for $45 million in February 2015.[70]

One legacy of the Teapot Dome scandal was a United States Supreme Court opinion, *McGrain v. Daugherty* (1927), holding that Congress could compel witnesses' testimony. Several defendants had refused to testify before the Senate committee investigating the oil leases owing to a lack of jurisdiction. The high court laid the matter to rest, deciding that each chamber of Congress has the power to compel a private individual to appear before it or one of its committees and provide testimony needed to enable Congress to exercise a legislative function under the United States Constitution.[71]

Perhaps the most enduring legacy was the indelible image of political corruption created by Teapot Dome. From the 1920s until the 1970s, when the Watergate cover-up eclipsed it in the national lexicon, the term "Teapot Dome" became a well-known shorthand designation for malfeasance by public officials. Warren G. Harding had been a beloved president when he died in August 1923, but within a few years his name became synonymous with a weak president who allowed his friends to run roughshod over him as they cashed in on government service. Harding was reputed to have said, "In this job, I'm not worried about my enemies. It's my friends, my Goddamned friends, who are keeping me awake nights." Thanks to men such as Albert B. Fall and Edward L. Doheny, the Harding administration and Teapot Dome were reminders that a government is only as virtuous and devoted to public service as the people who occupy its offices and do business with its agencies.[72]

# "I Am the Only Candidate Inspected by the United States Government and Found to Be 100 Percent Pure."

## WILLIAM "WILD BILL" LANGER

William "Wild Bill" Langer was a larger-than-life character. First elected governor of North Dakota in 1932, Langer developed a reputation as a heavy-handed political operative, a man unafraid of ruffling feathers and engaging in mischief. He became embroiled in a major controversy when he required state employees to contribute funds to a weekly newspaper friendly to his gubernatorial administration. This practice was not unheard of in North Dakota at the time, but Langer ran afoul of federal law when he extended the requirement to highway department employees. Because those employees were paid through federal relief programs, Langer was charged with engaging in a criminal conspiracy to defraud the United States government.

Two of Langer's strongest political opponents prosecuted the case, and, not surprisingly, the governor and five coconspirators were convicted. Owing to the felony conviction, the North Dakota Supreme Court ordered that Langer be removed from office and Lieutenant Governor Ole H. Olson be sworn in as his replacement. Defiant in the face of the court order, Langer refused to leave office. Instead, he barricaded himself in his office, declared martial law, and proclaimed the state of North Dakota an independent political entity. He said he would not surrender until the state supreme court met with him. In time, he reluctantly acceded to the court order and vacated the governor's office.

Langer's conviction was overturned on appeal. He was retried twice and even faced another trial for allegedly committing perjury in a motion he filed to ask the original trial judge to recuse himself in the future. After the litigation ended, Langer ran for governor again and, incredibly, won reelection.

Langer ran for the United States Senate in 1938 but lost. Two years later, he campaigned for North Dakota's other Senate seat and won with a plurality of 38 percent of the vote against two other candidates. When he came to Washington, DC, however, the Senate was concerned about his felony conviction. He was seated conditionally while his fellow senators investigated. The Committee on Privileges and Elections determined that he was guilty of "moral turpitude" and concluded that Langer was unqualified to be a United States senator. The full Senate declined to follow the committee's recommendation, however.[1]

The so-called "Dakota Maverick" became a colorful figure in his state's history, but, as with many political leaders, his early years were inauspicious. German immigrants Frank Langer and Mary (Weber) Langer came to Minnesota before settling in Casselton, Dakota Territory, twenty miles west of Fargo. According to the 1880 census, the town sported a population of 361 souls. There, on September 30, 1886, their son William (Bill) was born in the Everest Township.[2]

Frank Langer was a prominent businessman and farmer who owned large tracts of land, operated a general store, served as a bank director, and became the principal shareholder in North Dakota's largest fire and hail insurance company. His activities were so extensive that the elder Langer depended on family members to assist in his operations. This situation required a young man like Bill to grow up quickly. At ten years of age, Bill Langer headed into town at his father's direction to recruit workers. At fifteen, Bill was hired out to a neighbor and served as the foreman on a work crew.

In addition to enjoying his family's wealth, Bill Langer lived a charmed life. He was a gifted athlete, playing center on his high school football team. The team won its final game by a score of 86–0. Although he was only an average student, young Bill Langer demonstrated the traits of a successful politician at an early age. He participated in high school oratory for the school's literary society. A classmate recalled that he was the best extemporaneous speaker she had ever heard. Langer also served as class president his senior year.

He decided that a career in law suited him well. In that era, an ambitious young man could attend law school without first earning a bachelor's degree from a college or university. In 1904, at age seventeen, Langer enrolled in the University of North Dakota Law School. It was a two-year program. When Langer arrived on the campus, the university had five hundred students, ninety-one of whom were enrolled in the law school. He graduated at nineteen and passed the state bar examination.

North Dakota required lawyers to be at least twenty-one years old before they practiced law. Because he was too young, Langer resolved to use his time wisely. He traveled to New York City and studied at Columbia University, graduating in 1910 with degrees in liberal arts and law. Unlike his earlier academic record, Langer's achievements at Columbia were impressive. He was senior class president, valedictorian, and voted "most likely to succeed."[3]

While he was enrolled at Columbia, Langer met the woman who would become his wife. Lydia Cady was the daughter of a New York City architect.

He supposedly saw her and announced, "That's the girl I am going to marry." Unaware of the prognostication, Lydia attended a concert with an escort. The escort was asked to step out from the concert and accept a telephone call, and Langer moved in. He had arranged the call so that he could sit beside Lydia and speak with her. It was the beginning of a seven-year courtship that eventually led to marriage.[4]

Langer might have remained in New York—he had an employment offer from Grover Cleveland's law firm—but he returned to North Dakota to launch his legal career. He accepted a position in Mandan, across the river from the state capital, Bismarck, with H. R. Bitzing, state attorney in Morton County. Not long after he started his job, the Morton County commissioners appointed him an assistant state's attorney. His political career had begun.[5]

He became a progressive in the mold of Theodore Roosevelt and Wisconsin's Robert M. La Follette Sr., joining the Young Progressive Republican League. His platform was to argue against economic monopolies and special privileges for rich elites. When Bitzing decided to run for the state senate and announced that he would not seek reelection as Morton County's state attorney, Langer threw his hat into the ring.[6]

Although he worked with Bitzing and might have been the heir apparent, Langer could not guarantee success in the race. To attract votes, he engaged in a hands-on campaign, demonstrating an affinity for retail politics. He genuinely enjoyed meeting constituents and displayed an indefatigable work ethic. Two days before the election, he was injured in a serious car accident. After spending the night in a hospital, Langer was back on the campaign trail the next day.[7]

When the votes were tabulated, he had won the Republican primary election. Because Morton County was predominantly Republican, Langer's primary victory normally would have been tantamount to capturing the seat. Establishment Republicans feared that the up-and-coming progressive was too liberal for their tastes, however, and they threw their support to the Democratic candidate. Facing strong headwinds, Langer tirelessly hit the road, visiting as many potential voters as possible. His remarkable ability to remember names and faces as well as his natural conviviality helped him win the election. He was twenty-eight years old.[8]

During the next two years, establishment Republicans in Morton County saw their worst nightmares come true. Langer received statewide attention for his progressive agenda. Prohibition was the law in North Dakota, and Langer demonstrated his zeal for enforcing the law. He also urged that taxes be increased on the Northern Pacific Railroad, and he pursued litigation against the company. A strong proponent of education, Langer enforced compulsory school-attendance laws.[9]

The ambitious young attorney set his sights on higher office. By 1916, Langer was prepared to run for the North Dakota attorney general's position. As he geared up for the contest, Langer sought and received an endorsement from the Nonpartisan League (NPL). Many organizations in American political life are labeled "radical," but the NPL was one of the few that lived up to the appellation. A political movement dedicated to assisting farmers, the league espoused openly socialist ideas, such as state control of banks, slaughterhouses, mills, and grain elevators. For a brief time in 1919, the NPL controlled all North Dakota's branches of government.[10]

With the NPL's help, Langer won the attorney general post in 1916. Always an excitable figure—he earned his nickname "Wild Bill" for his exuberance—he came into office determined to make a name for himself. He succeeded. A lifelong teetotaler, the new attorney general promised to enforce Prohibition laws vigorously. He had once commented that the warden at a North Dakota penitentiary "tells me that at least ninety percent of the fellows out there got there through liquor. I believe special stress should be placed on enforcement of the prohibition laws."[11]

One order of business was to clean up the town of Minot. Langer was a hands-on elected official. He dispatched fifty detectives into the town disguised as laborers, but he also went into the field with them. He lived in the town undetected for three weeks. As a result of a series of raids, Langer's men arrested 156 people, some of them prominent citizens. Langer later indicated that 153 of the defendants were convicted. To ensure that the first people arrested would not alert others, Langer's detectives cut the town's telephone lines.[12]

Langer turned his attention to Grand Forks after Minot. Deputized as a United States marshal, he, along with his men, raided a brewery in Grand Forks for engaging in illegal liquor sales. The brewery never reopened.[13]

Although Langer had numerous supporters, his detractors howled that he was overzealous in enforcing the state's blue laws. He was unapologetic. The attorney general was unafraid to prosecute powerful parties. He even turned on his friends, including the NPL. Langer agreed with the league's goals for government, but he was disturbed by the group's expansion into private businesses. In 1919, the year after he was reelected as attorney general, Langer publicly broke with the NPL.[14]

He longed to move into the governor's mansion. On March 23, 1920, Langer announced the start of his campaign. Downplaying his personal ambition, he insisted that he was answering a clarion call. "Influenced by the petitions of more than 20,000 citizens of the state," he said, "I accede to their wishes, and I will become a Progressive Republican candidate for governor."[15]

Fellow Republican Lynn Frazier was the NPL choice, and he was a formidable candidate. Despite the challenges of running against such a strong foe,

Langer was undaunted as he continued his attack on the league: "I would rather be the most humble practitioner of law in the state of North Dakota than be attorney general or governor in this state and be subject to the domination of an over-lord."[16]

As usual, Langer threw himself into the campaign, traveling widely—some twenty-five thousand miles between March and June, delivering seventy speeches to fifty thousand people—and drawing enthusiastic audiences. His well-honed oratorical skills and love of voters served him well. Yet he had made too many enemies among the NPL and its allies. For all his advantages as a candidate, Langer lost the primary—which, in effect, was the election for the officeholder—by approximately fifty-four hundred votes.[17]

He remained attorney general until the end of his term on January 3, 1921, but he was at a crossroads in his career. When his term ended, he no longer held high office. He had lost an election for the first time, and he had made bitter enemies within the still-powerful NPL. At the same time, Langer enjoyed widespread name recognition across the state, he had become a skilled campaigner and elected official, and he was a relatively young man. He understood intuitively that he might yet become governor, but he needed an image makeover.[18]

First, he had to recast himself as a populist. Langer entered private law practice and set out to distinguish himself in the courtroom. His efforts paid handsome dividends. The firm soon became one of the most successful law practices in the state. Out of sight did not necessarily mean out of mind. Always interested in politics, Langer used his wilderness years to good effect. He wrote to numerous public officials, celebrities, and common folk. He often penned a quick note to seniors graduating from high school. Although eighteen-year-olds could not yet vote, their parents could. It was clear that Langer was positioning himself for a future foray into elective politics.[19]

Reflecting on his fractured association with the Nonpartisan League, Langer understood that he had to repair the damaged relationship if he hoped to reenter the political arena. Owing to his improved financial condition resulting from his burgeoning law practice, Langer provided more than $21,000 to the NPL between 1928 and 1932. The funds did much to restore amicable relations. In fact, the NPL supported Langer's unsuccessful bid to become attorney general in 1928.[20]

Some losing candidates retreat in humiliation and despair, but Langer was playing a long game. He recognized an opportunity to remake the NPL to become a potent faction inside the Republican Party. The organization would propel him into the governor's mansion. Slowly and methodically, he rebuilt the organization from the precinct level up. By 1932, the NPL was, in effect, the "Langer League." It was a shrewd, sophisticated organizational triumph. Along with support from the Farmers' Union and the Farmers' Holiday Association,

Langer and his NPL supporters rode to victory in 1932. He was the only Republican elected governor that year as Democrat Franklin D. Roosevelt defeated the Republican incumbent president, Herbert Hoover.[21]

Like many states, especially states with large numbers of farmers, North Dakota in 1933 was suffering from the unprecedented economic devastation of the Great Depression. The new governor realized that bold, decisive action was necessary. As attorney general more than a decade earlier, he had already demonstrated his willingness to act without fear of overreach.

As soon as he came into office, Langer announced a moratorium on all debt, although later he revised his proclamation to forbid foreclosures on real property. A month later, he exempted foreclosures by federal agencies. He also slashed state appropriations across the board, except for funding for primary and secondary education. Confronted with a crisis involving the collapsing price of wheat, Langer placed an embargo on out-of-state wheat in the fall of 1933. The price increased by five cents on the first day following the embargo. By December 5, the price had risen repeatedly. A federal district court in Minneapolis struck down the embargo, but it had served its purpose. As prices for agricultural commodities rose, Governor Langer claimed credit.

Farmers loved Langer for his policies, which had saved many a farm from foreclosure. Neighboring South Dakota had twelve thousand more foreclosures than North Dakota, which was partially attributable to Langer's policies. He had achieved his long-held ambition to become governor, and he was at the apex of his influence and popularity. During this time, however, "Wild Bill" engaged in a series of incidents that landed him in legal trouble.[22]

It was not uncommon for a public figure to receive substantial support from friendly newspapers. At a time when President Roosevelt and his numerous backers in the state were Democrats, Langer, a Republican, found little support. To counterbalance the Democrats' favorable news coverage, Langer created a newspaper under the NPL's auspices. *The Leader* would express support for the governor and ensure that he received the laudatory coverage he deserved.[23]

Financing the newspaper during the Great Depression was not an easy chore. Shortly after assuming office in January 1933, Langer had cleaned house in the state's executive departments, removing longtime employees and replacing them with loyalists. This kind of spoils system was hardly unique in the annals of American state politics. What was novel was the governor's newspaper financing plan. Because many state employees were expected to demonstrate their fidelity to the man who had provided them with jobs, Langer openly solicited funding for the newspaper by inviting employees to subscribe to *The Leader* for an amount equal to 5 percent of the employee's annual salary. Employees need not bear the cost, however; enterprising state employees could recoup the salary loss by selling subscriptions on their own.

As a legal and ethical maneuver, the plan was questionable, but as a fund-raising mechanism, it was an exceptional effort. *The Leader* soon eclipsed its rivals, enjoying the largest circulation of any weekly newspaper in North Dakota. At a time when few people had money, Langer's subscription drive netted $58,751. This scheme, as ethically challenged as it appears, might have raised nothing more than eyebrows but for one unpleasant statistic. Of the amount raised, $469 came from relief employees who administered federal funds from the United States government. Their salaries were paid with federal dollars channeled through the state's coffers. Federal law prohibited soliciting money from federal employees.[24]

Langer insisted that his newspaper subscription plan was a legitimate fund-raising tactic, but he faced stiff opposition from North Dakota Democrats. Writing to President Roosevelt to complain, a state Democrat observed, "In this state there is a federal relief fund—it is a Governor Langer relief fund, and all the employees connected with it are Republicans." In 1934, prosecutors indicted Langer on charges of "soliciting and collecting money for political purposes from federal employees and of conspiring to obstruct the orderly operation of an act of Congress." Although the United States Justice Department had found in a similar case from Ohio that federal money became state money after a state received it, the prosecutor, an anti-Langer man named P. W. Lanier, pursued the case.[25]

Langer was not the sole defendant. The prosecutor also went after the state highway commissioner, employees of *The Leader*, and various state employees. According to the indictment, one or more defendants engaged in twenty-eight "overt acts" that made up a criminal conspiracy. The trial commenced on May 22, 1934, in Bismarck.[26]

Although nine defendants were on trial, all eyes were on Langer. He adopted a nonchalant attitude as he sat in court chewing on an unlighted cigar with the cellophane still attached. At one point, Langer enraged the trial judge when a juror, Les Hulet of Mandan, was walking by the defense table. During voir dire, Hulet had admitted that he knew Governor Langer, but he assured the court that he would be fair and impartial in the trial. Incredibly, he had been impaneled. Seeing his acquaintance pass by, Langer stood and draped his arm around the man in full view of everyone in the courtroom. "Hi, Les," he said. "How are you?"[27]

Langer eventually took the stand and admitted that he had relied on state employees to fund *The Leader*. When he learned that the salaries of federal employees had been solicited, he directed that the solicitations cease, and their money be returned. He said he was baffled by the indictment because he thought the matter had "been cleared up." Concerning a charge that he had transferred funds from *The Leader* to his personal account, Langer explained that he had used his own money to create the newspaper and was seeking reimbursement. The NPL owed him $20,000, he said.[28]

The trial lasted until June 17, 1934. After three days of deliberations, the jury rendered its verdict: guilty. The judge sentenced Langer to eighteen months in jail and a $10,000 fine. The governor immediately appealed. Among other errors, he argued that the trial judge was biased against him and was therefore predisposed to rule against Langer.[29]

State law mandated that anyone convicted of a felony could not serve as governor. In such a case, the lieutenant governor would serve in his stead. Ole Olson, North Dakota's lieutenant governor in 1934, came to Bismarck to assume control. He landed in the middle of a clash of wills and ideology. The state attorney general, P. O. Sathre, ruled that when Langer filed an appeal the legal maneuver stayed the conviction until the proceedings ran their course. Olson appealed Sathre's ruling to the state supreme court, which disagreed with the attorney general.[30]

"Wild Bill" Langer had sacrificed much to become governor, and he would not leave without putting up a fight. When Olson arrived at the governor's office, he encountered the National Guard. Langer had barricaded himself in his office and posted sentries. A large crowd had gathered outside, and Langer said the National Guard was necessary to keep the peace. Olson and his allies, however, believed that Langer was using his office to retain power. It was only the intervention of Adjutant General Earle Sarles that convinced Langer to submit to the state's authority. He left the office reluctantly.[31]

Langer believed that he should not have been removed from executive office except through impeachment, and he said as much. His opponents in the state legislature moved to institute such proceedings, but both chambers lacked a quorum. The impeachment initiative went nowhere.[32]

Temporarily booted out of office, Langer was in dire straits. The felony conviction had stripped him of his civil rights, which meant that he could not practice law. He had hoped to run again for governor in 1934, but the conviction precluded that option. He could put his wife, Lydia, in the race, however, and he did exactly that. Unfortunately for Langer, she lost the election to Thomas Moodie.[33]

Langer was as wily as ever. Realizing that Moodie was a Minnesota native, Langer investigated the new governor's background. Much to his delight, he discovered that Moodie had voted in the 1930 election in Minneapolis, which meant that he had not met North Dakota's residency requirement for governor. When Langer presented this information to the state supreme court, the court disqualified Moodie as governor. He had served for less than a month. For the second time in six months, North Dakota's legal system had removed a sitting governor.[34]

Moodie's successor, Walter Welford, expressed his gratitude to Langer for helping clear the way for Welford's accession. In the meantime, Langer pursued his appeal in federal court. Much to his relief, on May 7, 1935, the Federal Circuit Court of Appeals reversed Langer's conviction and ordered a new trial. Several trials involving the original charges followed. A conspiracy trial resulted in a hung jury. Langer received a "not guilty" verdict in a perjury trial. A second conspiracy trial found him not guilty as well.[35]

By 1936, Langer had cleared all the legal hurdles and was ready to campaign again in the upcoming gubernatorial election. He found that Welford, who had made a full recovery from his severe case of gratitude, was happy in the governor's office and refused to step aside. Langer now could count on the reconstituted NPL to back his campaign. Anti-Langer Leaguers, known as rumpers, were defiant. They refused to run on a ticket with "Wild Bill" Langer. Not surprisingly, the rumpers held their own convention and nominated Welford as the Republican gubernatorial candidate. Of the 180,000 votes cast in the Republican primary in June 1936, Welford bested Langer in the primary election by a paltry 695 votes.[36]

With support from the NPL, Langer thought he could still win the seat, and so he filed to run in the fall general election as an independent. As a result, three candidates entered the field: Welford, the Republican; John Moses, the Democrat; and Langer, the independent. It was an especially bitter campaign, with each candidate attacking the other repeatedly. Rampant corruption in the Langer administration was a constant refrain. Welford charged that Langer "lives for politics. He doesn't live for farmers, nor does he live for anybody unless he can get them in his clutches."[37]

Never a shy, retiring type, Langer went on the offensive, accusing Welford of raising taxes and increasing state appropriations by $9 million while the Langer administration had reduced taxes by $5.5 million. As for corruption in his administration, Langer sought to turn the multiple lawsuits to his advantage. "The federal government spent nearly a million dollars to find me honest," he boasted. "I am the only candidate inspected by the United States government and found to be 100 percent pure."[38]

Langer's gambit worked. He narrowly defeated Walter Welford, earning 36 percent of the vote. It was the first time an independent candidate had been elected governor of North Dakota. He triumphantly returned to the office he had left more than two years earlier.[39]

Langer entered office in 1937 amid the bitter feelings of his detractors. He had amassed many political enemies during his political life. Shrugging off criticism, he focused on helping North Dakota farmers suffering from the Great Depression. He strong-armed the legislature to appropriate $6 million for welfare at precisely the moment that the state's coffers were almost depleted. In 1937, when wheat prices fell from eighty-nine cents to thirty-seven cents per bushel, Langer directed the state-owned mill to pay thirty-five cents per bushel over the new market price, claiming he had saved the state's farmers more than $12 million. He repeated the action a year later.[40]

Farmers appreciated the governor's actions, but stories of corruption in the administration soon circulated, reinforcing the stories about Langer's ethical and legal laxity. Three of the governor's friends had profited from purchasing county bonds at a discounted price and selling them to the Bank of North Dakota at full face value. In 1938, the State Board of Equalization reduced the assessment on Great Northern Railroad property by $3 million around the time that a railroad attorney bought $25,000 of worthless Mexican land stocks from the governor and never sought delivery of the stock certificates.[41]

Even when Langer was not directly involved, he found himself embroiled in scandal. After the board of administration fired the president of the North Dakota Agricultural College (AC) in Fargo and dismissed several faculty members, the AC lost its accreditation. The American Association of University Professors censured the institution. Because many members of the board of administration were Langer supporters, the governor received criticism for his willingness to politicize education and risk AC's accreditation for his own political ends.[42]

Against this backdrop, Langer set his sights on his next political goal—winning a seat in the United States Senate in 1938. The problem was that Gerald P. Nye, the incumbent Republican, had no intention of vacating the office without putting up a fight. Langer believed (rightly, as it turned out) that his nemesis Nye had pushed for Langer's prosecution in the 1934 and 1935 trials. Defeating the incumbent in the 1938 election would be sweet revenge. Unfortunately for Langer, Nye won both the Republican primary and the fall general election. Langer would have to wait until North Dakota's other Senate seat was up for election in 1940.[43]

After gearing up for a fight, Langer was ruthless during the 1940 campaign. Using his leverage with the NPL, Langer maneuvered to oust the incumbent senator, Lynn J. Frazier. It worked. Langer captured the Republican nomination. In the fall election, Langer won the Senate seat by more than one hundred thousand votes.[44]

As with so many things in Langer's political life, the election victory was not the end of the story. When the senator-elect arrived in Washington, DC, on January 3, 1941, to swear his oath of office, the Senate majority leader, Democrat Alben Barkley of Kentucky, acknowledged that the Senate had received a petition from several North Dakota citizens alleging that Langer had engaged in bribery in leasing government property, received kickbacks, and collected fees for services that he had not provided. In short, he was unfit to be seated as a United States senator owing to his "moral turpitude."[45]

Barkley recommended that Langer be seated "without prejudice" and his case be referred to the Committee on Privileges and Elections, chaired by Senator Tom Connally of Texas, for a judgment. Sixteen members served on the committee, including Gerald P. Nye and California's Hiram Johnson. Both Nye and Johnson asked to be excused.

Because Langer was seated without prejudice, the Senate could rule on his admission by a majority vote as opposed to the two-thirds vote required for expulsion. Langer swore his oath; afterward, Senate leaders submitted the petition to the committee, which created a subcommittee to hold hearings on the matter. The investigation and debates lasted for more than a year.[46]

With the allegations hanging over his head, Langer felt compelled to send an open letter to his constituents. On May 24, 1941, he wrote, "During my public life, my political enemies have charged me time after time with crookedness, dishonesty and corruption. Although the United States government spent many thousands of dollars, and my political enemies many thousands more, bringing some twenty-odd civil and criminal cases against me, the courts and juries have invariably established my innocence in every criminal case." He assured the voters that the charges were not well founded, but he would cooperate so that his name could be cleared.[47]

The full committee considered allegations spanning the entire length of his public career from state attorney in Morton County to governor. They elicited testimony from North Dakota and beyond. Even Langer testified, insisting on his innocence in uncompromising terms that some critics characterized as arrogant.[48]

On January 29, 1942, the Committee on Privileges and Elections, with a new chairman, Senator Theodore F. Green of Rhode Island, presented its majority report. The committee agreed that Langer met the constitutional requirements of age and citizenship, and he had not acted in a disorderly manner, but he lacked the "moral fitness to be a senator" and should be excluded from the Senate if a majority voted against him. Having listened to testimony about Langer's activities throughout his public career, a majority of committee members expressed outrage at Langer's "lawlessness, shot-gun law enforcement, jail-breaking," as well as the man's tendency to obstruct the administration of justice. Langer's behavior, the majority concluded, demonstrated "a continuous, contemptuous, and shameful disregard for the high concepts of public duty."[49]

One especially bizarre instance of malfeasance was scarcely believable, but the committee reported on it nonetheless. Witnesses recalled an episode that occurred in 1932, when Langer was practicing law. According to their accounts, Langer represented a man, Jacob Oster, who was charged with murder. His wife, Emma, was the sole witness. While Oster was held without bail in the Hazelton, North Dakota, jail, Emma obtained a divorce. A wife cannot be compelled to testify against her husband, but the privilege does not apply to an ex-wife.

Recognizing that his client was at risk, Langer persuaded his friend, the sheriff, to deputize him and release Oster into his custody. Langer transported Jacob Oster and Emma Oster, along with two witnesses, to McIntosh, South Dakota, so Jacob and Emma could remarry. Langer assured Emma Oster that he would obtain a free divorce for her after trial. As a postscript, Emma Oster later married another man on the assumption that Langer had obtained the divorce for her, although he had not.[50]

The minority report objected to the tone of the majority report. According to the minority, the senators had never before reviewed the entirety of an elected official's career. They suggested that the witnesses were unreliable, and

**North Dakota governor William "Wild Bill" Langer was a larger-than-life character. (*Elwyn B. Robinson Department of Special Collections, Chester Fritz Library, University of North Dakota*)**

the alleged evidence was little more than unsubstantiated hearsay compiled by Langer's political opponents.[51]

The committee voted 13–3 not to seat Langer, which meant that the issue would come before the full Senate for adjudication. On March 9, 1942, floor debate opened, and it lasted two weeks. Langer watched as his colleagues argued over whether he was guilty of "moral turpitude," as the term was loosely defined. His supporters vehemently defended his right to serve, arguing that the voters should decide on whether he was qualified. To disqualify a senator based on supposed moral turpitude was to change the meaning of the United States Constitution, which imposed no such prohibition.[52]

Langer's case came down to whether he should be denied his seat based on a majority vote or a two-thirds vote. A Senate majority decided that refusing to set him was tantamount to expulsion, and expelling a senator required the higher standard. In any case, Langer's opponents could not even muster a simple majority. In the final vote, which occurred on March 27, 1942, fifty-two senators agreed to seat him, and thirty-two voted against Langer. On September 17 of that year, the Senate agreed to pay $16,500 in attorney fees to reimburse Langer for the defense of his seat.[53]

He retained his position in the United States Senate, becoming a vocal isolationist during World War II. At war's end, Langer was one of only two senators to vote against adoption of the United Nations charter. To his legion of political opponents, he was a corrupt, unprincipled, outlandish figure, but North Dakota voters loved him. They repeatedly reelected him, and he served until his death in 1959.[54]

Late in his career, when asked what drove "Wild Bill" to act in sometimes baffling ways, Langer disputed the idea that he was a political enigma. "I am the most predictable damn fellow in the United States Senate," he claimed. "I am always on the side of the underdog." Until the day he died, William Langer was proud of the appellation that was sometimes applied to him: "fighter for the people."[55]

CHAPTER 7

# "Nobody Sat Down in Front of Me with a Suitcase of Money."

## SPIRO AGNEW

Spiro Agnew, President Richard M. Nixon's vice president, began his political career in Baltimore, Maryland, as a county executive. He served as governor of Maryland before Nixon picked him to be vice president. In 1973, while the Watergate crisis was engulfing the Nixon presidency, the United States attorney in Maryland was investigating corruption involving state construction kickbacks. He discovered evidence implicating Agnew. The vice president denied any involvement, but as the evidence mounted, he agreed to a plea bargain. Agnew promised to resign his office instead of facing impeachment and/or multiple criminal indictments. To avoid further litigation, Agnew pleaded no contest on federal income tax evasion charges. He received a $10,000 fine and was sentenced to probation for three years. The Maryland court of appeals stripped him of his law license. The Agnew corruption case was especially egregious because, coupled with the Watergate imbroglio, it reduced public faith in government and the honesty of American political leaders.[1]

Under the terms of the Twenty-Fifth Amendment to the Constitution, Nixon selected a new vice president. He chose a Michigan congressman, Gerald R. Ford, the House minority leader who was known for his honesty. Ten months later, Nixon resigned from the presidency to avoid impeachment, and Ford became the thirty-eighth president of the United States. Had Agnew avoided corruption charges, he might have stepped into the presidency in Ford's stead.[2]

In later years, Agnew was remembered as a divisive, sleazy, self-serving politician, an intellectually challenged, morally obtuse attack dog for Nixon, who was one of the most corrupt presidents of all time. In his early years, however, Agnew's story was uplifting. He was the son of Greek immigrants who traveled to America in search of a better life and thereby embodied the American dream.[3]

Theophrastos Anagnostopoulos arrived in the United States around age twenty, in 1897, and settled in Schenectady, New York. As with so many immigrant families, he chose to Anglicize his surname. He called himself "Agnew." He eventually opened a diner before moving to Baltimore, Maryland, where he bought a restaurant. Agnew became friends with the city's meat inspector, William Pollard, because Pollard and his wife, Margaret, were frequent customers. After William Pollard died, Agnew courted Margaret. The two eventually wed. On November 9, 1918, their son Spiro Theodore Agnew was born. Margaret Agnew also had a son from her first marriage.[4]

Young Spiro graduated from public school in 1937 and entered Johns Hopkins University. He majored in chemistry, but Agnew was not a good student. Choosing to change direction, he entered the unaccredited Baltimore Law School, working as a clerk for an insurance company during the day while he studied at night.

When World War II erupted, Agnew attended Army Officers Candidate School. He married his girlfriend, Elinor Isabel Judefind, three days after he graduated. The couple eventually had four children. In the meantime, Agnew served as a company commander in the Tenth Armored Division in the European theater of World War II. He won a Bronze Star for his service.

After the war, Agnew returned to law school. He had been apolitical for most of his life. When pressed, he said he followed his father's example as a Democrat. When Agnew clerked for a Baltimore law firm, a senior partner advised him to become a Republican. Baltimore politicians were mostly Democrats, and it was difficult for an ambitious young man to distinguish himself from the crowd. Republicans were comparatively rare, so it was easier to stand out, especially in the suburbs. Acknowledging the wisdom of this advice, Agnew moved his growing family to Lutherville, a Baltimore suburb, in 1947. From that moment, Spiro Agnew considered himself a Republican, unintentionally demonstrating the ruthless expediency that would always be his political lodestar.

Agnew's road forward was rocky. He earned his law degree in 1947, passed the Maryland bar examination, and commenced a law practice in downtown Baltimore. It failed. He worked for a while as an insurance investigator before becoming a store detective for Schreiber's supermarket chain. After a brief return to the service in the Korean War, Agnew practiced law again.[5]

During the 1950s, he settled into a comfortable middle-class existence in the Maryland suburbs. He served on the parent–teacher association (PTA) and avoided any contacts or behavior that could be labeled radical or nonconformist, eventually gravitating toward politics. According to his wife, "Ted got into politics through the PTA. He kind of spread out."[6]

In his initial foray into elective politics, Agnew resolved to become a Republican candidate for the Baltimore County Council. After party leaders rejected his bid, Agnew campaigned for the Republican ticket. When Republicans won an unexpected majority on the county council, party elders reassessed Agnew. He had been helpful and effective. As a reward for his work, he won an appointment to the county zoning board of appeals. The prestige of the appointment bolstered his struggling law practice. In time, party elders reappointed Agnew, and he served as the board chairman.[7]

By 1960, he was anxious to move up to a higher position. He sought election to the county circuit court, but he lost, finishing fifth in a field of five candidates. Democrats prevailed in many Baltimore races, including on the county council. After the opposition party was in control, its members removed Agnew from the zoning board. The defeats initially appeared to be major setbacks for Agnew, but news stories about the solitary Republican standing up to the Democratic hordes raised his profile and cast him as the victim of a political vendetta.[8]

Agnew was savvy enough to use his emerging reputation as an up-and-coming Republican to good effect. He tried to persuade party leaders that he was the right man for a congressional seat in the 1962 election cycle. Despite Agnew's enormous potential as a shining star in Republican circles, the nomination went to a more experienced candidate, J. Fife Symington. Republicans asked Agnew instead to campaign for the county chief executive post, a position held by Democrats since 1895. Taking advantage of a split in the Democratic ranks, Agnew won the election. After Symington lost his congressional bid, Spiro Agnew became the highest-ranking Republican elected official in the state of Maryland. He was on his way up the political ladder.[9]

For all his later infamy as a reactionary vice president, Agnew's stint as the county executive was surprisingly progressive. An antidiscrimination bill passed, requiring the desegregation of public accommodations such as restaurants, one of the first measures of this type in the United States. During Agnew's tenure, the county built new schools, increased teacher salaries, reorganized police departments, and improved water and sewer systems.[10]

Even as he was hailed as a visionary county official, Agnew proved to be on friendly terms—perhaps *too* friendly—with local real estate developers. He awarded county contracts to developers with whom he enjoyed close personal relations, and their chumminess appeared to be improper. Years later, this relationship presented problems for Agnew.[11]

As the 1960s became more tumultuous, Agnew's progressivism suffered. He became a "law and order" man, blanching whenever demonstrators took to the streets. He simply could not understand why activists would march in open defiance of the law, even for a peaceful protest. In Agnew's view, marching in the streets, regardless of the reasons or the circumstances, undermined law and order and could not be tolerated.[12]

By 1966, as Agnew pondered his political future, he realized that he probably could not be reelected as the county executive. Democrats were united and likely to defeat him if he threw his hat into the ring. He was faced with a crucial decision, and the time seemed right for him to seek the governorship. As a leader in his party, Agnew easily won the April Republican primary.[13]

The general election promised to be a difficult campaign, although once again the Democrats provided Agnew with an electoral gift. Three factions battled for the Democratic gubernatorial nomination before George P. Mahoney, an avowed segregationist, emerged as the victor. Mahoney was unabashedly racist, and he promoted his opposition to integrated housing with his campaign slogan: "Your Home Is Your Castle. Protect It." Despite his occasional flirtations with progressive causes, Agnew would never be mistaken for a political liberal. Nonetheless, political liberals flocked to his defense, rightly viewing the Democratic alternative as the greater of two evils. Agnew won the race by 81,775 votes.[14]

Critics attacked Agnew later for failing to report three bribery attempts from slot machine industry representatives during this time. The governor-elect shrugged off the criticism because he had not accepted the bribe. "Nobody sat down in front of me with a suitcase of money," Agnew explained. He also came under fire for his landholdings at a site adjacent to a planned bridge over Chesapeake Bay. Recognizing that his cozy relationship with land developers created at least an appearance of impropriety, Agnew disposed of his holdings.[15]

During his two-year tenure as governor of Maryland, Agnew developed a reputation as a competent, if uninspired, governor. His agenda included initiatives on tax reform, ensuring clean water, and repealing laws that prohibited interracial marriage. Progressives applauded his programs for improving access to higher education and improving job opportunities for lower-income citizens.[16]

Agnew had received support from civil rights leaders, but he eventually disappointed them. Protesters were becoming increasingly violent as they turned out to demonstrate against the Vietnam War and in favor of civil rights protections for people of color. When a presidential commission produced a report indicating that white racism was a major cause of black violence, Agnew balked at the conclusions. "It is not the centuries of racism and deprivation that have built to an explosive crescendo," he remarked. The problem was "that lawbreaking has become a socially acceptable and occasionally stylish form of dissent." On another occasion, Agnew said that it "is not evil conditions that cause riots, but evil men."[17]

Following the assassination of Dr. Martin Luther King Jr. on April 4, 1968, riots broke out in cities across the country. A few days later, fires erupted in Baltimore, and they lasted for three nights. Governor Agnew responded immediately, declaring a state of emergency and dispatching the National Guard.

By the time the ordeal ended, six people had died and more than four thousand had been arrested. Officials indicated that the fire department had extinguished twelve hundred fires. Looting was widespread.[18]

On April 11, Agnew summoned black leaders to the state capitol. Instead of a dialogue about how they might work together to improve the situation, which is what the leaders expected, Agnew upbraided them for their inability or unwillingness to control the radicals who had burned the city. In no uncertain terms, the governor insisted that the civil rights leaders either were cowards for refusing to rein in the lawbreakers or were complicit in the crimes. It was a stinging rebuke, and the black leaders, incensed, walked out. No one ever accused Spiro Agnew of harboring progressive ideals again.[19]

The black community denounced Agnew's histrionics, comparing him to the ardently racist governor of Alabama, George Wallace, but they missed the point. The stunt had achieved its purpose. The governor knew that he would never be a darling of the left despite his progressive accomplishments during his first two years in office, so he did not try. Instead, by hewing to the law-and-order line, he established his bona fides among reactionary Republicans and others worried about rioting in the streets. White suburbanites especially appreciated Agnew's unflinching support for punishing criminals and malcontents. Phone calls, letters, and telegrams of support inundated the governor's office, and more than 90 percent of the nine thousand contacts supported Agnew's strong stance.[20]

Agnew's uncompromising position attracted attention from another man who appreciated law and order. Richard M. Nixon, the former vice president campaigning for the 1968 Republican presidential nomination, saw in Spiro Agnew a potential running mate who might sign on to a southern strategy playing on white citizens' fears of an ascendant black radical class. The Maryland governor's ability to attract newspaper headlines for attacking liberals and radicals was impressive.[21]

Before 1968, Agnew had been a liberal Republican in the mold of New York governor Nelson Rockefeller, whom Agnew originally supported in the 1968 presidential campaign. After Rockefeller's withdrawal, Agnew searched for a new candidate. He met with Nixon in March 1968, and the two men discovered that they had much in common. Although Agnew publicly insisted that he intended to serve the remainder of his four-year term as governor of Maryland, he knew that he had moved on to Nixon's short list of vice-presidential running mates.[22]

Agnew arrived in Miami Beach for the Republican National Convention as Maryland's favorite son. Chosen to place Nixon's name in nomination for president, Agnew remained a top contender for the vice-presidential slot. For many Americans, the Maryland governor was not yet a national figure. Agnew's competitors—John Lindsay, mayor of New York City, and Ronald Reagan, the up-and-coming governor of California—were far better known, but these men also had amassed political enemies during their time in the spotlight. Nixon feared that either figure might split the Republican Party, not to mention that these men were more charismatic than he was. He risked being eclipsed by Lindsay or Reagan. Agnew, however, would eclipse no one. He was half a step above a nonentity, and he possessed the necessary obsequiousness to suit Nixon's purposes.[23]

On August 8, 1968, after he won the nomination on the first ballot, Nixon told party leaders that Agnew was his choice for vice president. He announced it to the press shortly thereafter. For his part, Agnew expressed astonishment. "I am stunned," he said. "I had no idea that this would happen. It's like a bolt from the blue."[24]

Agnew was not the odds-on favorite to be Nixon's running mate, but it was hardly a bolt from the blue. He had positioned himself to become vice president, and his law-and-order rhetoric served him well as Richard Nixon's attack dog. Agnew proved himself willing and able to join the team as a ferocious defender of all things Nixon.[25]

He made the news as he campaigned throughout the fall, leading a reporter to comment on Agnew's "offensive and sometimes dangerous banality." His casual racism was jarring to some admirers of his earlier pro–civil rights record. He referred to a Polish gentleman as a "Polack" while dismissing a Japanese American reporter as a "fat jap." Remarking on poor neighborhoods in racially diverse areas, Agnew shrugged. He told reporters that "if you've seen one slum, you've seen them all." As the head of the ticket, Nixon might have stopped Agnew's outbursts, but he did not. Nixon understood his running mate's appeal in parts of the South. Right-wing populism resonated with white citizens fearful of rising crime rates, "uppity blacks," and antiwar opposition among hippies and other young people. Moreover, Nixon stole votes from George Wallace, the enthusiastic segregationist running as a third-party candidate, without directly appealing to out-and-out hatred. The Nixon-Agnew team could appeal to soft bigotry with a wink and a nod, always ready to deny their lurking racism should they be called to account.[26]

Critics dismissed Agnew as an intellectual and a moral lightweight, the king of malapropisms and clichés with little depth to his character. A campaign commercial produced by Hubert Humphrey, Nixon's Democratic opponent, featured a television set displaying the words "Agnew for Vice President?" accompanied by an off-camera man laughing hysterically until he choked. The tagline read, "This would be funny if it weren't so serious."[27]

Even as he ascended into the upper echelon of politics, Agnew's past came back to haunt him. The *New York Times* created an existential crisis for the would-be vice president in October 1968 when the newspaper published a series of articles on his suspect financial transactions in Maryland. Remembering his own close call with scandal when he ran as Dwight Eisenhower's running mate in the 1952 election, Nixon defended his vice-presidential candidate in no uncertain terms. The presidential nominee chided the *Times* for engaging in "the lowest kind of gutter politics." Agnew stayed on the ticket in 1968, but his Maryland business dealings would remain a problem.[28]

The Nixon-Agnew ticket eked out a narrow victory on November 5, 1968. They won by just over five hundred thousand votes out of seventy-three million cast. In the all-important Electoral College, the contest was not quite as close. Nixon won 301 electoral votes to 191 for Humphrey and 46 for George Wallace. Spiro Agnew had risen in a relatively short time from a local official to a state governor to vice president of the United States.[29]

Nixon knew that the vice presidency was an ill-defined constitutional position in American government. Perhaps recalling his own indignities while serving in that office, the new president initially promised that Agnew would have a substantive role in the new administration. To some extent, Nixon fulfilled his promise. He assigned Agnew responsibility for heading the Office of Intergovernmental Relations and the National Space Council. Because Agnew had served as governor, Nixon asked him to work with state governors on an anticrime initiative. These assignments sounded more impressive than they were. Nixon preferred foreign policy, leaving domestic affairs to aides stationed outside his inner circle.[30]

Agnew accepted Nixon's promises at face value, which showed how much he misunderstood his place within the administration. He had an office in the West Wing of the White House, which he assumed meant that his opinions were valued and desired. He soon learned the error of his ways. The vice president had the temerity to speak up on a foreign policy issue during a cabinet meeting early in his tenure. Irked at the intrusion, Nixon dispatched his chief of staff, Bob Haldeman, to inform Agnew that he was not to offer an unsolicited opinion in the future. So much for requesting substantive input from his vice president.[31]

Desperate to carve out a niche where he could influence policy formulation, Agnew spent much of his time in the United States Senate. The Constitution establishes the vice president as the president of the Senate, but he can only vote in the case of a tie. Because a tie vote is relatively rare, vice presidents appear in the Senate to sit on the dais on infrequent occasions. Agnew was the exception that proved the rule. He was happy to appear and fraternize with senators. Although he was visible to the press and affable among elected officials, most of Agnew's work was symbolic, and it was clear that he exercised little genuine political power despite Nixon's assurances to the contrary.[32]

Nixon softened his rhetoric after he became president, but he occasionally dispatched Agnew to handle the dirty work. The vice president spoke on numerous occasions about the sorry state of the nation owing to agitators and radicals. For all his obvious deficiencies, Agnew excelled at railing against elites such as liberal intellectuals and their favored newspapers, including the *New York Times* and the *Washington Post*. The vice president's alliterative denunciations against his enemies made for good copy. He dismissed the "nattering nabobs of negativism" and the "effete corps of impudent snobs," as well as "pusillanimous pussyfooters" and "hopeless hysterical hypochondriacs of history." In return for these heroic efforts, faithful conservatives displayed signs saying "God Bless Spiro Agnew" along with "I Like Spiro" bumper stickers.[33]

The press corps became Nixon's favorite villains, and he unleashed Agnew on them repeatedly during the administration's first year. Although Nixon eventually shied away from direct attacks, his (and Agnew's) willingness to attack liberal media bias resonated with many conservatives. Decades later, when President Donald Trump branded the mainstream press the "enemy of the people," he was building on the foundation constructed during the Nixon-Agnew years.[34]

Agnew became a visible symbol of the Nixon administration. Inside the White House, he was seldom consulted or appreciated, but in Republican Party gatherings outside of Washington, he was a much-beloved figure. Speaking invitations poured in from across the country. Agnew traveled frequently, engaging friendly Republican audiences whenever he could, possibly with an eye toward his own presidential bid in 1976.[35]

To Democrats and detractors outside of Republican circles, Agnew had betrayed the progressive agenda of his gubernatorial career. He was a divisive, narrow-minded, bigoted spokesman for a corrupt, secretive, obstructionist presidential administration. Many citizens saw him as a pompous, bloviating bore who frequently spoke in a soft monotone, spewing out a series of stale clichés. It became fashionable among the smart set to ridicule Agnew's intellect.

In 1970, a joke circulated among college students that Mickey Mouse wore a Spiro Agnew watch, implying that Micky Mouse, a cartoon character, was making fun of Spiro Agnew, a fellow cartoon character. In response, Dr. Hale E. Dougherty, a California physician, had a Spiro Agnew wristwatch designed so he could sell it. The design became such a hit that Agnew watches became a cultural phenomenon. Everyone had to have one, actress Elizabeth Taylor and rock musician John Lennon among them. Agnew claimed that he found the affair funny, but he eventually sued to stop the distribution. He was not a man known for his self-deprecating humor.[36]

Nixon had a love-hate relationship with Agnew. On one hand, he dispatched his vice president to deliver a speech or handle an unpleasant task, such as attending foreign funerals of dignitaries, that Nixon did not care to handle. On the other hand, Agnew's independent streak and popularity among rank-and-file conservatives made Nixon suspicious that his second-in-command was insufficiently loyal. As the 1972 election approached, Nixon debated replacing Agnew as his running mate, perhaps with John Connally, a conservative Democrat who had served as governor of Texas and was Nixon's treasury secretary. Ultimately, Agnew remained on the ticket, but neither Nixon nor Agnew was happy about their partnership.[37]

When burglars with ties to Nixon's reelection campaign broke into the Democratic National Committee's headquarters in the Watergate office building in Washington, DC, Agnew learned of the event through the news. For the first time in his tenure, he benefited from his ostracism from the president's inner circle. Yet Agnew was not outraged by the break-in. A veteran of hardball politics, he assumed that both political parties spied on each other and engaged in dirty tricks. In Agnew's opinion, however, the break-in was ridiculous and unnecessary. The Republican Party enjoyed enormous momentum heading into the fall election season. Nixon operatives did not need inside information on the Democrats' operations. The Democrats of 1972 were in such disarray that their amateur political plans were irrelevant to the Nixon juggernaut. Moreover, it was doubtful that any useful information would be uncovered even if someone decided to break the law and burglarize an opponent's offices.[38]

Watergate became a problem for Nixon, but Agnew stayed away from the scandal. He had his own developing scandal to worry about. As he and Nixon geared up for the 1972 election season, George Beall, the United States attorney for the District of Maryland, launched an investigation of corruption in Baltimore County. Beall believed that many current officials in the county were implicated in criminal enterprises with local construction companies. His investigation stretched into 1973. By that time, Nixon and Agnew had won reelection handily. It was one of the most decisive presidential elections in American history. Nixon and Agnew won forty-nine states and the District of Columbia, capturing more than 60 percent of the popular vote and 520 electoral votes.[39]

Safely reelected, Agnew believed that he could look ahead to 1976 and a possible presidential bid. When he learned of Beall's investigation in February 1973, he was alarmed. The bad press generated by a corruption investigation could sink his presidential prospects before he even launched his campaign. Agnew asked Attorney General Richard Kleindienst to contact Beall. The vice president also sent his personal lawyer, George White, to discuss the issue. Beall understood the need for discretion. Because Agnew had not been the county executive for more than five years, Beall believed that the statute of limitations for prosecuting Agnew had expired even if evidence of wrongdoing were discovered. Accordingly, Beall assured White that Agnew was not a subject of the investigation.[40]

The legal analysis changed when Beall discovered that Agnew had received illegal payments from an engineering firm while he was governor. In June 1973,

Beall learned, to his astonishment, that the kickbacks continued even when Agnew was vice president. The statute of limitations had not expired on these offenses. Beall informed the new attorney general, Elliot Richardson, that Agnew was under investigation for tax fraud and corruption.[41]

Believing that the best defense is a good offense, Agnew tried to get ahead of the story. As Beall's investigation became public, Agnew insisted that he was innocent of all charges. He explained that the payments were legal campaign contributions. Nixon supported his vice president in public, but behind the scenes it was a different matter. The president instructed his chief of staff to meet with Agnew and suggest that Agnew "take action" before an indictment was handed down. Nixon was already engulfed in the unfolding Watergate scandal, and he did not need another corruption investigation to dominate newspaper headlines.[42]

Even as leaks circulated through Washington, DC, during August and September 1973, Agnew defied his critics. The drumbeat for his resignation was incessant, but he would not yield. "I will not resign if indicted," Agnew told the press on September 29, 1973. "I will not resign if indicted!"[43]

When witnesses came forward to testify that Agnew had accepted cash bribes, his fate was sealed. Still, he resisted, arguing that a sitting vice president could not be indicted. He asked Speaker of the House Carl Albert to launch a congressional investigation, but Albert demurred. It would be improper for Congress to intervene in a matter that was being adjudicated in the courts. Rebuffed, Agnew filed a motion to block an indictment because the vice president's interests had been prejudiced by leaks in the press. He also delivered a series of speeches to rally support.[44]

When those efforts failed to resuscitate his cause, Agnew's lawyers met with the prosecutors to discuss a plea bargain. Understandably, Agnew did not want to serve time in prison. The two sides reached an accommodation in early October. Agnew agreed to lodge a *nolo contendere* ("no contest") plea to a single charge of failing to pay taxes on income he received as governor of Maryland in 1967. He would resign the vice presidency in exchange for serving no jail time. As Agnew explained later, he resolved to enter the plea because he wanted to end the matter quickly and spare his family additional pain and embarrassment. By pleading "no contest," he was not admitting guilt.[45]

Agnew met with President Nixon in the White House on October 9 and told him of his decision. The next day, Agnew stood in a federal courtroom in Baltimore. Aside from resigning his office, Agnew agreed to pay a $10,000 fine and serve three years of unsupervised probation. His resignation letter, effective immediately, was dated October 10, 1973.[46]

A forty-page summary of the evidence detailed Agnew's financial woes. He accepted bribes and kickbacks, he said, because he was not a wealthy man, and

**Spiro Agnew served as vice president under Richard M. Nixon from 1969 until 1973. He resigned his office as part of a plea bargain to avoid serving jail time for bribery. (*Biographical Dictionary of the United States Congress*)**

he needed funds to live the kind of lifestyle he believed a man in his position should live. He insisted, however, that these payments were not illegal; they were monies he was owed for his professional expenses. Considering the overwhelming evidence against him, the arguments were unpersuasive.[47]

Spiro Agnew lived until 1996. He spent the rest of his life seeking to rehabilitate his public image. He was not a greedy politician on the take, he argued to anyone who would listen, but a good man unfairly maligned. All but the most partisan hacks rejected such self-serving statements. A man who once exhibited seemingly limitless promise as a relative anomaly—a politically conservative progressive governor—became a symbol of corruption and venality during the Nixon years, a time when corruption appeared to be a way of life.[48]

# "I Am Not a Crook."
## THE WATERGATE SCANDAL

Watergate has become the scandal by which all other American scandals are judged. Whenever an elected official is caught in a compromising situation, his or her actions are often compared to Watergate. The suffix "gate" suggests that malfeasance occurred on a massive scale. When an attorney general–designee confessed that she had not paid Social Security taxes for her caregiver, the episode was dubbed "Nannygate." When it became clear that the Reagan administration traded arms for hostages, it was "Iran-gate." President Barack Obama wore a light tan suit to a public event, and his Republican critics pounced, labeling his attire choice "tan-gate." When conspiracy theorists concocted a phony story that Democratic presidential candidate Hillary Clinton and her allies were conducting a child sex trafficking enterprise inside a pizza parlor, the hoax was labeled "Pizzagate."[1]

The original Watergate episode began on June 17, 1972, as a "third-rate burglary attempt," in White House press secretary Ron Ziegler's words. Police officers apprehended five men in business suits breaking into the Democratic National Committee headquarters in the Watergate building in Washington, DC. Investigators learned that the men had ties to the Committee to Reelect the President (CRP, sometimes mockingly known as CREEP), an organization formed on behalf of Richard M. Nixon. As the police and press investigated, so, too, did the United States Congress. Investigators ultimately learned that the Nixon administration had engaged in a multitude of illegal activities.[2]

The president was not aware of the initial Watergate break-in, but when he learned of the incident, he orchestrated a cover-up. Nixon had installed a taping system inside the Oval Office, and several tape recordings captured his plans to hide the actions of his White House "plumbers" (who were supposed to fix the information leaks coming from the White House). Although he was reelected president by a landslide in 1972, Nixon's political viability slowly eroded as Congress and a special prosecutor investigated his behavior. In one especially dramatic development, on October 20, 1973, Nixon ordered his attorney general, Elliot Richardson, to fire the special prosecutor, Archibald Cox. After Richardson resigned rather than comply with the order, Nixon ordered Deputy Attorney General William Ruckelshaus to fire Cox. Ruckelshaus resigned as well. Solicitor General Robert Bork, the Justice Department's number three official, fired Cox, although later Bork was forced to appoint a new special prosecutor, Leon Jaworski.[3]

In response to a subpoena, Nixon initially refused to release his Oval Office tape recordings to investigators, citing executive privilege. In a case that went to the United States Supreme Court, *United States v. Nixon*, the judiciary ordered the president to release the tapes. It was little wonder that Nixon fought to prevent the release of the tapes, as several conversations demonstrated that the president had been involved in the cover-up from the earliest days following the Watergate burglary.[4]

Faced with certain impeachment and probable conviction, Nixon resigned as president, effective August 9, 1974. As of this writing, he is the only president of the United States to resign before his term of office ended. The term "Watergate" has entered the American political lexicon as the benchmark of political scandals. Whenever anyone describes a political scandal, the speaker often claims that the event is "worse than Watergate."[5]

That a sitting president of the United States could be brought down by such a seemingly inconsequential series of events remains a topic of endless fascination. Watergate was far more than a "third-rate burglary attempt," however; it was part of a long pattern of lawlessness in the Nixon administration. Nixon had always been a practitioner of the "dark arts" of politics. He had made his career as a Red-baiting demagogue in the late 1940s. When he went after a career State Department officer, Alger Hiss, Nixon played on citizens' fears of encroaching Communism. A proponent of realpolitik, Nixon believed that "dirty tricks" were fair game in American elections.[6]

It should come as no surprise, therefore, that Nixon's men acted in unethical and illegal ways with relative impunity. Even if President Nixon did not order them to engage in mischief, they understood that he was unconcerned about lawless behavior in service of his reelection. A president sets the tone of his administration.

The tone was set in 1971, after the *New York Times* published excerpts from a series of top-secret documents that came to be known as the Pentagon Papers. President Nixon expressed his fury in no uncertain terms. The papers showed that officials in the Kennedy, Johnson, and Nixon administrations had lied about progress made during the Vietnam War. White House staffers realized that something must be done to plug the leaks inside the administration and the bureaucracy. They were especially incensed at Daniel Ellsberg, a former State Department and RAND Corporation analyst who had copied the records and turned them over to the *Times*.[7]

President Nixon's chief domestic policy analyst, John Ehrlichman, tasked his subordinates Egil "Bud" Krogh and David Young with establishing an informal group, the "White House Plumbers," to plug leaks inside the administration. Krogh and Young enlisted G. Gordon Liddy, finance counsel for CRP, as well as a former Central Intelligence Agency (CIA) operative, E. Howard Hunt, to conduct a "covert operation" to gather information about Ellsberg's mental state. The plan was to discredit the whistleblower. Demonstrating a notable lack of scruples, the informal group decided to burglarize the office of Dr. Lewis Fielding, Ellsberg's psychiatrist, and rifle through his files in search of damaging information on their nemesis. Ehrlichman authorized the project provided it was "done under your assurance that it is not traceable."[8]

On September 3, 1971, Liddy and Hunt, accompanied by CIA agents Eugenio Martínez, Felipe de Diego, and Bernard Barker, broke into Dr. Fielding's office and located Ellsberg's file. It did not contain damaging information. The men subsequently debated whether they should break into Dr. Fielding's home, but Ehrlichman refused to authorize the operation.[9]

The Fielding burglary was important because it showed the Plumbers that they could engage in illegal campaign activities with the blessing of the Nixon White House. Although they found no usable information during the initial break-in, the secrecy of the deed ensured that the group would continue its "dirty tricks." In short, the Fielding break-in was a blueprint for subsequent operations.[10]

Throughout late 1971 and early 1972, Nixon's men devised various plots to aid Nixon's reelection campaign. On January 27, 1972, Liddy met with Attorney General John Mitchell, presidential counsel John Dean, and Jeb Stuart Magruder, CRP's acting chairman, to discuss future operations. Liddy had developed an ambitious plan to obtain information from Democrats using illegal surveillance. According to Dean, this meeting represented "the opening scene of the worst political scandal of the twentieth century and the beginning of the end of the Nixon presidency."[11]

John Mitchell, the nation's highest-ranking law enforcement officer, should have reacted with righteous indignation, insisting that no one would engage in such blatantly criminal activity while he was in office. He should have thrown the men out of his office and threatened them with criminal prosecution if they ever entertained such ideas again. He did not. Instead, he rejected Liddy's plan as unworkable.[12]

Liddy returned two months later with a scaled-down version of the surveillance plan. This time, he proposed breaking into the Democratic National Committee headquarters housed in an office building, the Watergate complex, to photograph documents and install listening devices—"bugs," in the parlance of the day—on the committee's telephones. Mitchell approved this plan.[13]

Liddy and his men got to work, relying again on E. Howard Hunt. They also brought in James W. McCord Jr., a former CIA man who was serving as CRP's security coordinator. In turn, McCord recruited other operatives, including Alfred C. Baldwin III, a former agent of the Federal Bureau of Investigation (FBI), who would carry out the wiretapping and monitor telephone conversations.[14]

The group rented a room at the Howard Johnson's motel across the street from the Watergate complex. On May 28, after several failed attempts, the burglars broke into the Democratic National Committee headquarters without being detected and installed listening devices on two telephones. Unfortunately for the operatives, the devices malfunctioned. They resolved to return and fix the defects.[15]

The second break-in became the most infamous burglary in American history. Shortly after midnight on June 17, 1972, Frank Wills, a twenty-four-year-old private security guard in the Watergate office building, noticed a piece of duct tape placed on a door lock adjacent to the underground parking garage as he made his rounds. The tape prevented the door from latching shut. It was an odd occurrence. The Watergate building was considered so safe that security guards did not even carry guns. Thinking it was strange but not criminal, Wills removed the duct tape and continued patrolling the building.[16]

Approximately thirty minutes later, Wills returned to the door and saw that the duct tape had been replaced. He distinctly recalled removing the tape during his earlier patrol. Realizing that someone else was inside the building, Wills scampered over to a lobby telephone and called the police. Within minutes, three plainclothes District of Columbia police officers—Sergeant Paul W. Leeper, Officer John B. Barrett, and Officer Carl M. Shoffler—arrived on the scene in an unmarked cruiser. The officers were on "bum patrol," which required that they dress as hippies and attempt to buy drugs from street pushers.[17]

The burglars had arranged for a lookout to keep watch from the Howard Johnson's motel across the street, exactly as he had done during the first burglary. The man, Alfred Baldwin, was watching television and never saw the police car. Even if he had, it was unmarked and might not have aroused suspicion. In the meantime, the officers turned off the elevators and locked the entrance and exit doors from the building. Wills accompanied the officers as they methodically searched each office on each floor.[18]

When Wills and the police officers searched the sixth floor, where the Democratic National Committee offices were located, Baldwin saw the activity from across the street and tried to alert his confederates via walkie-talkie. It was too late. The officers discovered five men wearing business suits carrying burglary tools inside an office. These middle-aged men were not ordinary burglars. They carried $2,300 in cash (mostly in $100 bills with sequential serial numbers), a shortwave radio receiver to pick up police communications, two 35-millimeter cameras, forty rolls of unexposed film, and three small tear gas guns. The officers immediately arrested the men, later identified as Virgilio Gonzalez, Bernard Barker, James W. McCord Jr., Eugenio Martínez, and Frank Sturgis. Police charged them with attempted burglary and attempted interception of telephone and other communications.[19]

By Sunday, June 18, White House officials knew they were in trouble. It was only a matter of time before the police traced the five defendants to the White House. G. Gordon Liddy had been instrumental in establishing the Plumbers, and he now was instrumental in concealing White House involvement in the crime. He called Jeb Magruder on June 18 to initiate a cover-up. However, they had a major problem: E. Howard Hunt's name appeared in the address book of two of the burglars. Several White House staffers destroyed files in Hunt's safe to conceal any links with the burglary.[20]

Judging by comments that Nixon made to his chief of staff, H. R. Haldeman, which were captured on the White House taping system, the president had not known of the burglary before it occurred. He did know, however, that his men were willing and able to carry out "black bag jobs." Despite his lack of advance knowledge, Nixon soon learned the details. Instead of expressing outrage that a member of his administration had broken the law, on June 23, 1972, the president asked Haldeman, "Who was the asshole that did this thing?" He was referring to the break-in. When he learned that the FBI was investigating the burglars' funding source, Nixon ordered Haldeman to have the CIA block the investigation. Thus, within a few days of the break-in, Nixon obstructed justice.[21]

The president's men had their marching orders: Watergate was to be kept as far away from the White House as possible. The strategy was to stonewall and deny all facts and inferences. To that end, White House press secretary Ron Ziegler blithely dismissed the incident as a "third-rate burglary attempt." Nixon himself later stated publicly that he had directed his White House counsel, John Dean, to investigate the Watergate burglary. On August 29, 1972, Nixon reported that, based on Dean's investigation, "I can say categorically that . . . no one in the White House staff, no one in this Administration, presently employed, was involved in this very bizarre incident." Dean later admitted that he had not launched an investigation into the episode.[22]

No matter how hard the administration attempted to distance itself from Watergate, the trail led back to the White House. When the press asked whether it was true that one of the burglars worked for the CRP, John Mitchell, the former attorney general who had resigned to head up the president's reelection committee, denied involvement in the break-in. The denials proved to be false. In August, investigators located a $25,000 check in Bernard Barker's account.

It was a campaign contribution from Kenneth H. Dahlberg to the Committee to Reelect the President. Dahlberg's check, among others, was a lawful contribution, but it had been used to pay for supplies used in the administration's covert operations. A check from a political donor found in a Watergate burglar's account was the first tangible link between the break-in and the Nixon administration. Other revelations followed in due course. Within a few months, it was clear that the administration had used a secret fund to finance a series of intelligence-gathering operations designed to help Nixon in his reelection bid.[23]

In the meantime, a grand jury indicted the five burglars. Hunt and Liddy had been tied to the operation, and they were indicted as well. They entered guilty pleas or were convicted at the conclusion of the trial on January 30, 1973.[24]

James W. McCord Jr. eventually wrote a letter to the federal district court trial judge, John J. Sirica, explaining that the burglars had been pressured to remain silent about who had financed the break-in. He said that the defendants had perjured themselves. Sirica believed that the White House was behind the enterprise, but the central question was how high the conspiracy went. Did President Nixon know of the operation, and if so, when did he know?[25]

As the scandal deepened, Nixon's White House counsel, John Dean, debated ways that he, Haldeman, and Ehrlichman might save President Nixon from impeachment and possibly a post-presidential criminal prosecution. Nixon was thinking along these lines as well. If he fired these three aides, he might yet save his presidency. The narrative would be that it was his assistants, not the president, who had authorized the series of unlawful acts. Nixon had been overwhelmingly reelected in November 1972. Now he had to hold on to his victory, even if it meant sacrificing the men who had helped him win high office.[26]

As Nixon increasingly engaged in the cover-up, his men, some facing substantial prison time, cooperated with the authorities. Magruder eventually told prosecutors that he had perjured himself when he testified at the burglars' trial. He implicated John Dean and John Mitchell. Dean had been willing to fall on his sword to save Nixon's presidency, but it dawned on him that he would be a scapegoat—perhaps the sole scapegoat—for the cover-up. During a White House meeting on April 15, 1973, Dean sensed that his conversation was being tape-recorded, although he did not know for certain that Nixon had installed a secret taping system in the White House. Two days later, Dean confessed to Nixon that he, Dean, was cooperating with the United States Attorney's Office.[27]

The president was becoming increasingly desperate. On April 30, 1973, he asked that Haldeman and Ehrlichman resign along with Attorney General Richard Kleindienst. He also fired John Dean as White House counsel. Explaining his actions in a televised address, Nixon claimed that with these personnel changes, it was time to put the Watergate scandal behind the nation. The implication was that these men were the perpetrators and he, as president, had cleaned house. He named a new attorney general, Elliot Richardson, that same day.[28]

Nixon hoped that Watergate would fade from the headlines, but he was under tremendous pressure to authorize the appointment of a special counsel. He reluctantly agreed that Attorney General Richardson possessed authority to investigate the matter. In May 1973, Richardson appointed a Harvard Law School professor, Archibald Cox, as a special counsel tasked with getting to the bottom of the scandal.[29]

Congress eventually investigated the episode as well. On February 7, 1973, the United States Senate voted 77–0 to approve a resolution creating a select committee to investigate the matter. A North Carolina senator, Sam Ervin, served as chairman. A white-haired, amiable self-styled "country lawyer" who spoke with a thick southern accent, Ervin (a Democrat known for his politically conservative views on race) could be counted on to support the administration whenever possible. That was the initial impression, in any case. Nixon would soon learn to his detriment that Ervin's fidelity to his country and to the facts of the case trumped his conservative ideology.[30]

The committee held televised hearings from May 17 through August 7, 1973, and they became riveting entertainment for millions of Americans. John Dean appeared before the committee and proved to be a devastating witness as he meticulously outlined the administration's malfeasance. Other witnesses provided fascinating testimony as well. Alexander Butterfield, a relatively low-level assistant, revealed that the White House contained a system that automatically tape-recorded conversations in the Oval Office, the cabinet room, and Nixon's private office in the Old Executive Office Building. This revelation electrified the country. Immediately following Butterfield's testimony, members of Congress and the special counsel sought access to the tapes as part of their concurrent investigations.[31]

Archibald Cox recognized that the tapes likely held information that would aid his investigation. Not surprisingly, he subpoenaed the tapes. Similarly, Senate investigators subpoenaed the tapes. Citing executive privilege, Nixon refused to release the recordings. The president could do nothing about the congressional subpoena because it was issued by a separate branch of government, but Cox reported to the attorney general, who was part of the executive branch. Accordingly, Nixon ordered Cox to drop his subpoena.[32]

It was a breathtakingly audacious act. The president was interfering in an investigation launched by the special counsel to delve into the president's alleged abuse of power in covering up the Watergate break-in. Directly defying the president, Cox refused to drop the subpoena. Accordingly, on October 20, 1973, Nixon ordered Attorney General Richardson to fire the special prosecutor. Richardson declined to follow the order. Instead, he resigned in protest. Nixon ordered.the next man in line, Deputy Attorney General William Ruckelshaus, to fire Cox. Rather than comply, Ruckelshaus resigned as well. The number three man in the United States Department of Justice, Solicitor General Robert Bork, fired Cox.[33]

The sordid episode, which became known as the "Saturday Night Massacre," had the opposite effect of what Nixon had intended. He had badly misjudged public reaction to his decision to fire Archibald Cox. He thought this act would relieve public pressure, but it only exacerbated tensions. Defending his actions a few weeks later, Nixon assured the press, "Well, I am not a crook." To illustrate the truth of this assertion, he allowed Bork to appoint a new special prosecutor. Bork tapped Leon Jaworski, a prominent Texas lawyer.[34]

If Nixon believed that a new special prosecutor would somehow be less diligent in investigating the scandal, he was mistaken. Jaworski plowed forward, picking up Cox's investigation where it had left off. He, too, sought access to the White House tapes.[35]

Even as Congress and the special prosecutor investigated Nixon's behavior, his aides faced parallel court proceedings. On March 1, 1974, a grand jury in Washington, DC, indicted seven of Nixon's men: H. R. Haldeman, John Ehrlichman, John Mitchell, Charles "Chuck" Colson, Robert Mardian, Gordon C. Strachan, and Kenneth Parkinson. Richard Nixon was an unindicted coconspirator. If he had not been a sitting United States president, he probably would have been indicted and convicted of one or more crimes.[36]

Confronted with mounting calls to release the White House tapes, Nixon understood that he faced a dilemma. If he did not release anything, he faced increasing scrutiny from all quarters. If he released all the tapes, it would be damning evidence of criminality. Aside from the legal jeopardy he faced, he knew that the American public would be outraged by the numerous instances of profanity as well as racial and ethnic slurs scattered throughout the recordings.

After much debate among administration officials, Nixon decided to release edited transcripts with the comment "expletive deleted" from places where someone (mostly Nixon) used vulgar language. All national security information would be redacted. Perhaps the transcripts would satisfy the numerous investigators.

To sell this solution, the president delivered an address to the nation on April 29, 1974. He pointed to a series of notebook binders to indicate that he was releasing a large volume of information. He hoped that the sheer volume of material would mollify his critics and halt the momentum that seemed to be headed toward impeachment.[37]

Initially, the release of the edited transcripts appeared to achieve Nixon's purpose. He had supplied investigators with sufficient material to argue that he had complied with the law and should no longer be pursued for additional information. Nixon's men argued that they had released more than enough

**Richard Nixon is pictured here at a press conference on April 29, 1974, with edited transcripts of his tape-recorded conversations from the White House. He hoped that the transcripts would convince investigators (and most of the American public) to drop the Watergate investigation, but they did not. (National Archives & Records Administration)**

information to meet the president's constitutional obligations to Congress. To require more was to hamper presidential effectiveness and upset the balance of power among the branches of government.

Nixon again failed to appreciate public opinion. As citizens and congressional leaders delved into the transcripts, the mood shifted. The behind-the-scenes Nixon who emerged from the tapes was a mean, vindictive, petty, and profane man. The Senate minority leader, Hugh Scott, was reluctant to criticize the leader of his party, but even he denounced Nixon and his aides as "deplorable, disgusting, shabby, immoral." Facing voters in the fall 1974 elections, Republican members of Congress distanced themselves from the embattled president.[38]

A renewed call for release of the unexpurgated tapes met with stiff resistance. Publicly, Nixon sought refuge in executive privilege, but only the most partisan hack believed that the president's stance was a principled defense of an implied constitutional power. Nixon knew what was in the tapes. Worse than revelations of his thuggish behavior were conversations demonstrating that, contrary to his assurances, Nixon was in fact a "crook." He had to hold the line at all costs.

The new special prosecutor, Leon Jaworski, was not satisfied with the transcripts. He wanted access to the tapes. Nixon's lawyers filed a motion in federal court to prevent their release, but Judge Sirica denied the motion in the federal district court. The tapes, he ruled, were necessary to the defense of Nixon's men facing trial for their roles in the Watergate affair. Sirica set a deadline of May 31 for Nixon to produce the tapes. In an appeal filed directly in the United States Supreme Court, Nixon's lawyers contended that the dispute was not a matter for the courts. Because Nixon and Jaworski were members of the executive branch, they could resolve the matter without involving the judicial branch. Moreover, Nixon argued that Jaworski had not demonstrated that the requested materials were necessary evidence in the ongoing trial of the seven Watergate defendants. Finally, the president's lawyers reiterated the executive privilege claim.[39]

It was a weak performance. Nixon's claims were tantamount to an argument that the president was above the law and that he need not comply with subpoenas or judicial orders that he deemed inconvenient. On July 24, 1974, the United States Supreme Court ruled 8–0 in *United States v. Nixon* that the president must release the tapes.[40]

Writing for the court, Chief Justice Warren E. Burger concluded that although a president can protect some material under a claim of executive privilege, the privilege is not inviolable. In this case, the judiciary's interest in providing a fair trial to the Watergate defendants outweighed the president's interests in keeping the tapes secret. The court ordered Nixon to deliver the subpoenaed tapes to Judge Sirica in the federal district court.[41]

The moment the high court instructed Nixon to deliver the tapes, his presidency was all but over. The tapes contained incriminating statements that could not be excused. During a conversation with John Dean on March 21, 1973, for example, Nixon's counsel described the Watergate cover-up as a "cancer on the presidency." It threatened to metastasize and engulf the White House. Referring to the decision to pay hush money to the burglars to keep them from testifying truthfully, Dean succinctly summarized the paramount problem. "That's the most troublesome post-thing," he said, "because Bob [Haldeman] is involved in that; John [Ehrlichman] is involved in that; I am involved in that; Mitchell is involved in that. And that's an obstruction of justice."[42]

When Dean told the president that E. Howard Hunt was attempting to blackmail the White House with ever-increasing demands for money, Nixon sounded unfazed by the illegality. He responded that the money should be paid, and he, Nixon, knew where they might obtain the funds. It was one of several "smoking gun" statements: the president of the United States was on tape saying that he knew where he and his advisers could find money to bribe burglars to lie under oath, or at least remain silent, in a criminal case.[43]

During several subsequent conversations, Nixon reiterated his agreement that the hush money should be paid. Not every conversation survived, however. In one infamous example, investigators discovered an eighteen-and-a-half-minute gap in one recording. The White House provided a convoluted explanation: Rose Mary Woods, the president's loyal, longtime personal secretary, had accidentally erased part of the tape when she pushed the wrong pedal on the Dictaphone while she answered a telephone call. The media had a field day when photographs showed that Woods had to strain her body to answer the phone while her foot remained on the pedal. It was highly unlikely that she could have accidentally erased the tape.[44]

Somehow Nixon's presidency limped on, but his political fortunes declined precipitously throughout 1974. Early in the year, the House of Representatives passed a resolution allowing the House Judiciary Committee to launch an impeachment investigation. On July 27, three days after the Supreme Court announced its decision in *United States v. Nixon*, the Judiciary Committee voted 27–11 to recommend as its first article of impeachment a charge of obstruction of justice. Two days later, the committee recommended a charge of abuse of power against Nixon. The vote was 28–10. On July 30, the committee charged Nixon with contempt of Congress for defying eight Judiciary Committee subpoenas from April through June 1974. The committee vote was 21–17.[45]

It did not appear that matters could grow worse for Nixon, but they did. On August 5, 1974, the White House released a tape from June 23, 1972, just a few days after the Watergate break-in had occurred. On the tape, Nixon and his chief of staff, H. R. Haldeman, discussed the FBI investigation of the break-in. After admitting that the bureau's investigation potentially "goes in some directions we don't want it to go," Haldeman recommended that Nixon order the director of the CIA to contact the director of the FBI and tell him to "stay the hell out of this." If Nixon had been the law-and-order leader he claimed to be, he would have expressed shock and outrage at the recommendation. He did not. He enthusiastically approved the recommendation. Referring to Haldeman's statement that the CIA should obstruct the investigation, Nixon said, "You call them in. Good. Good deal. Play it tough. That's the way they play it and that's the way we are going to play it."[46]

Anticipating a public backlash from the tape, Nixon insisted that his comments did not constitute obstruction of justice. He simply wanted the CIA to inform the FBI that the spy agency believed that national security issues were involved in the Watergate investigation. This explanation fooled no one. Even Nixon's lawyers, Fred Buzhardt and James St. Clair, understood that their client had lied to them as well as to Congress, his supporters, and the American people.[47]

Nixon could not survive the public reaction. Even his most committed supporters recognized that their man was politically doomed. On August 7, 1974, House minority leader John J. Rhodes, Senate minority leader Hugh Scott, and Arizona senator Barry Goldwater (the 1964 Republican presidential nominee and a revered elder statesman in the party) filed into the Oval Office to deliver bad news to their leader. They told him that he had virtually no congressional support. Rhodes bluntly said that the House was certain to vote in favor of the articles of impeachment. Perhaps only 75 of the 435 House members would oppose the articles. The senators told him that no more than 15 of their colleagues would vote for acquittal, leaving 85 senators to vote for conviction. Nixon needed at least 67 senators to retain his office.[48]

Facing overwhelming opposition, Nixon had no viable options. Although the congressional Republicans had not specifically counseled resignation, the president decided to resign before he could be impeached and convicted. In a televised address on August 8, 1974, announcing his decision, Nixon explained:

> I have never been a quitter. To leave office before my term is completed is abhorrent to every instinct in my body. But as President, I must put the interest of America first. America needs a full-time President and a full-time Congress, particularly at this time with problems we face at home and abroad. To continue to fight through the months ahead for my personal vindication would almost totally absorb the time and attention of both the President and the Congress in a period when our entire focus should be on the great issues of peace abroad and prosperity without inflation at home. Therefore, I shall resign the Presidency effective at noon tomorrow. Vice President Ford will be sworn in as President at that hour in this office.[49]

It was a stunning, historic address. Richard M. Nixon was the first president to resign in the nation's history. For his supporters, it was akin to a Shakespearean tragedy. Nixon was a brilliant foreign policy strategist who had opened the country to China and improved relations with the Soviet Union. Watergate was indeed a third-rate burglary, and while the president showed poor judgment in attempting to cover up his aides' malfeasance, it should not have been grounds to end his presidency.[50]

Nixon's legion of detractors believed that "Tricky Dick" was a morally bankrupt human being who did not hesitate to abuse his power in his quest for political power. He was unfit to serve as president, and his removal from office was necessary to preserve the integrity of the American system of government. With his departure, it was time for the country to heal.[51]

Nixon met with his staff in front of the television cameras in the East Room of the White House on the morning of August 9, 1974. In a rambling, maudlin speech, he reflected on his time as president, his parents' sacrifices, and the hardships that presidents such as Theodore Roosevelt suffered in their lives. He concluded by advising his staff that "the greatness comes not when things go always good for you, but the greatness comes when you are really tested, when you take some knocks, some disappointments, when sadness comes; because only if you've been in the deepest valley can you ever know how magnificent it is to be on the highest mountain." In advice that might have saved his own political career, Nixon said, "Always give your best; never get discouraged; never be petty. Always remember others may hate you, but those who hate you don't win unless you hate them, and then you destroy yourself."[52]

With that, Nixon and his family boarded a helicopter and departed from Washington. The Nixon presidency had ended ignominiously. Gerald R. Ford, his vice president of ten months, became the thirty-eighth president of the United States.[53]

A month later, Ford pardoned Nixon for crimes he had "committed or may have committed or taken part in" as president in hopes of healing a divided nation. Nixon accepted the pardon but insisted that he had done nothing wrong. He went to his grave almost twenty years later insisting that his only mistake was "in not acting more decisively and more forthrightly in dealing with Watergate, particularly when it reached the stage of judicial proceedings."[54]

Ford suffered extensive political damage for pardoning his predecessor. Skeptics wondered whether there had been a quid pro quo. Nixon had appointed Ford as vice president, with congressional approval, following Spiro Agnew's resignation in October 1973. In the days leading up to Nixon's resignation, Ford had met with Nixon's chief of staff, leading critics to observe that Ford might have traded the promise of a pardon in exchange for Nixon's agreement to leave office quickly and quietly. Ford denied that such an arrangement existed. When Ford died in 2006, even his most vocal critics conceded that his decision to pardon Nixon was an act of political courage. In issuing the pardon, Ford had harmed himself politically, but he had acted to move beyond Watergate. In his inaugural remarks, Ford observed that "our long national nightmare is over."[55]

Watergate remains the quintessential example of political corruption in American history because the venality was so clear. Burglarizing an opponent's office building to collect campaign intelligence to assist in the president's reelection efforts is unquestionably illegal. Nixon did not know about the crime beforehand, but he established the conditions necessary for his men to engage in such behavior with impunity. When he learned of the break-in, Nixon could have denounced the activities of his men and demanded justice. Instead, he sought to cover it up lest his law-and-order message be exposed as hypocrisy and his reelection bid suffer. He was willing to use the executive branch bureaucracy in service of the conspiracy. Throughout his political career, Nixon had lived by a simple maxim—the ends justify the means—and he demonstrated his adherence to that motto in the Watergate affair.[56]

# CHAPTER 9

# "Money Talks in This Business, and Bullshit Walks."

## THE ABSCAM SCANDAL

It sounded like something out of a poorly written crime novel. The United States Federal Bureau of Investigation (FBI) launched an operation known as Abdul scam, or Abscam, aimed at preventing the trafficking of stolen property. In time, the operation evolved into a sting to identify corrupt elected officials. Posing as Arab sheiks representing a fictional Arabian company, FBI agents approached numerous elected officials, many of whom were serving in Congress, asking for favors. The "sheiks" lured their targets to hotel rooms and other private properties and then offered them bribes. Agents videotaped their unsuspecting prey. For members of Congress, the sheiks promised cash payments if the representative would introduce a private immigration bill into the appropriate committee. These secret meetings occurred in the late 1970s and early 1980s.

By the end of the investigation, the FBI had snagged thirty political figures. Seven members of Congress—one senator and six House members—were convicted of accepting bribes. In addition, one New Jersey state senator; the mayor of Camden, New Jersey; several members of the Philadelphia city council; and an Immigration and Naturalization Service inspector were ensnared in the sting.

When the operation came to light, the public expressed mixed reactions. A majority agreed that it was necessary to root out corrupt public officials. A minority, however, expressed misgivings about the FBI engaging in a series of clandestine meetings designed to entrap elected officials in a scheme that would not have occurred but for the FBI's active participation. Amusing anecdotes emerged as well. One congressman facing charges, Florida's Richard Kelly, claimed that he had not really accepted a bribe. He was conducting his own undercover investigation of the sheiks, and the FBI had intervened to spoil Kelly's investigation. Congressman John W. Jenrette Jr., of South Carolina, obviously inebriated, was videotaped uttering these immortal words when asked whether he would accept a bribe: "I've got larceny in my blood. I'd take it in a goddamn minute."[1]

The operation originated in February 1978 when Melvin Weinberg, a con man and swindler who had previously served as an FBI informant, agreed to assist in recovering stolen paintings. Facing three years in prison for their participation in a fraudulent real estate scam, Weinberg and his girlfriend Evelyn Knight knew their only hope to avoid incarceration was to join the scheme. It was one more con in a life filled with cons.

Weinberg was fifty-three years old in 1978. He had barely made it out of grammar school, preferring to rely on his street smarts rather than finishing his education and pursuing a conventional career. He had devoted his life to the exciting world of white-collar crime. In a thirty-five-year career, Weinberg had hustled men and women from all walks of life on six continents in a series of schemes and scams from real estate to bogus gold contracts. He was not much to look at—short, mostly bald, with tufts of hair sprouting from portions of his head, and a gray beard—and his thick New York accent identified him as Brooklyn born and bred. Still, Weinberg was a con man extraordinaire. Like all talented grifters, he understood the psychology of the easy mark.

His dreams and schemes were legendary. Even at an early age, Weinberg could talk his way out of almost any scrape or persuade even the most educated and sophisticated clients to invest in his enterprises. He had an amazing capacity to concoct a plausible story that his mark would buy with little, if any, suspicion. Sometimes Weinberg's façade failed him, though, as on one memorable occasion when he was wining and dining a mark in a French restaurant during his first trip to Europe. Posing as a wine connoisseur, Weinberg held up his glass as the waiter poured a small portion to be tasted. Observing the tiny amount of wine, Weinberg misunderstood what he was supposed to do. He snapped at the waiter, "Fill it up, ya fuck. Whaddya think I'm payin' for?"[2]

The FBI Abscam operation in the late 1970s required Weinberg to create a fake company, the sort of subterfuge that was his specialty. It was called Abdul Enterprises and was headed by two fictional Arab sheiks, Kambir Abdul Rahman and Yassir Habib, who claimed to have invested millions of dollars in the United States. To provide legitimacy for the company, the FBI funneled $1 million into a Chase Manhattan Bank account. Although several FBI agents worked on the sting, one agent, Anthony "Tony" Amoroso, became strongly associated with the operation owing to his portrayal of Sheik Habib.[3]

The operation evolved from its inception. The original purpose was not to ensnare elected officials in a bribery scheme, but that eventually became the goal. The FBI decided to approach elected officials, especially members of Congress, and ask for favors in exchange for cash. Specifically, the "ask" was for the member to sponsor a private immigration bill allowing foreigners affiliated with Abdul Enterprises into the country. The company representatives—the undercover "sheiks"—also asked for building permits and casino licenses in Atlantic City.[4]

The FBI invested much time and money in the operation. The bureau had been tainted by public revelations in the mid-1970s of a series of illegal and unethical activities undertaken during the decades-long tenure of the former director, J. Edgar Hoover. Anxious to rehabilitate its public reputation, the FBI was determined to make an airtight case whenever an elected official accepted a bribe. The agents resolved to go by the book. Tape recordings of telephone conversations and videos of the officials accepting bribes became standard operating procedure.[5]

John Good was the agent in charge. Tireless, dedicated, and streetwise, Good had the sense to partner with Weinberg. The operation would never have succeeded without a gifted swindler and con man at the helm. The notion of an Arab sheik approaching elected officials with promises of ready cash sounds far-fetched and ridiculous, an obvious ploy to entrap them in a crazy, illegal scheme. Yet Good and Weinberg engineered a sting that succeeded beyond what they or anyone thought possible at the outset.[6]

Angelo Errichetti, the Democratic mayor of Camden, New Jersey, as well as a New Jersey state senator, was the first elected official to take the bait. Seemingly unencumbered by ethical qualms, Errichetti promised the sheiks' representatives that "I'll give you Atlantic City." Taking him down was easy. The mayor was a criminal wannabe who had crossed the line, agreeing to guarantee a casino license for $400,000. "Angie Errichetti was one helluva guy," Weinberg recalled. "I really liked the man." It was no wonder that Weinberg felt a connection with Errichetti. The two men were kindred spirits, always seeking out deals, legal or otherwise. "He always looks relaxed, but his mind's goin' a mile a minute," Weinberg said with a touch of admiration. "He's got deals goin' on all over the place and he's always lookin' for a new one."[7]

The FBI offered Errichetti a deal he could not refuse. If he helped bureau operatives in their sting, they would recommend that the judge provide a reduced prison sentence for his crimes. The mayor readily agreed. He was well connected in New Jersey and beyond, and he promised to prepare a list of politicians who would be willing to accept bribes.[8]

From these humble beginnings, Abscam expanded. As the operation unfolded, several FBI agents as well as Weinberg and Errichetti arranged meetings in a house in the Washington, DC, Foxhall neighborhood, on a Florida yacht, and in hotel rooms in Pennsylvania and New Jersey. Typically, Weinberg arranged the meetings through third-party contacts with access to the elected official. Agent Amoroso, posing as the fictional Sheik Habib, handled the negotiations during the meeting while cameras recorded the scene. As an experienced FBI agent, Amoroso knew the right questions to ask to establish that a federal crime had been committed. Throughout 1979, the agents met with a litany of elected officials and went through the spiel. Cash sometimes exchanged hands on the scene. On other occasions, payment came later.[9]

As the operation expanded, Errichetti took to his role with gusto. He offered up two Pennsylvania congressmen, Michael (Ozzie) Myers and Raymond Lederer, both of whom represented districts encompassing the Philadelphia area. As the scheme unfolded, undercover FBI agents approached the two congressmen with a simple proposition: each man would receive $100,000 if they agreed to help the two fictional sheiks stay in the United States.

Congressman Myers accepted $50,000 from Agent Amoroso in a Travel Lodge suite near Kennedy Airport on August 22, 1979. Myers later complained that he thought the agreed-on price was $100,000. The money was important to Myers, who was videotaped commenting that "money talks in this business,

The FBI's Abscam investigation, a high-level sting targeting public corruption, captured numerous crooked public officials. In this undercover video, United States congressman Michael Myers (second from left) holds an envelope containing $50,000 that he just received from undercover FBI agent Anthony Amoroso (left). Also shown in the photo are Angelo Errichetti, mayor of Camden, New Jersey (second from right), and convicted con man Melvin Weinberg. (Balfore Archive Images / Alamy Stock Photo)

and bullshit walks." For his part, Congressman Lederer accepted the $50,000 bribe without complaint.[10]

New Jersey senator Harrison "Pete" Williams, a Democrat, was arguably the most prominent elected official caught in the Abscam sting. Williams repeatedly met with FBI agents, supposedly to discuss a titanium operation. The plan was for Williams to receive shares of the fictional company's stock; in return, the senator agreed to steer government contracts to the company. After he was indicted in October 1980, Williams argued that he was not technically bribed because the stock was worthless. He also argued that he was targeted for the scam because he supported Massachusetts senator Ted Kennedy for president over the incumbent, Jimmy Carter. Finally, he complained that he was entrapped by FBI agents, and he would not have engaged in this behavior but for the bogus offers made by the phony sheiks.

A jury did not believe his defenses. After deliberating for twenty-eight hours, the jurors convicted Williams of nine counts of bribery and conspiracy. Sentenced to serve three years in prison, he appealed the convictions, but they were upheld. After the Senate Ethics Committee voted to censure Williams, it was possible that he might be expelled from the Senate. To prevent a vote on expulsion, Williams resigned his seat.[11]

Another New Jersey lawmaker, Congressman Frank Thompson, met with the "sheiks" and promised to assist certain individuals in circumventing immigration laws. Thompson's constituents loved him. He had served the district for a quarter century, but that fact no longer mattered. Faced with possible expulsion after the indictments became public, Thompson resigned his seat. Like Pete Williams, Thompson was convicted and sentenced to three years in jail. Both he and Williams served two of the three years behind bars.[12]

As typically occurs in criminal investigations, a defendant charged with breaking the law has a strong incentive to cooperate with investigators. Congressman Thompson knew that aiding law enforcement officers might mitigate his sentence. He introduced investigators to Congressman John Murphy of Staten Island, chairman of the Merchant Marine and Fisheries Committee. According to the charges filed against him, Murphy agreed to receive an "unlawful gratuity." Convicted of the crime, he served three years in prison.[13]

The only Republican lawmaker caught in Abscam, Congressman Richard Kelly of Florida, insisted that he had not accepted a bribe. He was conducting his own investigation, he said. He won points for chutzpah, if nothing else. In 1982, he won a temporary victory when the court overturned his conviction, accepting his entrapment defense. On appeal, however, the conviction was reinstated. Kelly served thirteen months in prison.[14]

John W. Jenrette Jr., an up-and-coming South Carolina congressman and a member of the powerful House Appropriations Committee, was a notorious alcoholic. While under the influence of alcohol, he agreed to accept a bribe as he uttered the provocative statement that he had larceny in his blood. The Justice Department was already investigating a Jenrette real estate venture. Anxious to lay the land deal to rest, Jenrette stipulated that he would accept a $50,000 bribe if the department dropped the investigation. He also sought a loan from the Arabs because his finances were in disarray.

Jenrette's saga was especially colorful, capturing headlines in South Carolina and around the country. When he was indicted for his Abscam involvement, Jenrette resigned from the House of Representatives before he could be expelled. As he appealed his conviction, his wife, Rita, left him to pursue a career as an entertainer. A comely blonde with aspirations of becoming a singer and actress, she appeared nude in *Playboy* magazine in 1981. The accompanying article was almost as revealing as the photographs, as Rita alleged that she and Jenrette had enjoyed sexual intercourse on the steps of the US Capitol Building. She later wrote a tell-all book, *My Capitol Secrets*, about her escapades with Jenrette. The comedy troupe known as the "Capitol Steps" adopted their name from Rita Jenrette's revelations. John and Rita eventually divorced. Evidence of his perfidy showed Jenrette to be a garden-variety crook, but his wife's shenanigans transformed him into an object of national ridicule and scorn. A 1989 shoplifting conviction further sullied his reputation. In his dotage, a former congressional bad boy had become a pathetic has-been to a skeptical, snickering public.[15]

Other elected officials escaped prosecution. Congressman John Murtha of Pennsylvania refused to accept a bribe, thereby avoiding conviction, but he did not have clean hands. He talked with the agents repeatedly and came close to breaking the law when he solicited business investments for his congressional district. Although prosecutors never charged Murtha with a crime, he was named as an unindicted coconspirator. Murtha eventually testified against Frank Thompson and John Murphy. Emerging from the scandal with his reputation mostly intact, Murtha served as a well-respected congressman for thirty-six years before his death in 2010.[16]

Senator Larry Pressler, a South Dakota Republican, met with the agents but, unlike many of his colleagues, refused to accept money or anything of value. After he heard that he might be given funds in exchange for favors, he halted the conversation. "Wait a minute," he said, "what you are suggesting may be illegal." When the exchange subsequently became public, some commentators, including legendary television anchor Walter Cronkite, called him a "hero." Pressler demurred. "I do not consider myself a hero," he said. "What have we come to if turning down a bribe is 'heroic'?"[17]

Pressler had a point. Few participants in any phase of Abscam deserved the label "heroic." Even the FBI agents who ran the operation came under fire for their willingness to rely on a criminal con man as their principal adviser. The entrapment defense, while rarely successful in a court of law, proved to be far more controversial in the court of public opinion. The elected officials caught in the scandal would never pass as paragons of virtue, but most of them had not sought out a criminal enterprise. They had been recruited to participate. They would not have joined a conspiracy or accepted a bribe in that time and place but for the actions of aggressive FBI agents. It was a sordid affair for everyone involved. If the role of law enforcement officers is to investigate criminal activity, critics contended that those same officers should not engage in criminal activity, even if—especially if—that activity was designed to compel others to commit crimes.[18]

Despite its notoriety in the early 1980s, Abscam was largely forgotten by the public within a decade. The investigations and convictions never garnered the same level of media attention as Watergate, but that fact was not surprising. Watergate centered on the president of the United States, the most powerful man in the world and arguably the leader of the free world, while Abscam involved legislators, mostly members of Congress who were not famous outside the Beltway of Washington, DC. Moreover, considering the salacious scandals that preceded and succeeded it, Abscam was not the type of malfeasance to capture the public imagination. Watergate played out in news coverage and televised hearings over many months, presenting an array of fascinating characters, from nerdy White House counsel John Dean to the folksy North Carolina senator Sam Ervin, who chaired the committee investigating the affair, to the bow-tie-wearing Harvard law professor Archibald Cox, to the famously shifty president of the United States himself, Richard Nixon. Abscam's central characters—Melvin Weinberg, Angelo Errichetti, and Anthony Amoroso—were seldom seen and almost never heard. Their images were mostly available only on grainy videos or in photographs buried in the back pages of the newspapers.[19]

Despite the episode's relative obscurity, Abscam was not completely lost to history. Hollywood produced a 2013 film, *American Hustle*, loosely based on the scandal. As with most things in Hollywood, however, the writers took numerous liberties with the facts, producing a film that garnered generally favorable reviews and captured award nominations but bore only a passing resemblance to the actual Abscam investigation. The film did little to elevate attention to the scandal beyond a small group of diehards interested in the era of the late 1970s.[20]

As for Abscam's legacy in law enforcement, on January 5, 1981, Attorney General Benjamin Civiletti issued "The Attorney General Guidelines for FBI Undercover Operations" to provide guidance on appropriate procedures for conducting criminal stings. After Abscam became public, the bureau struggled to defend the legitimacy of its undercover operations. The Civiletti guidelines tacitly acknowledged the need to formalize federal law enforcement guidelines and procedures to avoid future controversy. The guidelines have been updated many times.[21]

Congress also investigated the bureau's Abscam activities. Beginning in March 1980, the House Subcommittee on Civil and Constitutional Rights held hearings to determine whether additional steps should be taken to police FBI undercover activities. The subcommittee's final report, issued in April 1984, addressed important issues raised by the Abscam scandal—namely, whether law enforcement officers should undertake operations that could damage the reputation of innocent individuals. The report also expressed misgivings about the loss of privacy suffered by private parties who were never indicted or convicted in the operation.[22]

Not surprisingly, the elected officials who accepted bribes ruined their careers. Worse, they undermined trust in government and its officials. Along with the Watergate scandal and the Church Committee hearings on FBI and Central Intelligence Agency abuses, Abscam demonstrated to wary Americans that, to paraphrase Ronald Reagan, government is not the solution to the nation's problems—government *is* the problem. It was a conclusion that remained with many citizens long after Abscam had faded from the headlines.[23]

# "I Have Been in Government Long Enough to Know That You Don't Have to Ask the Question Explicitly to Know What the Message Is."

## THE SAVINGS AND LOAN SCANDAL

Among the political and financial scandals during the latter half of the twentieth century, the savings and loan (S&L) crisis has been almost forgotten, but in its day it attracted its fair share of media coverage. From 1986 until 1995, more than 1,000 of the 3,234 savings and loans associations in the United States failed. The failures were attributed to numerous causes, including poor management and lax regulatory oversight. The S&L crisis of that era is the story of an evolving industry that relied on the good graces of members of Congress who were overly anxious to assist their constituents, resulting in billions of dollars of taxpayer bailouts—estimated at between $150 billion and $175 billion—for an industry that should have been scrutinized to a greater degree.[1]

S&Ls—sometimes referred to as thrift banks, savings banks, or savings institutions—resemble commercial banks in some respects. S&Ls provide traditional services such as deposits, loans, mortgages, debit cards, and checks, but they focus on residential customers whereas commercial banks generally focus on corporations and large businesses. S&Ls initially were established to service individuals' needs, especially the needs of customers in communities where the S&Ls were built. Commercial banks typically are managed by a board of directors hired by stockholders who are far away from the individual customer base. S&Ls, however, are either owned by depositors and borrowers or governed by a consortium of stockholders who possess a controlling share of the S&L stock.

As S&Ls were conceived in England during the eighteenth century, they were, in effect, "the poor man's commercial bank." An S&L was a not-for-profit cooperative designed to aid working-class men in buying a home. S&L owners and operators invested time and money in the local community. The creation of S&Ls in England, and later the United States, reflected the increasing demand for affordable housing, especially in the years following World War II.

S&Ls grew by leaps and bounds, with apparently no end in sight. To attract depositors, S&Ls sometimes engaged in rate wars with commercial banks. As the wars increased, Congress stepped in to set rate limits in 1966. A decade later, S&Ls faced unprecedented challenges owing to stagflation, an unusual phenomenon. Traditional economic theory posits that high interest rates, accompanied by inflation, occur when the economy is growing and the demand for loans is rising. Conversely, low growth reduces demand—hence it results in lower inflation. During the 1970s, however, the American economy was caught in a period of slow growth, high interest rates, and inflation. The resultant stagflation almost decimated S&Ls.[2]

Regulators strictly controlled the rates that thrift banks could pay on deposits, which meant that in a time of rising interest rates, depositors had an incentive to withdraw their funds in search of an investment that paid a higher dividend. In the meantime, customers who wanted to qualify for a mortgage found it difficult to do so because the low economic growth often translated into lower wages at precisely the time that higher interest rates required them to pay more for a home. These economic conditions reduced the demand for single-family home mortgages, which in turn undercut the bottom line for many S&Ls.[3]

To remain solvent in this rough economic climate, S&L managers sought creative means of increasing revenue. Some S&Ls offered interest-bearing checking accounts and alternative mortgages. Lobbyists for the industry insisted that S&Ls were overregulated and that relief must be provided if the industry hoped to survive. As the 1970s progressed, S&Ls increasingly failed.[4]

The Federal Savings and Loan Insurance Corporation (FSLIC), an institution dating from the Great Depression, administered deposit insurance for S&Ls. As the institutions failed, FSLIC supplied replacement funds, but the agency's resources were limited. By 1983, FSLIC had $6 billion in capital to insure S&Ls, but the cost of providing funds for failed institutions was approximately $25 billion. Realizing that Congress would not provide additional funds, regulators had few viable options. They were forced to allow insolvent S&Ls to operate in hopes that the institutions would eventually generate enough revenue to stay in business. It was a bold gamble on the financial health of weak, often poorly managed, and undercapitalized institutions.[5]

Even as regulators struggled with the problem of how to handle insolvent S&Ls, Congress debated the virtues of deregulating the industry so that institutions could offer a larger array of services. It was a curious response to a looming problem. Rather than fret over the means of bailing out bankrupt S&Ls, Congress debated whether it should allow the institutions to expand their services in hopes of outgrowing their financial woes.

In the early 1980s, Congress enacted new statutes to provide a lifeline to S&Ls. The first new law, the Depository Institutions Deregulation and Monetary Control Act of 1980, signed by President Jimmy Carter on March 31, 1980, was designed, in the words of the statute, "to facilitate the implementation of monetary policy, to provide for the gradual elimination of all limitations on the rates of interest which are payable on deposits and accounts, and to authorize interest-bearing transaction accounts." In the Garn–St. Germain Depository Institutions Act of 1982, Congress deregulated S&Ls and allowed them to provide adjustable rate mortgages. The industry hailed the laws as exactly what thrift banks needed to overcome their problems. With reduced regulatory oversight, the ability to offer more services, and the elimination of the minimum number of stockholders required to form an S&L, even undercapitalized, poorly managed institutions were free to go after new business.[6]

Deregulation had the desired effect. S&Ls grew rapidly between 1982 and 1985—more than twice as fast as commercial banks during that same time. Compared with commercial banks, S&Ls benefited from less regulation; indeed, they had enormous incentives to maximize profits by participating in risky, high-yield investments. In fact, the only way that S&Ls could grow as rapidly as they did was to pursue risky financial opportunities. Times were good, though, and few S&L managers thought the bubble would burst.[7]

Unfortunately, all bubbles eventually burst. As S&Ls increasingly funded home mortgages for customers who were less financially stable than a traditional borrower, the institutions became vulnerable to any market deviations or interest rate fluctuations. Predictably, their losses mounted, and they failed in ever larger numbers. L. William Seidman, a former chairman of the Federal Deposit Insurance Corporation (FDIC) and the Resolution Trust Corporation (RTC), remarked that the "banking problems of the '80s and '90s came primarily, but not exclusively, from unsound real estate lending."[8]

As the 1980s progressed, the mounting problems with S&Ls became readily apparent to anyone who examined the failures. Many institutions held portfolios replete with risky investments. Managers often had little appreciation of how undercapitalized their thrift banks had become, nor did they understand the role of new technology in allowing other types of financial institutions to compete directly with S&Ls. The lack of effective regulation and the willingness of some S&L operators to take advantage of loopholes in existing regulations ensured that a financial collapse was increasingly likely.[9]

From 1986 through 1989, FSLIC closed almost 300 S&Ls, requiring the agency to reimburse depositors for the loss of $125 billion in assets. Later, the RTC, another agency created to oversee S&Ls, was forced to reimburse depositors for an additional 747 S&Ls from 1989 until 1995. When state insurance funds failed, the federal government had to bail out some state S&Ls as well.[10]

Although more than one thousand institutions failed in the 1980s and 1990s, the failures seldom made the news. Eventually, some S&Ls captured headlines owing to the unmitigated venality and high-profile activities of the participants. As an example, a federally chartered S&L, the Midwest Federal Savings & Loan, failed in 1990. It became infamous when the chairman, Hal Greenwood Jr., and his daughter, Susan Greenwood Olson, along with former executives Robert A. Mampel and Charlotte E. Masica, were convicted on racketeering charges. Midwest's collapse cost taxpayers $1.2 billion.[11]

The collapse of the Silverado S&L attracted press attention in 1988 because Neil Bush, son of Vice President George H. W. Bush, served on the institution's board of directors. Critics charged that Neil Bush had accepted a loan from Silverado, but he insisted that he was innocent of all charges. A subsequent investigation found that Bush had, in fact, engaged in "breaches of his fiduciary duty involving multiple conflicts of interest." Bush did not face criminal charges, but he and his fellow directors fought a civil suit filed by the FDIC, eventually settling the case. Silverado directors also settled an RTC lawsuit, this time for $26.5 million. In the final accounting, the Silverado S&L failure cost taxpayers $1.3 billion.[12]

Arguably, the worst S&L failure—and certainly the most infamous—concerned the Lincoln S&L. Five United States senators were accused of improperly contacting the Federal Home Loan Bank Board (FHLBB), the agency that regulated the S&L industry (and administered FSLIC) at the time. The senators acted on behalf of Charles H. Keating Jr., chairman of the Lincoln Savings and Loan Association. Lincoln failed in 1989, costing American taxpayers more than $3 billion and leaving twenty-three thousand Lincoln customers holding worthless bonds.[13]

The debacle originated in 1985, when FHLBB chairman Edwin J. Gray instituted a new rule allowing S&Ls to hold no more than 10 percent of their assets in "direct investments," which limited their ability to own certain financial instruments. The purpose of the rule was to prevent S&Ls from continually taking on risky investments, declaring bankruptcy, and requiring taxpayer-funded bailouts.[14]

Keating was an especially aggressive S&L officer. He had taken advantage of a multitude of risky deals to build Lincoln S&L into a powerhouse institution. Along the way, Keating had knowingly violated the FHLBB's rules, including Gray's prohibition on holding more than 10 percent of the S&L's assets in direct investments. Keating was politically well connected, and he sought to use those connections to repel a FHLBB inquiry into Lincoln's practices.[15]

With an eye toward staffing the FHLBB with friendly regulators, Keating had persuaded President Ronald Reagan to appoint a real estate developer and Keating confederate, Kee H. Henkel Jr., to the bank board using a recess appointment. Keating also commissioned a study from Alan Greenspan, who was then a private economist but later served as chairman of the Federal Reserve Board, to demonstrate that direct investments by S&Ls were safe and secure.[16]

The measures were insufficient to insulate Lincoln S&L from the regulators' scrutiny. Henkel was forced to resign from the FHLBB when news broke that he had financial ties to Lincoln, having accepted loans from the institution. Frustrated with the results of his maneuvers, Keating knew that he must take additional steps to hobble the regulators.[17]

Following the 1986 congressional elections, the Republicans no longer controlled the United States Senate, but that was not a problem. Keating had contacts in both political parties. He approached Senator Alan Cranston, an influential Democrat from California, to ask that the senator remove Ed Gray from the FHLBB. If Keating could not persuade agency personnel to see things his way, he would facilitate a change in personnel. Lincoln S&L was in California, which meant that the S&L was technically a Cranston constituent. Keating spread his money around, donating $39,000 to Cranston's 1986 reelection campaign as well as $850,000 to organizations allied with Cranston's various pet projects. Moreover, Keating contributed $85,000 to the California Democratic Party.[18]

Keating's efforts did not stop with Cranston. He also contributed $55,000 to the 1988 reelection campaign of Senator Dennis DeConcini of Arizona. Because Keating lived in Arizona, he was DeConcini's constituent. Later, after Keating came under fire for his actions on behalf of Lincoln, the senator returned the contribution.[19]

Senator John Glenn of Ohio, a legendary former astronaut-turned-lawmaker, received $34,000 in donations from Keating and his allies for his 1984 reelection campaign, followed by $200,000 donated to a political action committee that Glenn owned. Keating operated an Ohio-based business, which provided the necessary link to claim Glenn as his senator.[20]

Senator John McCain, an Arizona Republican, had known Charles Keating socially since 1981. Over a five-year period starting in 1982, Keating and his associates had contributed $112,000 to McCain's campaign fund. Aside from the campaign, McCain's family members had invested in a real estate deal with Keating. McCain had traveled on Keating's private jet and stayed as a visitor at a Keating vacation home. When the trips became public news, McCain quickly reimbursed Keating for the travel costs.[21]

Keating also contributed $76,000 to Donald Riegle, a Michigan Democrat, for Riegle's 1988 Senate campaign. Because Keating owned a hotel in Michigan, he could claim to be Riegle's constituent. The senator eventually returned the contribution.[22]

These five senators became known as the "Keating Five" because of their cozy relationship with the financier and because they were willing to intervene with the FHLBB on Keating's behalf. Of course, Charles Keating had not contributed funds to the senators' reelection committees and cultivated the relationships because he enjoyed their company or marveled at their sparkling wit. He knew that one day he might need a favor.[23]

The day came when Keating called in the favor. Facing the possibility that the FHLBB would seize Lincoln S&L for insolvency, Keating told Ed Gray that "some senators out west are very concerned about the way the bank board is regulating Lincoln Savings." It was a thinly veiled threat, but one that Keating intended to follow through on if Gray and his associates at the FHLBB did not relax their scrutiny. When Gray appeared unfazed by the comment, Keating assured him that "you'll be getting a call."[24]

DeConcini was amenable to intervening on Keating's behalf, but McCain initially balked. Recognizing the political peril, the Arizona senator did not want to besmirch his public reputation or face legal recriminations. An angry Charles Keating insisted that his longtime friend owed him assistance. Keating and McCain exchanged heated words, but the senator relented.[25]

On April 2, 1987, Ed Gray met with Senators DeConcini, Glenn, Cranston, and McCain in DeConcini's office. The senators' staffers were not present. When DeConcini mentioned "our friend at Lincoln," Gray told them that he was not personally involved in the Lincoln S&L case but that he could put the senators in touch with the appropriate FHLBB regulators.[26]

Exactly a week later, the Keating Five met with the FHLBB regulators in DeConcini's office. "We wanted to meet with you because we have determined that potential actions of yours could injure a constituent," DeConcini said at the outset. Recognizing that the meeting could be characterized as lawmakers unduly influencing federal regulators, the senator hastened to add that "I wouldn't want any special favors for them." After stumbling through more excuses, he explained that "I don't want any part of our conversation to be improper." Everyone understood the disingenuousness of DeConcini's remarks.[27]

Following the Arizona senator's dithering, John Glenn got to the point. "To be blunt," he said, "you should charge them or get off their backs."[28]

It was an awkward moment. Finally, the FHLBB representatives broke the silence. To ensure that the senators understood how risky their position was, the regulators said that they were pursuing a criminal investigation against Lincoln Savings and Loan. The meeting suddenly took on a new, ominous tone. Five United States senators were interceding into a pending criminal case against a constituent. John McCain understood how vulnerable he was. After the session concluded, he severed all ties with Charles Keating and his businesses.[29]

FHLBB regulators subsequently wrote a report recommending that the United States government seize Lincoln owing to the institution's unsound financial practices. Ed Gray's tenure was ending, so he deferred action on a criminal referral to the United States Department of Justice (DOJ). Later, Gray's successor, M. Danny Wall, expressed sympathy for Lincoln. Consequently, he refused to act on the report. In May 1988, the FHLBB negotiated an agreement with Keating and did not refer a criminal case to the DOJ.[30]

Despite their precarious positions, Cranston, DeConcini, and Glenn continued their efforts on Keating's behalf even after they knew about the possible criminal charges. The senators set up multiple meetings with influential members of Congress, including House majority leader Jim Wright, who later became speaker of the House and experienced his own problems with the S&L issue. The senators' actions blurred the thin line between conscientious constituent services and improper influence peddling.[31]

It was many years before the S&L crisis became a salient political issue. The complex nature of the transactions and the closed-door meetings with tight-lipped participants ensured that the facts were easily concealed. An aggressive press corps eventually brought the facts to light.

When the stories emerged, the Senate Ethics Committee investigated the Keating Five and arranged for varying punishments. Cranston received the harshest penalty: the ethics committee publicly reprimanded him. The committee also criticized Riegle and DeConcini for acting improperly but stopped short of issuing a public reprimand. John Glenn and John McCain escaped punishment for improper actions, but committee members concluded that the two men demonstrated poor judgment. Of the five, Glenn and McCain successfully ran for reelection, and McCain eventually became the Republican nominee for president of the United States in 2008. Looking back on the affair, McCain called the Keating Five investigation the low point of his life. In the meantime, according to public opinion polls, the S&L crisis reinforced citizens' views that members of Congress could not be trusted to act appropriately in the public interest.[32]

Even as the Keating Five faced ethics complaints in the Senate, House Speaker Jim Wright faced his own set of challenges involving S&Ls. Like his Senate colleagues, Wright had accepted campaign contributions from Charles H. Keating Jr. It did not stop there. Wright had also assisted other constituents in their efforts to manipulate the actions of the FHLBB.[33]

Ed Gray vividly recalled the day when Wright called to say he wanted to "come talk" with him about a constituent, his "friend Tom Gaubert," a man sometimes described as an "S&L kingpin." No stranger to political pressure, Gray reflected that "I have been in government long enough to know that you don't have to ask the question explicitly to know what the message is, and I knew what the message was. My impressions were that he was interfering with the regulatory process on behalf of friends, and I thought this was a violation of his job as one of the highest-ranking members in the United States government."[34]

**Speaker of the House Jim Wright, pictured here, resigned to avoid a prolonged ethics investigation into influence-peddling charges for, among other things, attempting to have William K. Black fired as deputy director of the Federal Savings and Loan Insurance Corporation. (*Office of the Clerk, United States House of Representatives*)**

Wright's critics charged that the speaker intervened in numerous instances to assist S&L owners and operators, ostensibly because they were his constituents. As a result, he delayed or deterred regulatory oversight that might have prevented bankruptcies costing taxpayers billions of dollars. After S&Ls failed in increasing numbers and the failures captured headlines, the issue gradually became a scandal. Jim Wright became the face of that scandal, although it was not his S&L interventions alone that sealed his political fate.[35]

He became the focus of ethics investigations alleging that he had used bulk purchases of a book he had written to circumvent House rules on outside earnings by members. Wright also allegedly used improper influence to have the FSLIC deputy director, William K. Black, fired. Having accepted numerous campaign contributions from S&Ls, the speaker apparently acted at the behest of several savings and loans officers. Rather than face a formal inquiry from the House Committee on Standards of Official Conduct, however, Wright resigned from Congress in June 1989 after two and a half years of service as the speaker.[36]

The story of the rise and fall of S&Ls—and the members of Congress who sought to protect the industry—is clearly a story of venality and influence peddling. The moral of the story goes beyond those surface features, however. It is an indictment of the American campaign finance system.[37]

It is a cliché to argue that financing political campaigns is expensive, time consuming, and broken, but the well-worn observations are no less true because of their familiarity. It costs millions upon millions of dollars to win a seat in Congress. Most contributors do not write checks based on disinterested motives. At a minimum, a campaign contributor expects that his or her phone calls will be answered promptly. In some instances, the contributor seeks more than a return phone call.

Elected officials are expected to provide superior constituent service if they hope to remain in office for multiple terms. Yet the line between effective constituent service and an improper quid pro quo relationship can be exceedingly thin. Every member of Congress wrestles with this question. How much should a representative do for a constituent, especially a large campaign donor, and when should the member refuse to act regardless of the size of the check? The need to collect huge sums of money from contributors without selling access to the elected office places a public official in an untenable situation. The joke is that under the nation's campaign finance laws, members of Congress cannot be bought—but they can be rented for a little while.

This conclusion does not absolve elected officials of responsibility for their actions. Ethical practice requires individual responsibility and moral autonomy. It does suggest that elected officials must seek a middle path. On one hand, if they refuse to accept money from big-money donors, corporations, and political action committees, they place themselves at a severe electoral disadvantage. On the other hand, if they accept funding from multiple big-money sources, they can expect to be inundated with requests for favors after the election. If federal campaigns continue to be financed through private contributions from well-funded sources, scandals such as the S&L crisis of the 1980s and 1990s will remain a distinct possibility.[38]

CHAPTER 11

# "I Told the American People I Did Not Trade Arms for Hostages."

## THE IRAN-CONTRA AFFAIR

The Iran-Contra scandal occurred during President Ronald Reagan's second term in the White House. The affair started, as such affairs often do, with good intentions that led to abysmal, illegal results. Originally, the Reagan administration sought to free seven American hostages held in Lebanon by the terrorist group Hezbollah. The United States government had a long-standing policy of not paying ransoms for hostages, fearing that such transactions only encouraged extremist groups to kidnap Americans in exchange for payments. In the meantime, as the government debated a means of freeing the hostages in the Middle East, President Reagan expressed his support for the Contras, a group of right-wing rebels opposed to the Marxist Sandinista regime in Nicaragua. Under the Boland Amendment in American law, the United States government could not provide funding for the Contras. To circumvent this requirement, members of the Reagan administration, primarily members of the National Security Council (NSC), hatched a scheme to sell American arms to Iran, thereby relying on Iran's contacts with Hezbollah to hasten the release of the hostages in Lebanon. Afterward, the administration would use the proceeds from the arms sale to support the Contras.

It was unclear then, or later, how much President Reagan knew about the arms-for-hostages scheme. When the story broke late in 1986, the president publicly acknowledged that the weapons transfers had occurred, but he initially insisted that the government never traded arms for hostages. Later, he amended his statement as the facts came to light. Congress launched several investigations into the matter. A commission chaired by former Texas senator John Tower along with former secretary of state Edmund Muskie and former national security adviser Brent Scowcroft concluded that the director of the Central Intelligence Agency (CIA), William Casey, should have briefed President Reagan and informed Congress of the Iran-Contra matter. An independent counsel,

Lawrence Walsh, later indicted fourteen administration officials, including for-mer secretary of defense Caspar Weinberger and NSC aide Oliver North, for their roles in the matter. Some critics believed that President Reagan should have been impeached, but his popularity was too great and his role in the affair too murky to make a successful impeachment proceeding likely.[1]

The roots of the scandal stretched back to 1961, when the Marxist Sandini-sta government came to power in Nicaragua. It was the apex of the Cold War, and Americans feared that the spread of Communism threatened the safety and security of the Western Hemisphere. The incoming Kennedy administration invested much time and energy in combating the regime of Cuba's dictator, Fidel Castro. Administration officials thought that Central America and South America might succumb to Communism, exactly as Cuba had, and such an outcome was unfathomable. Kennedy's Alliance for Progress (Alianza para el Progreso) was designed to reach out to Latin America to bring vulnerable coun-tries into the community of noncommunist Western nations.[2]

The United States eliminated aid to Nicaragua when the Sandinistas ar-rived, but the government remained alert for opportunities to oppose any Marx-ist regime in Latin America. The leftist Sandinista government persisted for two decades. By 1981, a new American president, Ronald Reagan, was anxious to promote regime change in Nicaragua, although he preferred covert action to a full-blown military operation.[3]

Reagan had built a successful public career as a staunch, vocal opponent of Communism. He was criticized for a simplistic worldview—for Reagan, a coun-try was either anticommunist and pro-American or a Communist-sympathizing enemy—but he shrugged off his detractors' objections. Elected president in a landslide in 1980, Reagan believed that his anticommunist ideology enjoyed a mandate among the American people, and he would use his political capital to fulfill that mandate. His administration would resist Communism whenever and wherever it existed.[4]

The new president was convinced that the Nicaraguans were exporting their leftist politics to nearby El Salvador. To forestall further Communist gains in the region, Reagan authorized the CIA to assist a small group of anti-Sandinista rebels, the Contras, in their efforts to undermine the regime. In January 1982, he signed a top-secret National Security Decision Directive to funnel almost $20 million in military aid to the rebel group.[5]

In public, Reagan was circumspect. He did not advertise his desire for regime change. His secret actions in 1981 and early 1982 were justified, he thought, because the law allowed CIA covert action if the president reported to the House and Senate intelligence committees "in a timely fashion" that national security interests required such actions. The definition of timeliness was not altogether clear.[6]

As distasteful as the Sandinistas were to Reagan and other ardent anticommunists, the Contras were hardly paragons of virtue. They were a violent band of thugs who did not enjoy popular support. They also were poorly led, failing to win military victories against the Sandinistas. Apart from resisting the Sandinistas and spewing the sorts of anticommunist bromides that Washington officials loved to hear, the Contras had little to recommend the administration's continued support. Yet Reagan and his allies dug in their heels, refusing to give up on the group. The rationale was that no one in Nicaragua had clean hands, but the anticommunist Contras were the best of a bad lot. The enemy of my enemy is my friend.[7]

Democrats in Congress were worried that the Reagan administration was so reflexively anticommunist that the United States was being driven to defend indefensible causes, such as the dastardly Contras. Supporting a band of rabble-rousers was bad policy; it was one step removed from encouraging lawlessness. Some Democrats also questioned whether the United States government had any business interfering in the internal politics of a sovereign nation regardless of the circumstances. The success or failure of the Sandinistas did not threaten the national security of the United States.[8]

To drive home the point, in December 1982, Congressman Edward Boland of Massachusetts offered an amendment to a defense appropriations bill for Fiscal Year 1983 to prohibit federal funding "for the purpose of overthrowing the government of Nicaragua." The administration recognized a subtle distinction. The CIA could still assist the Contras, provided that the assistance was not aimed at overthrowing the Sandinistas. Anything short of regime change was permissible. Critics viewed this fine line as a distinction without a difference. The Democrats had sought to enact a comprehensive ban on all assistance to the Contras, but they did not have the necessary votes to pass such an amendment.[9]

In December 1983, Congress again modified the administration's relationship with the Contras by authorizing a paltry $24 million as a ceiling of financial support for the group. Shortly thereafter, members of Congress learned that the administration had authorized the CIA to lay mines in Nicaraguan ports without informing the House and Senate intelligence committees. Incensed, both chambers of Congress rejected an administration request for additional funding in Nicaragua. A second Boland Amendment expressed congressional intent to eliminate all funding for the Contras in the future.[10]

The Reagan administration and the conservative Heritage Foundation argued vehemently that the Soviets were attempting to gain a foothold in the Western Hemisphere. Supporting the Contras was the most effective means of countering Soviet aggression. To lose Nicaragua was potentially to lose much of Latin America to Communist infiltration. This argument was a revitalization of the domino theory in American foreign policy.[11]

First developed after World War II, the domino theory suggested that Communism was a figurative contagion that, like a virus, could spread easily from one country to another. If the nations of the free world did not oppose Communism as it arose in developing nations, the ideology would spread to the first world and eventually engulf nations such as the United States. It was preferable to fight Communists in the jungles of Vietnam, the thinking went, than to fight them on the beaches of Santa Monica or Miami.

By the 1980s, after America had spent billions of dollars and tens of thousands of soldiers' lives to fight Communism in the Vietnam War, the domino theory was largely discredited. "Losing" a nation to Communism did not necessarily mean that the United States and its allies were imperiled. Communism could and should be resisted in strategic areas, but the contagion metaphor was inaccurate and overwrought. Choices about when to fight Communism and when to leave it alone required a nuanced analysis on a case-by-case basis, with protecting America's national security as the cardinal objective. American leaders needed to have greater faith in the resilience of democratic institutions. Along these lines, a Bureau of Intelligence Research report produced for the State Department found that the Reagan administration's anti-Soviet stance in Latin America was exaggerated. Fighting the Sandinistas was not in America's national interest. The presence of a Marxist regime in Nicaragua, while certainly not desirable, posed no serious threat to the United States or its major allies.[12]

Reagan disagreed. He had spent his political career arguing against the supposed rapacity of Communists who were eager to gobble up territory for their own insidious ends. Now that he was in power, he would not relent. Consequently, it was clear that the administration would stubbornly persist in its belief that helping the Contras was in the country's national interest, contrary evidence or arguments be damned.[13]

To ensure that the administration was not emboldened to invest more resources into the fight, Congress approved a third Boland Amendment. It prohibited all aid to the Contras from any United States government agency, not just the CIA. The language provided that "during fiscal year 1985, no funds available to the Central Intelligence Agency, the Department of Defense, or any other agency or entity of the United States involved in intelligence activities may be obligated or expended for the purpose or which would have the effect of supporting, directly or indirectly, military or paramilitary operations in Nicaragua by any nation, group, organization, movement or individual." If the president issued a report to Congress after February 28, 1985, stating that further assistance was needed for "military or paramilitary operations" prohibited by the Boland Amendment, Reagan could spend $14 million in funds, provided that Congress passed a joint resolution expressing its approval for the expenditure.[14]

The exceptions helped the administration, but not much. Reagan believed that more had to be done, and soon. He flatly refused to admit defeat. On May 1, 1985, he tried a different approach, announcing that his administration considered Nicaragua to constitute "an unusual and extraordinary threat to the national security and foreign policy of the United States." This presidential finding allowed him to declare a "national emergency." Based on the declaration, the United States imposed a trade embargo on Nicaragua.[15]

Aside from the dispute between the president and Congress over aid to the Contras, the issue involved a broader question of the separation of powers. Reagan and his allies argued that the United States Constitution vests the president with power to conduct foreign affairs. As part of his duties, it was the president's prerogative to determine whether assistance to the Contras served a vital national interest. Congress had overstepped its constitutional authority in interfering with the president's duties as commander in chief.

His opponents contended that Congress shared power with the president as part of the constitutional checks and balances. Because appropriating money was a key congressional responsibility, the Boland Amendment's limitations on Contra funding were well within the scope of legislative authority. It seemed that both sides had reached an impasse.[16]

Recognizing that the Contras were desperate for aid, Reagan was anxious to find a means of meeting the group's needs without violating the letter of the law. If he could not rely on government agencies to accomplish the objective, he mulled over a novel option: the use of private organizations to fund the Contras. In short, the administration would outsource a portion of its foreign policy. That such an end run around Congress violated the spirit of the law, or that such circumvention created a dangerous precedent for subsequent cases of executive overreach, mattered little to a presidential administration in the heat of a partisan battle.[17]

Reagan's NSC created "the Enterprise," a network designed to smuggle arms to the Contras without congressional knowledge or authorization. Headed by retired United States Air Force major general Richard Secord, the Enterprise was characterized as a private-sector organization, but it was subject to NSC dictates. A Marine lieutenant colonel assigned to the NSC, Oliver North, had recruited Secord.[18]

North was fiercely loyal to the administration's goals, and he took to his duties with gusto. Recognizing that time was of the essence, North reached out to the CIA director, William Casey, to provide intelligence to the Contras as well as arrange for training in military tactics. North also arranged back-channel deals for the Contras to purchase covert arms supplied by countries outside of the United States. The rebels still needed money, but North's creative dealmaking provided the Contras with short-term assistance while he searched for long-term funding.[19]

One promising method was to approach American allies for support. The United States, a wealthy nation, did not customarily meet with allies to ask for money, but desperate times called for desperate measures. Reagan's national security adviser, Robert "Bud" McFarlane, approached King Fahd of Saudi Arabia to solicit funds. The Saudis were generous, initially supplying $1 million a month and eventually increasing their contribution.[20]

In the meantime, Oliver North, ostensibly acting under the auspices of an ambiguously named nonprofit organization, the National Endowment for the Preservation of Liberty (NEPL), made the rounds among wealthy private donors in the United States. He developed a polished pitch that generated dollars and controversy. Critics charged that the administration should not solicit private donations for America's public business, essentially treating government functions as a business operation subject to the traditional rules of commerce. North was unfazed. He explained to all who would listen that he and the administration had complied fully with the terms of the Boland Amendment. Congress could prohibit funding for the Contras, but foreign policy was well within the purview of the executive branch. If administration critics were dissatisfied with North's fundraising and the privatization of American foreign policy, they should pressure Congress to restore financial assistance to the Contras.[21]

North also stumbled on a means of funneling money to the Contras from Iran. At first blush, it seemed an odd choice. In the years since the Iranians had stormed the American embassy in Tehran and taken American hostages in 1979, the Iranian regime had been deemed hostile to the nation's interests. Yet the Reagan administration recognized the advantages in dealing with Iran behind the scenes while publicly continuing the American policy of treating the regime as anathema. Perhaps Americans could do business with Ayatollah Ruhollah Khomeini, Iran's religious leader, after all.[22]

Iran desperately needed arms as well as spare parts for its mostly American-made weaponry. Embroiled in a long, bitter war with Iraq, Iran was open to purchasing arms even from the "great Satan," the United States. The administration recognized an opportunity. If armaments could be transferred surreptitiously to Iran, the money from the sales could be channeled to the Contras. It was a creative means of circumventing American law without attracting undue public or congressional attention. This arms-for-hostages exchange was not the administration's original goal, but the policy developed after Congress closed off financial support for the Contras.[23]

During the summer of 1985, Bud McFarlane wrote a National Security Decision Directive calling for improved relations with Iran to prevent Tehran from acquiring military assistance from the Soviet Union. The directive allowed the

United States government to sell military equipment to Iran. When Secretary of Defense Caspar Weinberger saw the directive, he dismissed McFarlane's plan as "almost too absurd to comment on." Similarly, Secretary of State George Shultz reacted negatively, remarking on the incongruity of designating Iran as a state sponsor of terrorism while agreeing to sell arms to the country. CIA director William Casey was the sole high-ranking foreign policy member of the administration to support McFarlane's plan.[24]

The plan was predicated on the possibility that a moderate faction existed within the Iranian government. This was a difficult position for the Reagan administration to take without appearing hypocritical. When Reagan was campaigning for president in 1980, the candidate bitterly criticized the Democratic incumbent, Jimmy Carter. Carter was president when the Iranian revolution occurred and the Khomeini regime captured Americans inside the United States embassy. The ongoing hostage crisis showed how weak President Carter was, and Reagan continually blasted the administration for not adopting a tougher stance against Iran. If he were elected, Reagan would be a strong commander in chief, refusing to defer to foreign thugs. During a Reagan administration, the United States would not suffer such indignities.[25]

Reagan won the White House in a landslide. In public, he continued his hard line against Khomeini, repeatedly insisting that the United States would never negotiate with terrorists. Unlike his predecessor, this new president would not become yet another victim to a hostage crisis.[26]

Unfortunately for Reagan, Iranian-sponsored terrorists kidnapped Americans and held them hostage despite his bellicose rhetoric. Nothing as dramatic as the storming of the American embassy occurred, but Iranian-backed terrorist groups such as Hezbollah kidnapped hostages one at a time with apparent impunity. Clearly a tough stance alone did not solve the problem. When he heard personal stories of how the hostages were treated, Reagan expressed genuine concern. He longed for a means of securing their release without appearing to give in to terrorists.[27]

Perhaps members of the administration could forge a path forward by linking all these foreign policy problems together. America's great ally in the Middle East, Israel, was struggling to deal with the Iranian regime, and that nation had been supplying American-made spare parts for armaments to Iran since 1981. Building off its relationship with Israel, the Reagan administration arranged a convoluted scheme to rely on intermediaries. The United States would ensure that Israel acquired arms that would be supplied to Manucher Ghorbanifar, an Iranian arms dealer and former secret policeman. In theory, Ghorbanifar would then supply the arms to the moderate Iranians, who would use the weapons in the civil war with Iraq. In return, Iran would pressure

Hezbollah, the terrorist group that had kidnapped seven American hostages, to release them from captivity.[28]

Aside from violating the policy of not negotiating with terrorists, the proposal was risky. Nothing guaranteed success. Terrorist groups could not be trusted to honor their promises and release the hostages. Even if they did, nothing prevented them from seizing new hostages a week later. When he heard that President Reagan was considering this plan, Secretary Shultz warned him, as the secretary of state later recalled, that "we were just falling into the arms-for-hostages business and we shouldn't do it."[29]

Reagan ultimately resolved to move forward because he had faith that Akbar Hashemi Rafsanjani, the influential speaker of the Iranian parliament and Khomeini's likely successor, sought a rapprochement with the United States. If the United States government made the necessary overtures, Reagan believed that Rafsanjani would respond in kind. Administration officials had no doubt that Rafsanjani could order Hezbollah to produce the hostages. Whether Rafsanjani was genuine in his willingness to work with the Americans or was feigning good faith remains an open question to this day.[30]

The United States completed its first arms sale to Iran as early as 1981, but most transactions occurred from August 1985 through October 1986, for a total of nine exchanges. After the first sale, Bud McFarlane resigned as national security adviser, citing his desire to spend more time with his family. His successor, Admiral John Poindexter, came into office just as the administration modified its arms-for-hostages scheme. In lieu of working with the moderate civilian faction in Iran, the Reagan administration, still using Israel as an intermediary, tried to ensure that Iranian army officers received the arms.[31]

Reagan always insisted that "[w]e were *not* trading arms for hostages, nor were we negotiating with terrorists," but some members of his administration were skeptical. Aside from Shultz, Secretary of Defense Caspar Weinberger staunchly rejected the plan and its rationale. Reagan went ahead, though. He bypassed the State and Defense Departments, allowing the NSC to take the lead. The plan soon entered a new phase, with a new lead character at the helm.[32]

As soon as McFarlane resigned, Oliver North, still struggling to arrange financing for the Contras, offered a new plan. Rather than supplying arms to Iran through Israel, the sales should be made directly to the Iranian regime. The United States could insist on a price markup as well. North had been searching for funding to assist the Contras without directly violating the Boland Amendment, with limited success. Now, he thought he saw a way to accomplish multiple goals simultaneously. If funds from the Iranian arms sales could be diverted to assist the Contras, the administration would be well positioned to free the hostages in the Middle East *and* combat Marxism in Latin America.[33]

Admiral Poindexter, as the new national security adviser, might have halted the arrangement. Bud McFarlane was out of office, and a new man could have modified the plan, possibly convincing Reagan to find a safer, less risky alternative. Instead of reining in North, however, Poindexter provided his assistant with increased discretionary authority in the arms-for-hostages deal. Imbued with more power and responsibility than most lieutenant colonels possess, North charged forward, directing the scheme with virtually no oversight. Reagan had established general priorities, but the president did not know about the operational specifics. The lack of knowledge about the details gave Reagan plausible deniability if the operation failed.[34]

For their part, the Iranians initially scoffed at the suggested price markup for the armaments, but they could not hold out indefinitely. The Iranian army sorely needed the weapons. In February 1986, the United States delivered one thousand TOW (tube-launched, optically tracked wire-guarded) antitank missiles. Unfortunately, no hostages were released as a direct result of the sale.[35]

In May 1986, North and his former boss, Bud McFarlane, accompanied by an Israeli official, visited Tehran traveling under forged Irish passports. Their objective was to facilitate increased arms sales. The men were humiliated to discover that they would not meet with high-ranking Iranians. Instead, they were shepherded into sessions with mid-level bureaucrats. Incensed at the insult, McFarlane exclaimed, "[a]s I am a Minister, I expect to meet with decision-makers. Otherwise, you can work with my staff."[36]

From beginning to end, the trip was a debacle. In addition to keeping the Americans waiting, the Iranians increased their demands, insisting that the Israelis abandon the Golan Heights and arguing that spare parts for Hawk missiles must be shipped before any additional hostages were released. Disgusted, the group departed after four days. McFarlane advised President Reagan to discontinue his outreach to the duplicitous Iranians.[37]

The administration ultimately rejected McFarlane's advice. Although Reagan understood that the Iranians did not always act in good faith, his administration had invested much time and energy in the project. He directed his men to continue their efforts. In the meantime, at North's suggestion, the administration modified its previous policy, which had called for all the hostages to be released simultaneously. Under North's new plan, shipments would be sequential, with an arms sale following a hostage release.[38]

As the scheme changed, the American team expressed frustration with Manucher Ghorbanifar, the Iranian arms broker. Aside from the difficulty they experienced negotiating with the Iranians, administration officials came to see Manucher Ghorbanifar as a dishonest intermediary. He was supposed to assuage the concerns of both sides, but he appeared to be far more interested in misrepresenting everyone's position to seek an advantage for himself. To disentangle themselves from Ghorbanifar, the Americans, acting on Richard Secord's recommendation, found a second (and presumably more reliable) intermediary, Ali Hashemi Bahramani, Rafsanjani's nephew. North was pleased with the change. He invited Bahramani to Washington, DC, and provided him with a guided tour of the White House late at night.[39]

Much to the Americans' dismay, Bahramani eventually brought many more Iranians into the arms negotiations. This greater number of participants meant that the Americans were negotiating with hard-liners as well as moderates within the Iranian government. Moreover, with the increased number of participants, the possibility of public disclosure increased.[40]

The scheme encountered difficulties when it came to funding the Contras as well. Secord later testified that his group spent approximately $3.5 million financing the Nicaraguan rebels. Among other things, Secord's men used the money to purchase airplanes to deliver supplies to the Contras. The airdrops commenced in April 1986 and continued until the Nicaraguan army shot down a transport plane on October 5, 1986. Everyone on board died except for a loading specialist, Eugene Hasenfus, an American civilian captured by the Nicaraguans. At a press conference held shortly after his capture, Hasenfus revealed that he had flown supplies to several CIA hot spots around the world, including Nicaragua. His statements greatly embarrassed the Reagan administration. Worse was yet to come.[41]

On November 3, 1986, a pro-Syrian Lebanese magazine, *Ash-Shiraa*, reported on the arms-for-hostages plan, including details about timing and shipments. The story even revealed McFarlane's and North's secret Tehran visit. Although the article did not reveal the source of the information, the Americans believed that the disgruntled Ghorbanifar probably leaked the material. Mehdi Hashemi, a high-ranking member of the Islamic Revolutionary Guard Corps, was another possible source.[42]

The Reagan administration initially denied the stories of an arms-for-hostages plan, but with the Hasenfus press conference and the *Ash-Shiraa* story coming so close together, it was impossible to conceal American involvement. In the meantime, angry members of Congress demanded answers. Faced with few good options, President Reagan spoke to the American people on the subject.[43]

In a televised address from the Oval Office on November 13, 1986, Reagan explained that for "eighteen months now, we have had underway a secret diplomatic initiative to Iran. That initiative was undertaken for the simplest and best of reasons: to renew a relationship with the nation of Iran, to bring an honorable end to the bloody six-year war between Iran and Iraq, to eliminate state-sponsored terrorism and subversion, and to effect the safe return of all hostages."[44]

As for a linkage between the arms sales and hostage negotiations, Reagan empathically denied the existence of a causal relationship. "The charge has been made that the United States has shipped weapons to Iran as ransom payment for the release of American hostages in Lebanon, that the United States undercut its allies and secretly violated American policy against trafficking with terrorists," he said. "Those charges are utterly false. The United States has not made concessions to those who hold our people captive in Lebanon. And we will not. The United States has not swapped boatloads or planeloads of American weapons for the return of American hostages. And we will not." Later in the speech, he reiterated that his administration was aboveboard. "To summarize: Our government has a firm policy not to capitulate to terrorist demands. That no concessions policy remains in force, in spite of the wildly speculative and false stories about arms for hostages and alleged ransom payments. We did not—repeat—did not trade weapons or anything else for hostages, nor will we."[45]

Whether Reagan knew on November 13 that his statements were not the truth, the whole truth, and nothing but the truth remains a point of contention. In any case, he did not mention a linkage among hostages in Lebanon, Iranian arms sales, and funding for the Nicaraguan Contras. The linkage would become public soon enough. In the meantime, if the president hoped that his speech would end the questions about the country's secret deals with Iran, he was mistaken. It did not.[46]

Six days later, Reagan held a press conference to address the issue again. In his opening statement, he insisted once more that the administration's policy was sound and that it had not violated long-standing American policy against negotiating with terrorists. He conceded one point. He said that "to eliminate the widespread but mistaken perception that we have been exchanging arms for hostages, I have directed that no further sales of arms of any kind be sent to Iran. I have further directed that all information relating to our initiative be provided to the appropriate Members of Congress." Following the press conference, the White House—forced to clear up one point (namely, Reagan's assertion that the negotiations had involved no third parties)—released a statement noting that the president had misspoken. A third party was involved, and it was soon clear that Israel was that party.[47]

Members of Congress, reporters, and the public reacted with outrage. With a potential scandal in the making, Attorney General Edwin Meese, a longtime Reagan confidant, conducted an internal investigation. It was an informal inquiry, and Meese did not provide a written report. The only document of substance he located was a memorandum that Oliver North wrote in April 1986 suggesting that money from the arms sales be diverted to finance the Contras' activities. North told the attorney general that he had written the memo, but he asked that it remain secret. Meese later claimed that he, Meese, told President Reagan about the memo on November 24, 1986.[48]

Meese's hasty, self-serving internal investigation satisfied no one. It was clear that the scandal would grow, and the entire scheme would become public knowledge. Consequently, between Reagan's November 19 press conference and the November 25 public disclosure of the administration's plan to divert funds from the Iranian arms sales to finance the Nicaraguan Contras, Oliver North and his secretary, Fawn Hall, removed NSC documents from the White House and shredded them. North later explained that he was trying to protect the lives of individuals involved in the plot who might be killed because of their assistance to the Americans. North also said that he personally witnessed National Security Adviser Poindexter destroy the signed version of a presidential action directive authorizing the CIA to ship a Hawk missile to Iran.[49]

On November 25, 1986, President Reagan appeared before the White House press corps to read a prepared statement about a "seriously flawed" policy. Admiral Poindexter had resigned, he said, and a White House review board was investigating the matter. After Reagan hastily departed, Attorney General Meese revealed the connection between Iranian arms sales and funding for the Contras. The public reaction was immediate—and devastating. The Reagan administration had violated the policy against dealing with terrorists in Iran, and it had circumvented the Boland Amendment by secretly funding the anticommunist rebels in Nicaragua. The lead story characterized the Reagan administration as lawless and the NSC and CIA as rogue, out-of-control elements within a rudderless administration. Following the Church Committee hearings in the 1970s, when the CIA was found to have engaged in extralegal activities in numerous countries, Congress had instituted changes to ensure that agencies within the executive branch, especially the CIA, would not overreach in the future. It appeared that the institutional controls had failed.[50]

The administration needed scapegoats, and it needed them immediately. Admiral Poindexter resigned as national security adviser, and Reagan fired Lieutenant Colonel Oliver North. That same day—November 25—Reagan announced the creation of a special review board to investigate the affair. Three well-respected leaders—former United States senator John Tower of Texas, former secretary of state Edmund Muskie, and former national security adviser Brent Scowcroft—agreed to serve.[51]

The Tower Commission, as it was called, convened on December 1, 1986, and published its report relatively quickly, on February 26, 1987. The commission was tasked with examining "the proper role of the National Security Council staff in national security operations, including the arms transfers to Iran," but the commission was not asked "to assess individual culpability or be the final arbiter of the facts. These tasks have been properly left to others." Owing to this limited mandate as well as a short time frame, the commission was not empowered to subpoena documents, compel testimony, or grant immunity from prosecution.[52]

During its brief tenure, the Tower Commission heard testimony from eighty-six witnesses and examined numerous NSC documents. In its final report, commission members criticized President Reagan's relaxed managerial style and aloofness from policy detail. Although he probably did not know about the diversion of funds for the Contras, Reagan should have known. He was too disengaged from the scheme to oversee his underlings effectively, the report concluded. The authors singled out Oliver North, Admiral Poindexter, and Defense Secretary Weinberger for withering criticism of their roles in the scandal.[53]

Often heralded as the Teflon President—because negative stories did not stick to him—and a great communicator, Reagan was accustomed to receiving mostly positive press coverage. The criticism stung him deeply. He introduced the Tower Commission report at a press conference but refused to answer questions.[54]

The report had criticized his chief of staff, Donald T. Regan, for allowing chaos to overtake the White House decision-making process. To demonstrate his willingness to correct deficiencies in his administration, Reagan fired Regan and replaced him with a well-respected former United States senator from Tennessee, Howard Baker. Baker promised to reform the White House and hold administration officials accountable for their actions. It was a classic example of a reform that was too little, too late.[55]

In any event, Baker commissioned another internal investigation to determine whether the president had any criminal exposure. To his immense relief, the results suggested that Reagan could not be implicated in criminal wrongdoing. Facing calls for additional external investigations, Baker became the voice of moderation, promising to cooperate with all inquiries.[56]

Reagan understood that the Tower Commission investigation would not satisfy public concern. Bowing to political pressure, he agreed to the appointment of an independent counsel. On December 19, 1986, a two-judge panel appointed a retired federal judge, Lawrence Walsh, to determine whether anyone involved in Iran-Contra should be prosecuted. That same month, the House of Representatives and the Senate select committees on intelligence conducted closed-door hearings.[57]

On January 6, 1987, the Senate formed an eleven-member Select Committee on Secret Military Assistance to Iran and the Nicaraguan Opposition, chaired by Daniel Inouye, a Democrat from Hawaii. The next day, the House created a fifteen-member House Select Committee to Investigate Covert Arms Transactions with Iran. Lee Hamilton, a Democrat from Indiana, and Dick Cheney, a Republican from Wyoming, cochaired the committee. Concern about the proliferation of committees eventually led the House and Senate to combine the two committees under Senator Inouye's chairmanship.[58]

The independent counsel was concerned that the congressional committees would interfere in his investigation and thereby jeopardize the possibility of securing criminal indictments. To accommodate Walsh's investigation, at least partially, the joint congressional committee limited its agenda and agreed not to drag out the hearings. In the end, the committee allowed for twelve weeks of testimony from thirty-two witnesses. Several witnesses received limited grants of immunity. Some testimony was offered on television, and some was delivered behind closed doors. Most important for the administration, Admiral Poindexter testified that he had never told Reagan about the scheme to funnel money from Iranian arms sales to the Contras. More than anything else, this testimony likely prevented the House from instituting impeachment hearings against the president.[59]

A heretofore obscure character in public, Lieutenant Colonel Oliver North emerged as a media darling when he testified before Congress in July 1987. Wearing a uniform decorated with medals, the ramrod-straight, buttoned-down Marine appeared on television and defiantly defended his actions. He admitted that he had misled Congress, but he explained that he had a noble purpose in mind when he did so. It was necessary to aid the Contras in the global fight against Communism. According to North, the Contras were "freedom fighters" valiantly resisting the dangerous Sandinista regime. As a loyal, patriotic American, he could not allow the freedom fighters to perish because America lacked the will to oppose the insidious forces of godless Communism. It was dramatic testimony that fed directly into right-wing myths of good versus evil on a global stage.[60]

North had shredded documents, he said, but he was acting on orders from CIA director William Casey. It was a convenient admission. Casey had died two months earlier, on May 6, 1987. North also claimed that Bud McFarlane had instructed him to alter official records so that any mention of funds diverted to the Contras was deleted. In short, Lieutenant Colonel North was a good soldier who had followed orders in service of a just, patriotic cause. For many conservative Republicans, a hero was born when Oliver North appeared before the cameras. He had violated the law, but he had done so in the service of a greater good.[61]

In the meantime, President Reagan knew that he must explain his actions in the wake of the Tower Commission report as well as the appointment of the independent counsel and the commencement of the congressional inquiries. Even before North testified, Reagan took to the airwaves to explain his administration's role in the affair. He had always been able to use his savvy public relations skills to good effect, and he resolved to do so now.

In this photograph, Lieutenant Colonel Oliver North testifies before Congress in 1987 regarding the Iran-Contra affair. (*Ron Sachs/CNP, ZUMA Press, Alamy Stock Photo*)

"A few months ago, I told the American people I did not trade arms for hostages," he said in a televised address on March 4, 1987. "My heart and my best intentions still tell me that's true, but the facts and the evidence tell me it is not. As the Tower board reported, what began as a strategic opening to Iran deteriorated, in its implementation, into trading arms for hostages. This runs counter to my own beliefs, to administration policy, and to the original strategy we had in mind. There are reasons why it happened, but no excuses. It was a mistake."[62]

He had to walk a fine line. On one hand, he did not want to implicate himself in criminal mischief by confessing to his centrality in the plot. On the other hand, Reagan had often been criticized for being a doddering old man, disconnected from public policy, and he did not want to reinforce the stereotype that he was not a decisive president firmly in charge of his administration. "I didn't know about any diversion of funds to the contras," he said. "But as President, I cannot escape responsibility."[63]

As for his management style, Reagan defended his hands-off approach: "The way I work is to identify the problem, find the right individuals to do the job, and then let them go to it. I've found this invariably brings out the best in people. They seem to rise to their full capability, and in the long run you get more done. When it came to managing the NSC staff, let's face it, my style didn't match its previous track record. I've already begun correcting this."[64]

Reagan never fully acknowledged his leadership failures in the Iran-Contra affair. He repeatedly said that he accepted responsibility for his administration's policies and actions, but he defended his own role as a minor failing owing to his excessive concern for the lives of the hostages. He seemed to believe that his only shortcoming was being too good hearted and suffering from an excess of empathy. Even after the joint congressional committee concluded that Reagan had not adequately supervised the NSC and had allowed staffers to bypass standard operating procedures designed to ensure accountability, the president did not admit that he was a poor leader. Moreover, his promise to reform the national security apparatus was perfunctory at best.[65]

Reagan might have faced impeachment proceedings. It was clear that his administration was out of control and lawless. Yet even Democrats never seriously considered preparing articles of impeachment in the House of Representatives. The reasons were never entirely clear. He was a popular president, but he was not so popular that he could survive a serious impeachment inquiry. Perhaps members of Congress worried that impeachment was too extreme for the transgressions in question. Inattentive mismanagement by an uninterested, ill-informed president did not rise to the level of a high crime and misdemeanor required by the United States Constitution. In addition, the facts were murky and convoluted. Without clear evidence of malfeasance, an impeachment inquiry would not serve anyone's interests.[66]

Long after Congress issued its reports, the independent counsel, Lawrence Walsh, submitted his final report. The date was August 1993, and the report followed a seven-year investigation. It was released to the public the following year. Walsh concluded that the Iran-Contra scheme was implemented with the approval of President Reagan and Vice President George H. W. Bush as well as Secretary of State Shultz, Secretary of Defense Weinberger, CIA Director Casey, and the two national security advisers, Bud McFarlane and John Poindexter.[67]

Reagan did not technically violate any laws, Walsh declared, but he knew of the arms-for-hostages plan beforehand. Despite repeated warnings by various officials, Reagan approved the plan, agreeing that his administration could mislead Congress to keep the arms sales and money transfers secret. The president of the United States swears an oath to ensure that the laws are faithfully executed, and Reagan failed to honor his oath.[68]

Unlike President Reagan, other participants faced indictments. A grand jury indicted Secretary Weinberger on five felony counts, which included one count of obstructing a congressional investigation, two counts of perjury, and two counts of making false statements. President George H. W. Bush eventually pardoned him. Bush also pardoned Bud McFarlane after the former national security adviser accepted a plea bargain in exchange for two years of probation.[69]

Admiral Poindexter was convicted of five felonies and was sentenced to serve six months in prison. He appealed. In November 1991, a federal appellate court overturned his convictions. Poindexter later started a software company.[70]

No one involved in the Iran-Contra affair received his or her comeuppance. Arms dealer Richard Secord entered a guilty plea for making false statements to Congress and received two years' probation. Fawn Hall, Oliver North's secretary, received immunity from prosecution for destroying documents. In exchange, she testified truthfully about her role in Iran-Contra. She later married Danny Sugerman, the former manager for the rock music group the Doors.[71]

Despite his riveting testimony and significant sympathy from right-wing administration supporters, Lieutenant Colonel Oliver North could not escape the legal consequences of his actions. He was indicted on sixteen felony counts in March 1988. His trial commenced in February 1989, and on May 4, 1989, he was convicted on four charges. Sentenced to serve a three-year suspended prison term and two years of probation and required to pay $150,000 in fines and complete twelve hundred hours of community service, he served part of the community service before an appellate court overturned his sentence. North later ran unsuccessfully for a United States Senate seat and served briefly as president of the National Rifle Association. He also became a frequent television commentator.[72]

The Iran-Contra affair demonstrated the perils of an out-of-control government overseen by a disengaged (and perhaps slyly manipulative) chief executive.

When a presidential administration found that Congress, exercising its constitutional role as a check on executive power, refused to fund support for the Nicaraguan Contras, Reagan and his men did not accept this result. Rather than explore potential policy options, administration officials resolved to circumvent the will of Congress in service of what they saw as a noble purpose. The ends justify the means, they concluded.[73]

A relatively junior NSC aide, Lieutenant Colonel Oliver North was vested with enormous discretionary authority to run an illegal operation out of the White House based on no principles save expediency. At the top of the hierarchy was a president who allowed his men to run amok. Was Reagan an ill-informed simpleton in over his head, or did he knowingly contravene the law to achieve his policy goals? The answer to that question remains a mystery.[74]

CHAPTER 12

# "All He Was Worried about Was Jack. Jack Has to Get His Next Big Check."

## JACK ABRAMOFF AND INFLUENCE PEDDLING

Jack Abramoff was a lobbyist whose name became synonymous with influence peddling and financial corruption in American politics. Many citizens mistrust lobbyists who cozy up to elected officials seeking access and special deals for their wealthy corporate clients. The rejoinder to objections about the lobbying profession is that interest groups necessarily must communicate with elected officials to ensure adequate and fair representation even if sometimes a few "bad apples" seek to influence public policy through bribes and payoffs.

Abramoff became the poster boy for bad apples, but he did not start out that way. He began his career as a lawyer-lobbyist legitimately working to represent his clients. Eventually, he engaged in a complex series of illegal practices to reap the enormous financial benefits that come from taking shortcuts. The list of his crimes was long: Abramoff provided financial bribes to members of Congress in express violation of federal campaign laws; he overbilled and defrauded Native American clients; and he hired ex-congressional staffers to lobby their former bosses in violation of the one-year ban on lobbying activity by former employees. In 2006, he agreed to plead guilty to three felony counts of conspiracy, fraud, and tax evasion. Abramoff's activities did not constitute the worst bribery offenses in American history, but his notoriety and numerous shady activities ensured that he would become an emblematic figure in the annals of American political scandals.[1]

Jack Allan Abramoff was born on February 28, 1959, in Atlantic City, New Jersey. His father, Franklin, was president of the Franchises unit of the Diners Club credit card company. In 1968, his family moved across the country, settling in Beverly Hills, California. At Beverly Hills High School, Abramoff played football and enjoyed weight lifting. He was reared to be competitive, and he hated to lose.

151

He attended college at Brandeis University in Waltham, Massachusetts, graduating with an English degree in 1981. Like his father, Jack Abramoff became a conservative Republican. In college, he became chairman of the Massachusetts Alliance of College Republicans. Owing to his father's contacts within Republican circles, young Jack became acquainted with influential party leaders at an early age.[2]

Following college graduation, Abramoff was elected chairman of the College Republican National Committee (CRNC), a national organization created to "recruit, train, mobilize and engage" young conservatives. He had already developed an uncompromising style of bare-knuckle politics, which he honed at the CRNC. "It is not our job to seek peaceful coexistence with the left," he wrote in the CRNC 1983 annual report. "Our job is to remove them from power permanently."[3]

During these years, Abramoff became friends with Grover Norquist, a Harvard MBA who founded Americans for Tax Reform (ATR), a lobbying group dedicated to preventing federal tax increases. The ATR was known for asking elected officials to adopt a taxpayer protection pledge. Along with another young conservative activist, Ralph Reed (who started as a CRNC intern and eventually became executive director of the Christian Coalition), Abramoff and Norquist formed the "Abramoff-Norquist-Reed triumvirate." The three young men remade the CRNC in their image as they purged dissenters. The triumvirate sought to remake Washington politics into a conservative bastion by engaging young men and women early and often.[4]

As CRNC chairman, Abramoff addressed the 1984 Republican National Convention. It was an auspicious start for a young conservative activist on the rise. The contacts he made during these years served Abramoff well. Many of the young conservatives of the 1980s were elected officeholders in the 2000s, and access to those people allowed Abramoff to develop a lucrative lobbying business.[5]

An unusually perceptive operative, Abramoff planted the seeds for his later success early. In 1985, he joined Citizens for America, an organization created to assist Lieutenant Colonel Oliver North in building support for the Nicaraguan Contras. A year later, Abramoff earned a law degree from Georgetown University Law Center, an impressive credential for an up-and-coming Republican lobbyist.[6]

Even as he learned his way around Washington politics, the young conservative understood the power of Hollywood in shaping public opinion. Along with his brother, he developed a story, "Red Scorpion," about a Soviet assassin dispatched to kill an African revolutionary. The would-be assassin witnesses Soviet abuses and changes his mind. The story became a 1989 film starring a prominent Swedish action star, Dolph Lundgren, and promoted a narrative favorable to the white South African regime. It was a controversial position owing to the regime's support for racist apartheid policies. Aside from the political controversy, *Red Scorpion* was hardly highbrow entertainment. One critic called the film "seriously God-awful," while another opined that the "movie's reflective moments belong to Mr. Lundgren's sweaty chest." Nonetheless, Abramoff was on his way as a budding manipulator of public opinion.[7]

In 1994, the lobbying firm Preston Gates Ellis & Rouvelas Meeds hired Abramoff owing to his close ties to important Republican elected officials. Abramoff used the resources and prominence of his new firm to propel him into the top ranks of Washington lobbyists. In 1995, he began his long association with Native American tribes when he represented the Mississippi Choctaw in the successful effort to defeat a congressional bill to tax Native American casinos. Texas congressman Tom DeLay, the House majority whip (and later House majority leader), led the effort to derail the bill, calling Abramoff one of his "closest and dearest friends."[8]

From the outset, Abramoff understood that he could influence federal legislation by arranging "goodies" for members of Congress. Journeymen lobbyists seek meetings with lawmakers to educate them on issues crucial to their clients' causes, but Abramoff largely eschewed such pedestrian tactics. Instead, he wined and dined members of Congress and other elected decision-makers with expensive meals, lavish trips and vacations, and hard-to-get tickets to concerts and sporting events. He also arranged for spouses and relatives of lawmakers to be employed in positions that paid handsomely without requiring much work—in effect, sinecures for the well connected.[9]

The Commonwealth of the Northern Mariana Islands (CNMI) hired Abramoff's firm to champion a policy exempting the CNMI from federal immigration and labor laws. From 1995 until 2001, the Islands paid $6.7 million for these services. To facilitate his actions, Abramoff secretly paid for prominent members of Congress to travel to the Marianas. He focused especially on three California Republican congressmen: Dana Rohrabacher, John Doolittle, and Ken Calvert.[10]

Abramoff advertised himself as a full-stop shop. Aside from providing lucrative trips, he and his staff prepared statements for congressmen to read on the floor of the House of Representatives. Congressman Ralph Hall, a Texas Republican, attacked a story offered by an escaped adolescent sex worker, "Katrina," in the Marianas with remarks that Abramoff ghostwrote.

Abramoff used Ralph Reed's marketing firm to send mailings to conservative Christian voters. He provided gifts to Roger Stillwell in the United States Department of the Interior. He arranged for Congressman Tom DeLay to visit Russia on a "fact-finding" trip before DeLay supported legislation to allow the International Monetary Fund to bail out the weak Russian economy.[11]

Abramoff operated on a global stage representing multiple industries, especially energy companies and the gaming industry. He had no qualms about taking on foreign governments as clients. During his career, Abramoff represented the governments of Malaysia and Sudan. No client was too repugnant or loathsome to represent—provided that the client paid exorbitant fees for Abramoff's services.[12]

He brought in millions of dollars for his firm, but not everyone was enamored of his business or his tactics. Some partners expressed unease at Abramoff's lack of concern for ethics and fair play. In 2001, he realized that it was time to move on from Preston Gates. He joined Greenberg Traurig, a prominent law firm and lobbying outfit that allowed him to assemble a crackerjack team to revamp the firm's lobbying practice. "Team Abramoff," as it was called, was composed of former congressional aides who used connections with members of Congress to ensure that the team leader enjoyed access within the highest circles of power.[13]

When George W. Bush entered the White House in January 2001, Abramoff was well positioned to cash in on his contacts to a degree he had never known before. He served on the administration's transition advisory team for the Department of the Interior and became friends with the department's incoming deputy secretary, coal lobbyist J. Steven Griles.[14]

The House Government Reform Committee later combed through Abramoff's records and found that the lobbyist had 485 contacts with the Bush White House during the first three years of the administration, including 345 meetings or face-to-face contacts. His influence was astonishing. Among other victories, Abramoff repeatedly persuaded senior administration officials to assist his clients in the Indian casino industry.[15]

Abramoff's high-flying lobbying business could not operate indefinitely without attracting the attention of law enforcement as well as congressional investigators. By late 2004, the latter were examining the lobbyist's work on behalf of Native American casinos. In September 2004, Abramoff appeared before the Senate Indian Affairs Committee but asserted his Fifth Amendment rights against self-incrimination rather than answer uncomfortable questions about his business dealings.[16]

Abramoff was wise to plead the Fifth. Records later revealed that he and partner Michael Scanlon, a former aide to Tom DeLay, conspired to bilk Indian casinos out of tens of millions of dollars in fees. Abramoff charged a huge retainer to four tribes—the Saginaw Chippewa of Michigan, the Agua Caliente of California, the Choctaw of Mississippi, and the Coushatta of Louisiana—to lobby for their interests in Washington, DC. When they realized that their fees might be in jeopardy, Abramoff and Scanlon orchestrated opposition to the casinos so they could convince their clients to keep the duo on retainer. In

November 2005, Scanlon entered a guilty plea to conspiring to bribe members of Congress and other public officials for his actions in the Indian casino matters. A few months later, Abramoff also agreed to plead guilty. As part of his sentence, the court ordered Abramoff and his codefendants to pay $25 million in restitution.[17]

Bernie Sprague, a representative of the Saginaw Chippewa of Michigan, expressed buyer's remorse for engaging Abramoff's services. "It totally destroyed our tribe," he said. "All he was worried about was Jack. Jack has to get his next big check."[18]

The quest for the next big check led Abramoff to pursue questionable business opportunities that a more cautious man would have avoided. His operations faced the most significant threat from his business dealings with Konstantinos "Gus" Boulis, a land developer, restauranteur—he created a popular chain restaurant, Miami Subs Grill—and casino operator. Boulis had discovered the profitable business of buying ships to escort patrons on a "cruise to nowhere." The cruise ship was a casino that sailed customers into international waters where Florida's gambling laws did not apply.

Boulis founded SunCruz Casinos, a gambling boat company, in 1994. Afterward, he ran afoul of zealous law enforcement officers in Hollywood, Florida. Undercover investigators found that he had allowed gambling on a SunCruz ship before entering international waters. After a contentious battle, Boulis avoided liability because the Hollywood authorities did not have probable cause to believe a crime had occurred when they launched their sting. Nonetheless, Boulis knew that the authorities had their eye on him. He grew weary of the scrutiny.[19]

By September 2000, he said he was ready to unload SunCruz. At the time, the company employed two thousand people and contained eleven ships. It brought in tens of millions of dollars in profits annually. Jack Abramoff and a partner, Adam Kidan, agreed to purchase the enterprise for $147.5 million. As part of the deal, Boulis would retain a silent 10 percent interest in the business. He also agreed to accept a $20 million promissory note instead of a $23 million down payment.

Abramoff and Kidan did not have the money necessary to complete the transaction, but they concocted an illegal scheme to get it. They faked wire transfers indicating that they had made the $23 million down payment, which allowed them to qualify to receive a $60 million loan.[20]

The fraud might have succeeded but for a series of unexpected developments. In December 2000, Kidan and Boulis became so upset with each other that they literally came to blows, with Boulis stabbing Kidan in the neck with a pen. In February 2001, someone murdered Boulis in his car. When the police rounded up three suspects, authorities discovered that Kidan had paid the men.

Kidan testified that he had hired Anthony "Big Tony" Moscatiello to protect him from Boulis and the mob, but he never asked Big Tony to kill Boulis.[21]

The cases dragged on interminably. After fourteen years of legal wrangling, the court concluded that Moscatiello killed Boulis on his own initiative. As a result of the murder, a jury sentenced Moscatiello to life in prison. His codefendant Anthony "Little Tony" Ferrari was convicted of murder and conspiracy and sentenced to serve a life sentence. The third defendant, James "Pudgy" Fiorillo, pleaded guilty to a conspiracy charge and was sentenced to serve six years in prison.[22]

With the scrutiny afforded the SunCruz deal, authorities uncovered the Abramoff and Kidan financing scheme. Abramoff realized that he had few options but to plead guilty to conspiracy and wire fraud, which he did in Miami on January 4, 2006. His plea agreement indicated that he would serve a maximum prison term of seven years, to run concurrently with a sentence he received the preceding day in a fraud, tax evasion, conspiracy, and bribery case. Prosecutors recommended that the sentence be reduced if Abramoff cooperated fully. In March 2006, Abramoff and Kidan received the minimum sentence of seventy months in prison and were ordered to pay $21.7 million in restitution.[23]

Aside from the SunCruz matter, Abramoff was involved in other activities with legal ramifications, although he emerged relatively unscathed. In 2002, Abramoff accepted a retainer to serve as a subcontractor for the Guam Superior Court to lobby against a proposal to place the superior court under the authority of the Guam Supreme Court. For his services, Abramoff received $324,000. The United States attorney for Guam, Frederick A. Black, initiated an investigation into the matter. A grand jury issued a subpoena requiring the Guam Superior Court administrator to release records about the contract. The investigation abruptly ended when the George W. Bush administration suddenly removed Black from office.

The matter appeared to be dead, but in 2005 a public auditor, Doris Flores Brooks, initiated a new investigation of the issue. Investigators found that the Guam Superior Court paid Abramoff's retainer by sending thirty-six checks of $9,000 each to Howard Hills, a constitutional lawyer who had advised the court for years. Hills had retained Greenberg Traurig, Abramoff's law firm, as a subcontractor. The structure of the deal and the amount of each check suggested that the Guam Superior Court sought to keep Abramoff's involvement a secret. Moreover, federal requirements for transfer payments require that amounts more than $10,000 to be reported to government authorities. By dividing up Abramoff's fee into thirty-six payments of less than $10,000, the court appeared to circumvent federal law. In addition, contracts more than $10,000 must be publicized through a competitive open bidding process, and that did not happen in this case.[24]

The Guam attorney general indicted Greenberg Traurig and Jack Abramoff in 2006. Fortunately for Abramoff, the case did not proceed to trial. The law firm returned the $324,000 fee in 2008, and the court dismissed the case. It had been a close call.[25]

By the time the courts disposed of the Guam case, Abramoff was serving his prison sentence for the SunCruz deal. He had already faced trial in another influence-peddling case. On September 4, 2008, a court in Washington, DC, found him guilty of supplying expensive gifts, meals, and trips to sporting events to legislators in exchange for favorable legislation, all violations of federal campaign finance laws. Because he had cooperated with prosecutors by detailing how he operated, the judge sentenced him to a reduced sentence of four years. He could have been sentenced to more than twelve years in prison.[26]

Addressing the judge in open court during his sentencing hearing, Abramoff exhibited the requisite contrition. He insisted that he had abandoned his profligate ways, telling the court that he was no longer the man "who happily and arrogantly engaged in a lifestyle of political corruption and business corruption." Summarizing his remorse, Abramoff declared that "I am sorry, so sorry that I have put everyone through this."[27]

Because of Abramoff's extensive influence-peddling operation, two dozen people were convicted of corruption or bribery, including Steven Griles, the former deputy interior secretary and the highest-ranking Bush administration official in the scandal. Griles pleaded guilty to obstruction of justice. Congressman Robert Ney, an Ohio Republican, received a two-and-a-half-year prison sentence for accepting bribes. William Heaton, Ney's former chief of staff, entered a guilty plea on a federal conspiracy charge involving a golf trip to Scotland, expensive meals, and tickets to sporting events between 2002 and 2004. David Safavian, a Bush administration procurement official, was sentenced to eighteen months in prison after he tried to cover up his relationship with Abramoff.[28]

With his myriad schemes brought to light and his lobbying career in shambles, Abramoff reported to the minimum security Federal Correctional Institution in Cumberland, Maryland, on November 15, 2006. He became inmate number 27593-112. Accustomed to earning millions of dollars in fees and retainers, he soon found himself working in the prison chaplain's office for twelve cents an hour. He also taught courses on public speaking and screenwriting to his fellow inmates. Always a film buff, Abramoff convinced the prison administration to institute a popular movie night for the inmates.[29]

On June 8, 2010, Abramoff moved from federal prison to a Baltimore, Maryland, halfway house. He worked as an accountant for a local pizzeria until his release from custody on December 3, 2010. After his release, he returned to lobbying.[30]

Despite his checkered past, Abramoff attracted a high-ranking clientele in Republican circles. In December 2016, he attempted to arrange a meeting between President-Elect Donald Trump and Republic of Congo president Denis Sassou Nguesso. Although the meeting never happened, it appeared that Abramoff was back in the game.[31]

By 2020, however, Abramoff was back in more ways than one. After a decade outside the limelight, his name returned to the headlines when federal prosecutors charged him and Roland Marcus Andrade—founder and chief executive officer of the NAC Foundation, also referred to as the "National AtenCoin Foundation," an organization that was created to develop and manage the new cryptocurrency AML Bitcoin—for making false statements to secure buyers. Abramoff also failed to register as a lobbyist, as required by the Lobbying Disclosure Act, after being retained. He agreed to plead guilty to the charges.[32]

Abramoff has become a cultural figure—and a controversial one at that. Hollywood cranked out a 2010 film, *Casino Jack*, about Abramoff's venality. Always a fan of movies, Abramoff must have been thrilled to learn that Oscar-winning actor Kevin Spacey (who subsequently became embroiled in a well-publicized sex scandal of his own) portrayed him in the film. Eager to cash in on

**Jack Abramoff, the lobbyist who "owned" Congress, is pictured in 2011. (Madeleine Ball, Lessig/Abramoff 5, Creative Commons Attribution)**

his notoriety, Abramoff appeared on television news programs as a commentator and blogged about his experiences as a lobbyist.[33]

In his 2011 book *Capitol Punishment: The Hard Truth about Washington Corruption from America's Most Notorious Lobbyist*, Abramoff reviewed his life as a high-flying influence peddler. He admitted that he had taken advantage of a notoriously weak and ineffectual system for policing lobbyists. Abramoff suggested that the only genuinely effective means of preventing corruption is to impose a lifetime ban on former officials serving as lobbyists. He also recommended prohibiting all gifts from lobbyists and lawmakers. In his view, term limits would prevent longtime elected officials from becoming ensconced in Washington.[34]

Although Abramoff was a single individual mired in corruption, his activities were emblematic of a broken political system. The American system of campaign finance, with its emphasis on raising large sums of money to fund the never-ending reelection cycle, all but encourages systematic abuse by politicians and the lobbyists who court them. Jack Abramoff was but one man; however, he came to symbolize the corrosive culture of political finance and manipulation in the United States.

# CHAPTER 13

# "Everybody's Trying to Get Me. It's Unfair. Now Everybody's Saying I'm Going to Be Impeached."

## 2016 RUSSIAN ELECTION INTERFERENCE

The most recent political scandal discussed in this book involves the 2016 presidential election, when the Russian Federation deliberately interfered in the American electoral process to sow seeds of discord and political instability for its historic adversary. Even before the November 2016 elections, American intelligence officials recognized that the Russian government had developed an ambitious scheme to hack computer systems operated by the Democratic National Committee (DNC) as well as systems used by Democratic operatives. The Russians specifically sought to harm Democratic Party candidate Hillary Clinton's chances of becoming president in favor of the Republican nominee, reality television star and real estate mogul Donald J. Trump, who was viewed as more favorably disposed to Russia and its authoritarian leader, Vladimir Putin, than Clinton and the Democrats would be.

After Trump staged a surprising come-from-behind victory in the presidential election, Congress and American intelligence agencies stepped up their investigations of Russian interference in the election. The incoming president was upset with these probes, apparently believing that charges of Russia's involvement were thinly disguised efforts to delegitimize his election. Trump so vigorously objected to American investigations that he undertook seemingly inexplicable actions, such as firing Federal Bureau of Investigation (FBI) director James Comey, presumably to impede the agency's Russia investigation. Following the Comey firing, the United States Department of Justice (DOJ) empowered a special counsel, former FBI director Robert Mueller, to investigate the affair. Mueller indicted several Trump associates for improper ties with Russia and he secured convictions, but he could not definitively conclude that Trump conspired—or "colluded," as Trump was wont to say—with Russia to win the 2016 election. It became one of numerous political scandals during the Trump era.[1]

The affair originated with hacking attempts by Russia, which had once been part of a superpower, the Union of Soviet Socialist Republics (USSR), commonly called the Soviet Union. The Soviet Union had opposed the United States and its allies in the Cold War for almost five decades. After the collapse of the Soviet Union in 1991, Russia suffered through a scramble for power and a search for an effective means of rebuilding its shattered economy.

A former intelligence officer, Vladimir Putin, emerged in the 1990s as a contender for the Russian presidency. Putin longed to restore Russia's place on the world stage, but he was working from a position of weakness. The once mighty superpower had been humbled, prostrated before the world. The United States was the sole superpower, although China was making rapid progress and might soon rival the Americans. In a desperate effort to strengthen Russia's position by undermining its adversaries, Putin approved a series of clandestine methods for attacking the United States and its electoral system.

United States intelligence agencies were confident that Russia coordinated cyberattacks against American interests in the 2016 presidential election cycle. Informed sources concluded that Putin personally authorized operations designed to undermine citizens' faith in democratic processes and institutions. Evidence suggested that Putin wanted the Republican presidential nominee, Donald J. Trump, to defeat Democrat Hillary Clinton in the election because Putin believed that Trump would ease economic sanctions against Russia and would not be a hard-line adversary. Putin was correct.[2]

Months before the 2016 election, the Internet Research Agency (IRA), a Kremlin-backed "troll farm" of computer hackers who were directed to use social media to talk up Trump's candidacy while castigating Clinton, launched a campaign to shape American public opinion. The IRA sought to stoke partisan, racial, and ethnic discord by posting messages denigrating groups based on negative stereotypes associated with their demographic traits.[3]

By 2016, the internet provided trolls with numerous social media platforms from which to spread their toxic messages. Facebook, Twitter, Reddit, Tumblr, Pinterest, Medium, YouTube, Vine, Instagram, and Google+ offered anyone in the world an instant, easily accessible forum for influencing opinions. The typical Russian tactic was to create a false organization, such as a fictional conservative interest group offering "dirt" on Hillary Clinton and the Democrats. Posting false news, manipulated videos and photographs, and derogatory messages captured voters' interest. The bogus conservative groups discovered how easy it was to garner media attention. In some cases, members of the Trump campaign reposted the damaging information with little concern about confirming its authenticity. The IRA trolls became experts at "astroturfing"—that is, disguising the sources of messages to make it appear as though it originated from average people with support from grassroots participants.[4]

2016 RUSSIAN ELECTION INTERFERENCE     163

Russian hackers also purchased advertisements on Facebook to reach ten million viewers. The trolls understood a crucial insight in generating effective propaganda: a lie repeated over and over, circulated, and shared online eventually became the conventional wisdom of public discourse. Attacks on Hillary Clinton's health and politics, DNC internal divisions, and policy failures in the Obama administration were especially potent topics.[5]

Aside from influencing opinions on social media, the Russians hacked into e-mail accounts associated with the Clinton presidential campaign as well as the Democratic Congressional Campaign Committee and the DNC. The hackers unearthed a treasure trove of damaging information, which they shared with the WikiLeaks organization. A person or organization using the nom de guerre "Guccifer 2.0"—probably a Russian hacker or someone closely associated with the IRA—also provided damaging information, as did the entity "DCLeaks."[6]

For all the sophistication of the Russian cyberattacks, their techniques were simple. Beginning in or around March 2016, the Glavnoye Razvedyvatel'noye Upravleniye (commonly abbreviated GRU), Russia's foreign military intelligence agency, targeted more than three hundred men and women associated with the Democratic Party and the Hillary Clinton campaign with a series of "spearphising" e-mails. When a target received the e-mail and clicked on a link or attachment, GRU operatives gained access to the target's computer system, including their e-mail files. This technique yielded thousands of e-mails and attachments that the Russians could use to damage the Democrats.

John Podesta, chairman of Hillary Clinton's campaign, received a classic phishing e-mail on March 19, 2016. The e-mail warned him that his computer system had been compromised, and he must change his password immediately. He clicked on the link and, in so doing, provided access to sixty thousand e-mails for the Russian hackers who had contacted him. The hackers recovered e-mails about the fees that Wall Street financiers paid to Hillary Clinton for her speeches, unguarded comments about potential vice-presidential nominees, and comments to and from staffers about celebrities and other candidates. The infamous Pizzagate conspiracy theory, which alleged that Democratic Party officials operated a child sex trafficking ring out of pizzerias in Washington, DC, originated because of the misinterpretation of information derived from these e-mails.[7]

The Russians timed the public release of e-mails at strategic points during the summer and fall general election campaign. On July 22, 2016, three days before the opening of the Democratic National Convention, the hackers released nineteen thousand e-mails and eight thousand attachments. As the Democrats headed into the convention in hopes of uniting myriad party factions, the newly released e-mails suggested that DNC officials had stacked the deck against Hillary Clinton's principal challenger in the primary elections, Vermont senator

Bernie Sanders. The Russians' goal in releasing the e-mails was to sow discord among Democrats at precisely the moment when the party faithful needed to coalesce behind their presidential nominee. The resultant brouhaha indicated that the hackers had achieved their goal. Members of the progressive wing of the Democratic Party complained that their candidate had been sabotaged by the party establishment. Owing to the public outcry about the national party's sharp practices, Congresswoman Debbie Wasserman Schultz resigned from her role as the DNC chairperson.[8]

A second release of e-mails, this one on October 7, 2016, distracted from the Obama administration's revelation that the Russians were interfering in the 2016 elections. It was a precarious time for the Trump campaign. A 2005 video-tape of Trump bragging about sexual assault to *Access Hollywood* television host Billy Bush was causing a furor among elected officials and the public. The new e-mails provided cover for Trump and his allies to divert attention from their candidate's damning admissions. Trump and his proxies dismissed the candidate's comments on the tape as "locker room talk" and insisted that the Democrats' e-mails were the real story.[9]

Critics charged that an eleven-year-old videotape and the Democrats' hacked e-mails were not the *real* story. Instead, Russia's nefarious hacking campaign should be the focus. When American intelligence officials issued their statement about the Russian election interference on October 7, they expressed high confidence that agents of the Russian government were responsible for the hacks. Moreover, they were reasonably certain that the e-mail leaks were designed to hurt Hillary Clinton's electoral chances. By publicizing internal Democratic polls, data analytics, and voter-turnout models, the hackers were influencing voters in favor of her opponent, Donald Trump.[10]

The ostensible source of the e-mail disclosures, WikiLeaks, was a nonprofit organization created in 2006 by an Australian activist, Julian Assange. Assange claimed that he was a free speech advocate who was dedicated to speaking the truth to power. In his view, governments were far too secretive, using their information monopoly as a means of suppressing dissent and oppressing the citizenry. By disclosing secret information, he was promoting the free exchange of ideas and exposing the ugly secrets of overbearing governments around the world.

These rationales served Assange well early in his career. He was a charismatic knave who aimed to clean up the dirt and grime created (and often hidden) by authoritarian governments. In agreeing to accept information supplied by disreputable sources that was obtained through illicit means, however, Assange showed that WikiLeaks was not the "white knight" enterprise portrayed by its founder. Assange detested Hillary Clinton, and his willingness to assist the Russian government—under Putin, hardly a bastion of transparent, participatory government—revealed him to be a hypocrite of the first order.[11]

Donald Trump was delighted by the Democrats' problems. A longtime celebrity and salesman for his brand, Trump hailed from the school of realpolitik. He had little use for traditional political or ethical considerations. He believed that politics was a zero-sum game: a participant either won or lost. He saw Russian interference in the election as another means to hurt his opponent and help his own campaign. When he learned of the WikiLeaks disclosures, Trump declared himself a Julian Assange fan, although he had disparaged the man and his methods previously. Trump insisted, however, that he had not coordinated or colluded with WikiLeaks or the Russian government.[12]

Hillary Clinton was already struggling to contain a brewing scandal involving e-mails when the WikiLeaks disclosures occurred. During her tenure as secretary of state in the first term of the Obama administration, she had merged her personal and State Department e-mail accounts, which meant that she possibly had transferred top-secret communications on an unsecure server, thereby violating departmental protocols and possibly federal law. The FBI launched an investigation. Clinton and her team sifted through thousands upon thousands of e-mails, deleting items that were private—perhaps as many as thirty thousand entries—and turning over e-mails containing State Department communications to the FBI. Although the agency found no evidence of criminality, the investigation created a giant public relations problem for the candidate. FBI director James Comey, in an unusual public announcement in 2016, indicated that no crimes had been committed, but he concluded that Clinton had been extremely reckless in her e-mail usage.[13]

The continuously negative press coverage was a godsend for the Trump presidential campaign. Trump was a stunningly weak candidate with a string of failed businesses and marriages to his credit. He had no experience in elective office, and as a loudmouthed, obnoxious, famously (and proudly) ignorant septuagenarian, he seemed to have little to recommend him for the position of president of the United States. Associates past and present marveled at his lack of judgment as well as his poor temperament for the job. His only hope of winning the election was to denigrate Hillary Clinton at every opportunity.

For all his deficiencies as a candidate and a human being, Trump was a master at negative campaigning. He possessed an uncanny knack for discovering an opponent's weaknesses and highlighting them incessantly. Because he was shameless and oblivious to other people's pain—his niece, Mary L. Trump, a clinical psychologist with a PhD, opined that he is a narcissist, adding that "the label gets us only so far"—Trump would stop at nothing to undermine, even humiliate a perceived enemy. With the ongoing news stories about Hillary Clinton's e-mails, he eagerly exploited the opportunities he had been afforded to attack the Democratic nominee.[14]

Purposely conflating Clinton's e-mail controversy with stories of Russian hacking of Democratic Party e-mails, candidate Trump appeared at a news conference on July 27, 2016, with a proposition. "Russia," he thundered to an approving crowd, "if you're listening, I hope you're able to find the 30,000 emails that are missing. I think you will probably be rewarded mightily by our press." Subsequently criticized for the comment, Trump insisted that he was joking. The comment and the situation did not appear funny to many observers worried about the integrity of American elections. Investigators later found that Russian operatives took up Trump's suggestion. On the same day that he uttered his "joke," hackers attempted to enter Hillary Clinton's electronic server for the first time.[15]

Throughout the campaign, Russian trolls sought to build up Trump's reputation and tear down numerous Democratic candidates' popular support by planting incendiary stories about Muslim terrorists, illegal immigrants, and strange people of color undermining the American way of life. The stories glossed over Trump's sexual affairs and broken marriages, his multiple bankruptcies, his numerous insults against women, his unbelievable lies about political opponents, his vicious attacks on Gold Star families, his draft dodging during the Vietnam War, and his long history of racism.[16]

Russian hackers were not satisfied with interfering in federal elections. They sought to influence statewide elections as well. If they could worm their way into databases containing voter registration information, the status of ballot applications, and lists of poll workers, perhaps they could sow chaos in the ranks and undermine public confidence in all American elections, not just at the presidential level. The FBI warned states to be on the lookout for hacking attempts. Two states, Illinois and Arizona, reported that information on registered voters was stolen.[17]

As American intelligence agencies learned of the Russian interference, the question was what they should do about it. Director of National Intelligence James Clapper included information on the attempt in the President's Daily Briefing (PDB) that he supplied to Obama. With the 2016 presidential election rapidly approaching, the president worried that any release of information about Russians trying to throw the election to Donald Trump would appear to be partisan manipulation of intelligence to make Trump look bad—"notice how much the Russians, our adversaries, want him to win"—and assist Hillary Clinton's campaign. Yet sitting on the intelligence was unfathomable. Allowing a foreign government to interfere in an American election with impunity would seriously harm the nation's electoral process.[18]

Central Intelligence Agency (CIA) director John Brennan recommended an "under-the-radar" response. Instead of the president making a prime-time public address castigating the Russians or ignoring a credible threat, Brennan said that he, Brennan, could approach Alexander Bortnikov, his counterpart in the Russian Federal Security Service (FSB), a successor of the infamous Soviet KGB. Brennan would tell Bortnikov that the Americans knew that the Russians were interfering in US elections. The Russians must immediately cease and desist. President Obama agreed that this was a wise approach, and he authorized Brennan to make the contact.

On August 4, 2016, Brennan did as he had been instructed. He reached out to Bortnikov and warned him that the American government would not tolerate continued Russian interference in the election. Bortnikov denied any Russian involvement. With a long record of disinformation and denial, the Russians' reaction was not surprising. At least the Obama administration had alerted them that the hacking had not gone unnoticed.[19]

In the meantime, DNI Clapper briefed members of Congress on the issue. Much to his dismay, the members reacted along party lines. Anxious to use the information to sully Trump's candidacy, Democrats asked multiple questions about the intelligence and seized on every detail as damning to Trump. For their part, Republicans did not want to hear about it. They seemed skeptical of the quality of the information and obviously did not believe, or want to believe, what Clapper told them. After a long career in intelligence, Clapper thought that all elected officials would be alarmed by the information, but he realized that he had been naive. Even intelligence data was seen through a partisan lens.[20]

President Obama understood that his administration needed to do more to discourage Russian hacking and election interference. In September 2016, the president spoke with Russian president Vladimir Putin privately while the two leaders were attending a G20 summit in China. Obama told Putin that the hacking had to stop. When it became clear that this conversation had no effect, Obama called Putin on the phone on October 31, 2016, and reiterated his concerns. Putin always denied that his country was responsible, but the denials no doubt helped buy him time. He knew that the Obama administration was on the way out of office. Putin could outlast the outgoing president in hopes of receiving preferential treatment from the incoming administration, which was the rationale for the hacking in the first place.[21]

Obama understood precisely what the Russian leader was doing. He instructed the American intelligence community to produce a report on the Russian efforts no later than January 20, 2017, the day his term of office ended. The president also instructed his intelligence officers to use overt and covert methods to foil the Russians, which would include American hacking of Russian computer systems.[22]

On December 29, 2016, less than a month before Obama left the White House, the United States government instituted a series of punitive measures against Russia for interfering in the election. The government sanctioned four high-ranking GRU officials and declared thirty-five Russian diplomats personas non grata, ordering the diplomats to leave the country within seventy-two hours. Vladimir Putin might have retaliated—typically, when one country expels diplomats, the other country immediately reacts with similar measures—but he did not. Putin knew that a Trump administration would be more hospitable to Russia than its predecessor. He could, and did, wait.[23]

Cyberwarfare is a relatively passive form of interference, and Putin sought an active response as well. Consequently, the Russians reached out to potential allies in the United States. Trump's campaign advisers had innumerable contacts with Russian nationals during 2016, but it was unclear whether the contacts were illegal. American intelligence officials were monitoring Russian government officials, a customary surveillance activity, when they heard their targets mention conversations with many Trump associates.

Paul Manafort, a prominent lobbyist for foreign governments, joined the Trump campaign in March 2016. Intelligence records indicated that Manafort met frequently with Russians before, during, and after his association with the Trump campaign. The most controversial Manafort-Russian contact during the 2016 campaign occurred on June 9, 2016, when he, Donald Trump Jr., and the president's son-in-law and adviser, Jared Kushner, met with a Russian attorney, Natalia Veselnitskaya, and other Russian nationals in Trump Tower. The purpose of the meeting became a matter of subsequent dispute. Eventually, it was clear that Trump's team sought damaging information on Hillary Clinton. Their defense was that nothing came of the meeting, and therefore the session was not evidence of a conspiracy between Russians and the Trump campaign to win the 2016 election.[24]

Manafort became Trump's campaign manager later in June, but he lasted only a few months. Because he carried so much baggage, he became a political liability. Trump accepted Manafort's resignation after several advisers, notably Kushner, told Trump that Manafort's overseas lobbying activities raised too many problems. In 2017, the United States District Court for the District of Columbia indicted Manafort on multiple charges for irregularities in his consulting work as well as tax and bank fraud.[25]

Michael Flynn, a former general who later served briefly as Trump's national security adviser, was another close Trump adviser who seemed cozy with the Russians. Flynn was seen in the company of Vladimir Putin in December 2015. He also had delivered a paid speech in Moscow without disclosing that fact, as required of former high-ranking military leaders. Intelligence intercepts revealed that the Russians believed Flynn's association with Trump could be used to good advantage. The general was another Trump enthusiast who started the campaign in the candidate's good graces but became a political liability and departed in disgrace.[26]

Jeff Sessions, a United States senator from Alabama who served as Trump's first attorney general before falling out of favor, also had Russian contacts, as did Roger Stone, a longtime Trump associate and informal adviser. Both men struggled to defend their associations after they initially lied about their contacts. Fearful of incurring Trump's wrath, on one hand, and violating federal law, on the other hand, Sessions and Stone walked a fine line that strained their credibility with all parties.[27]

An oil industry consultant and Trump associate, Carter Page, became the target of a United States Foreign Intelligence Surveillance (FISA) Court warrant because he was suspected of serving as a Russian foreign agent. While he was acting as a Trump foreign policy adviser, Page had contacts with the Russians that worried American intelligence officials. Trump's subsequent charge that the "deep state" within the United States government was spying on his campaign was because the FISA court had allowed intelligence officials to monitor Page's communications. Intelligence officials insisted that they were following leads and it was Page's contacts with the Russians, not his association with the Trump campaign, that made him the subject of the FISA warrant application.[28]

Because he was Donald Trump's son-in-law, Jared Kushner enjoyed a special relationship with the president. The relationship created and saved his White House career. When Kushner applied for a security clearance, he failed to disclose multiple meetings with foreign officials, including some Russians. He was denied the security clearance, but Trump overruled the decision. Any other White House staffer likely would have had to leave the staff and seek employment where a security clearance was not required.[29]

Michael Cohen, Trump's personal lawyer, also had contact with the Russians. When he testified before both chambers of Congress in 2017, Cohen admitted that he had reached out to contacts inside the Kremlin for assistance in building a Trump Tower property in Moscow. Unlike previous presidential candidates, Trump never divested himself of his business holdings, nor did he place them in a blind trust. This decision left Trump and his agents free to pursue business opportunities while he campaigned for president—and even after he won the post—but it also left him especially vulnerable to charges of self-dealing and manipulation by foreign entities.[30]

Furthermore, Trump appeared vulnerable to foreign influence according to a controversial source known as the "Steele dossier." In June 2016, Christopher Steele, a former agent of the British intelligence agency MI6, accepted an assignment from Fusion GPS, a research firm hired to provide opposition research on Donald Trump. Republican operatives originally hired Fusion GPS when Trump was running for the Republican presidential nomination. After he became the party's nominee, the Republicans ceased using the firm. The DNC and the Clinton campaign later hired Fusion GPS to continue the opposition research on Trump. Steele was tasked with producing information focusing especially on Trump's Russian connections.

Steele's report—the so-called "dossier"—alleged that the Trump campaign conspired with the Russians to steal the election from Hillary Clinton. The dossier contained salacious and unsubstantiated information suggesting that Russian officials possessed compromising information (*kompromat*) on Trump. The most outrageous claim intimated that the Russians possessed a tape of prostitutes urinating on Trump in a Moscow hotel room in 2013. Even the most die-hard anti-Trumper found this tidbit difficult to credit considering Trump's famous aversion to germs. (Of course, Trump could have watched the prostitutes urinate on the bed even if he did not venture close enough to make physical contact.)

As the dossier circulated, the issue for media outlets was how they should handle the information. Some sources freely reported material from the dossier, but most mainstream media outlets refused to do so because they could not corroborate many of the allegations. Trump's operatives insisted that everything in the report was fabricated by his enemies in a desperate attempt to derail his winning political campaign. The sheer outrageousness of the dossier made it difficult to credit the allegations as anything other than rumor and innuendo.

Of course, accurate or not, the information could serve multiple purposes. In October 2016, FBI agents used portions of the dossier—although it was not clear which portions—to obtain a FISA warrant in the Carter Page case. Trump and his allies attacked this fact as evidence that the deep state was out to get him and that the entire FBI investigation of Russian election interference was corrupt and therefore untrustworthy. The FBI responded that the dossier was only a small fraction of the material used to obtain the FISA warrant. According to the bureau, a FISA warrant probably would have been granted even without the Steele dossier.[31]

After Donald Trump won the presidency in one of the greatest upset victories in American political history, the question of how much the Russians had contributed to that victory remained crucial, although Trump did not care to hear it. As far as the president-elect was concerned, his victory was all that mattered. How he had gotten there, and whatever shortcuts he and his campaign staff had taken, were immaterial. He was ready to put allegations of Russian election tampering behind him by shutting down further investigations.

Because Trump could not separate his own private interests from the public interests, he did not see the value in uncovering Russian election interference to ensure the integrity of future American elections. As far as he was concerned, harping on Russia's role in the election accomplished nothing other than delegitimizing his own victory. He saw no point in dwelling on the election apart from referring to it as the most amazing accomplishment in American political history.[32]

Despite Trump's aversion to continuing the Russian investigations, the CIA issued a December 2016 report concluding that "individuals with connections to the Russian government" had provided material to WikiLeaks, including the e-mails hacked from John Podesta's e-mail account as well as the DNC e-mail account. The Republican National Committee account had been hacked as well, but that material was not disclosed. The report did not reach the conclusion that Trump, or his men, knew of the leaks, or had coordinated with the Russians, but their involvement was an open question.[33]

In addition to the CIA, the FBI investigated the Russian hacking episodes and any possible connections with the Trump campaign. Beginning in July 2016, when the DNC reported the theft, the bureau followed the trail from the Russian trolls to WikiLeaks. The FBI wanted to find out whether the Trump campaign had been in touch with the hackers or with WikiLeaks. It was possible that Trump had benefited innocently from a foreign government that wanted him to win for reasons unrelated to his participation, but it was also possible that Trump or someone associated with his campaign had been in contact with the Russians or their agents.

The bureau focused especially on a meeting between George Papadopoulos, a low-level Trump campaign adviser, and Alexander Downer, a prominent Australian politician and diplomat, in London in May 2016. During the meeting, Papadopoulos bragged about his advance knowledge of a release of e-mails damaging to Hillary Clinton. Papadopoulos had met with a Maltese academic, Joseph Mifsud, a few months earlier. Mifsud had shared his knowledge of the e-mails with Papadopoulos before the theft of the information from the DNC and the Clinton campaign was common knowledge.[34]

Despite the Papadopoulos connection, in the summer of 2016 the FBI was not certain that the Russians had interfered in the election to help the Trump campaign. It was possible that the interference was simply a general effort to spread disinformation and chaos. Later, intelligence professionals concluded that the Russians favored Trump's election. On July 31, 2016, the bureau launched "Operation Crossfire Hurricane," the code name for the FBI counterintelligence investigation into links between Trump associates and Russian officials. The goal was to determine whether Donald Trump's presidential campaign officials were coordinating, "wittingly or unwittingly," with the Russian government's efforts to interfere in the 2016 US presidential election.[35]

Although the newly inaugurated President Trump was not inclined to examine evidence of Russian interference in the election, other government officials sought information about what happened and how it could be prevented in future elections. Congress and American intelligence agencies launched multiple investigations. To preserve the legitimacy of his victory, Trump repeatedly and emphatically argued that whatever hacking Russia did in the election, if any, had not influenced the outcome. His CIA director, Mike Pompeo, agreed. As Pompeo understood it, the intelligence community concluded that Russian meddling had occurred, but it "did not affect the outcome of the election."[36]

Other officials disputed the administration's conclusions. James Clapper remarked that "it stretches credulity to think the Russians didn't turn the election." Trump barely won three key Midwestern states that traditionally vote Democratic—Wisconsin, Michigan, and Pennsylvania. As the well-known academic Kathleen Hall Jamieson observed, Russian trolls convinced enough voters to not vote for Clinton or not vote at all in at least these three states, which handed the election to Donald Trump.[37]

In response to the allegations of Russian interference, President Trump searched for ways to reassure the public of the legitimacy of his victory. He had always been a paranoid personality, but the barrage of stories about Russian interference only heightened Trump's deep-seated insecurities. He demanded loyalty from everyone in his administration, including executive branch appointees with fixed terms. When Trump did not receive sufficient guarantees from officials, he typically erupted in anger. In most cases, an errant appointee was dismissed.

FBI director James Comey was a case in point. Comey was a controversial public figure because he had assumed a higher profile than most of his immediate predecessors. His surprising comments about Hillary Clinton after the bureau decided not to charge her with a crime and, later, his abrupt decision to reopen the e-mail investigation shortly before the 2016 election incensed Democrats who believed that he had irreparably harmed their candidate. Donald Trump, of course, had been delighted. As president, he hoped that he could persuade Comey to become an ally, especially while the FBI investigated the Russian connection with the Trump campaign. Throughout his adult life, Trump had surrounded himself with loyal supplicants. The question was whether Comey would become another Trump sycophant, in which case he could stay in his position as FBI director—he was four years into a ten-year term—or whether he should be removed from his post.[38]

After Comey testified before Congress in January 2017 about Russian election interference, Trump publicly declared that he retained confidence in the FBI director. Their relationship turned sour, however, after Comey confirmed that the bureau was investigating a possible link between the Trump campaign and Russia. Comey also disputed Trump's unfounded allegation that the Obama administration had spied on Trump's campaign.

At the dawn of the Trump administration, the FBI was investigating General Flynn's connections with Russia. Although Trump had dismissed Flynn from the position as national security adviser, the president retained a soft spot for the general. Flynn had been an early and avid Trump supporter, appearing at rallies where the audience chanted "lock her up," a slogan alluding to Hillary Clinton's alleged crimes, and encouraging the crowd to support their man's demagoguery. At a one-on-one meeting with Comey on February 14, 2017, the president asked the FBI director to gloss over Flynn's possible malfeasance.

According to contemporaneous memoranda that Comey wrote shortly after the discussion, the president was unequivocal in delivering his message. "I hope you can see your way clear to letting this go, to letting Flynn go," Trump said. "He is a good guy. I hope you can let this go." It was a stunning conversation. The president of the United States was "suggesting" that a federal law enforcement officer drop the prosecution of a potential defendant in a criminal investigation. Unnerved but nonetheless resolute, Comey did not act on the recommendation.[39]

Three months passed following this encounter. By May 2017, Trump had grown disillusioned with Comey. The president was convinced that the myriad investigations into Russian interference in the election, and especially the focus on the Trump campaign, was a "witch hunt" that must be derailed. Comey's unwillingness to issue a public statement that Trump was not under investigation and his continued probing into sensitive subjects infuriated the president. Trump longed to sack the rogue FBI director and install a crony in his place.

Trump's advisers cautioned him against taking precipitous action. White House counsel Don McGahn fretted that firing Comey because of the investigation into Russian election interference would create untold political and legal headaches, not to mention establishing potential grounds for an impeachment inquiry. Chief strategist Steve Bannon, as usual, offered a blunt, earthy assessment. Though Comey was unpopular, even inside the FBI, dismissing the man from his position could backfire. "The moment you fire him he's J. fucking Edgar Hoover," Bannon explained. "The day you fire him, he's the greatest martyr in American history. A weapon to come and get you. They're going to name a special fucking counsel." These were wise, prescient words.[40]

Despite these admonitions, Trump would not be dissuaded. "Don't try to talk me out of it," he told his men, "because I've made my decision, so don't even try." He needed a pretext for dismissing Comey, and his advisers resolved to manufacture one.[41]

The deputy attorney general, Rod Rosenstein, agreed that Comey should be dismissed for his mishandling of the Clinton e-mail investigation. Seizing on this explanation, Trump directed Rosenstein to record his comments in writing. In response, the deputy attorney general produced a three-page memorandum titled "Restoring Public Confidence in the FBI." Using this memorandum as his stated justification, Trump relieved Comey of duty on May 9, 2017.[42]

In his termination letter, Trump disingenuously wrote that "I have received the attached letters from the Attorney General and Deputy Attorney General of the United States recommending your dismissal as the Director of the Federal Bureau of Investigation. I have accepted their recommendation and you are hereby terminated and removed from office, effective immediately." Before he received the letter, Comey saw news coverage of his firing on television while he was visiting the FBI's Los Angeles field office. The surprised former FBI director rode back to Washington, DC, on a bureau plane, although Trump later ranted that Comey should have been left in California to find his own way home. In "Trump World," when you were gone, you were gone for good, immediately.[43]

If Trump had hoped that the Russia investigation would disappear from the headlines because he dismissed Comey from his post, he was woefully mistaken. Newspapers and online sources blasted the president's decision. Trump undermined his position when he and administration officials offered conflicting reasons for firing Comey. One rationale for Comey's dismissal, the White House insisted, was because he had lost the support of rank-and-file agents, although Trump's press secretary later admitted that she had exaggerated this point. In one of his many explanations, Trump said that Comey "wasn't doing a good job."[44]

The president could not help himself when it came to defending his decision. While he was meeting with Russian foreign minister Sergey Lavrov and Russian ambassador Sergey Kislyak in the Oval Office on May 10, 2017, Trump sought to impress his guests. "I just fired the head of the FBI. He was crazy, a real nut job," he bragged. "I faced great pressure because of Russia. That's taken off." It was an extraordinary statement. The president of the United States was telling high-ranking Russian officials that he had fired the man who was investigating claims of Russian interference in American elections.[45]

During a television interview with Lester Holt of NBC News on May 11, 2017, Trump contradicted the other explanations, inadvertently revealing his true motivations. He fired Comey, he said, because of the FBI's investigation of Russian interference in the 2016 election: "I said to myself, you know, this Russia thing with Trump and Russia is a made-up story." The only way to stop the "made-up story" was to seek a different FBI director who, presumably, would not pursue leads with the same zeal as his predecessor—especially considering his predecessor's fate. Trump needed a loyal "yes man" to protect him from FBI investigations.[46]

In the wake of Comey's abrupt dismissal and the resultant public outcry, the FBI Russian election interference investigation was left in doubt. No one outside of the White House seriously thought that Comey's firing would shut down the investigation, but the path forward was unclear. A new issue arose: Should the firing be investigated as well?

Deputy Attorney General Rosenstein answered that question on May 17, 2017, when he appointed a special counsel to investigate Russian election interference and related matters, including Comey's firing. Steve Bannon's prediction had come true. Rosenstein appointed a well-respected attorney, Robert Mueller, to serve as special counsel. Mueller was an ideal choice. With a long-standing reputation as a straight shooter, the Republican Mueller had served as FBI director from 2001 until 2013, serving in Democratic and Republican presidential administrations. As special counsel, Mueller would have broad powers to hire staff, issue subpoenas for records, compel testimony, and prosecute any federal crimes he and his investigators uncovered.[47]

When he learned of the appointment of a special prosecutor, President Trump was apoplectic. "Everybody's trying to get me," he groused. "It's unfair. Now everybody's saying I'm going to be impeached." He claimed that Mueller had too many conflicts of interest to serve in the position. Mueller had once been a member of Trump's National Golf Club in Sterling, Virginia, and had engaged in a dispute over fees. He also said that Mueller had recently been to see Trump and lobbied for his old position as FBI director. Both comments were false. Mueller had resigned from the golf club because he never used his membership. He had requested a refund of his club fees, but he did not nurse any personal animosity over the issue. As for the position of FBI director, Mueller had visited Trump, but the president, not Mueller, mentioned the position. Mueller was not interested. He was working in a prestigious law firm and did not want to return to government service. Rosenstein had pressed him to accept the appointment as special counsel, and Mueller had reluctantly agreed to serve.[48]

The special prosecutor got to work. He assembled a team of dedicated, tenacious investigators and issued an order that they should not leak information to the press. In a town where leaks were common, the Mueller team became known for its deafening silence. The special counsel preferred to work through a grand jury and allow indictments to be his public voice.[49]

In October 2017, George Papadopoulos agreed to plead guilty in what became the first victory in the special counsel's Russia probe. Papadopoulos confessed that he had lied to the FBI, saying that he had not met with Russian agents when, in fact, he had. As part of his plea deal, Papadopoulos agreed to cooperate with investigators.[50]

That same month, former campaign manager Paul Manafort surrendered to FBI agents after he was indicted on multiple charges. His associate, Rick Gates, facing indictment, surrendered as well. Prosecutors tried to use the indictments to pressure Manafort and Gates to provide information implicating other members of the Trump inner circle, a common prosecutorial practice.[51]

In keeping with his preference for superlatives, President Trump frequently excoriated the investigation into Russian election interference as an unprecedented hoax, the most egregious "witch hunt" in American history. Yet evidence of Russian election meddling was incontrovertible. On February 16,

2018, a grand jury in Washington, DC, indicted thirteen Russian nationals as well as three Russian entities on federal charges of conspiracy to defraud the United States, conspiracy to commit bank fraud, and fraud with identification documents. The indictment outlined a pattern of social media activity designed to sow discord and damage Hillary Clinton's candidacy. Other indictments followed later in 2018.[52]

Two years after his appointment, Mueller's report on his investigation was the most highly anticipated development in the multiple Russian inquiries. Aside from occasional indictments filed in open court, his investigators had remained remarkably quiet in 2017 and 2018. During that time, President Trump had continually used social media and speeches to attack the special counsel and his "team of angry Democrats" for their unfair prosecutions as part of his effort to discredit their findings before the final report appeared.[53]

On March 22, 2019, Mueller transmitted his two-volume report, titled *Report on the Investigation into Russian Interference in the 2016 Presidential Election*, to Attorney General William Barr. It was the attorney general's decision as to whether he should release all, some, or none of the report to the public. Barr released a redacted version of the report on April 18, 2019. The redactions occurred pursuant to President Trump's claim of executive privilege.[54]

Volume 1 of the report found that insufficient evidence existed to conclude that the Trump campaign "coordinated or conspired with the Russian government in its election-interference activities." Nonetheless, the report concluded that the Russians interfered "in sweeping and systematic fashion" and that the purpose was to benefit the Trump candidacy. Moreover, several Trump campaign officials made false statements about their communications with individuals linked to the Russian government, and those same campaign officials obstructed investigations into the matter.[55]

Volume 2 highlighted the obstruction of justice issue in detail. According to a long-standing DOJ Office of Legal Counsel (OLC) opinion, a sitting United States president is immune from criminal prosecution while he is in office because such proceedings would preempt impeachment proceedings. Accordingly, the special prosecutor believed that he must not accuse Trump of a crime because the president would not have the opportunity to defend himself at trial. In arguably the most befuddling statement in the report, Mueller's team wrote that the investigation "does not conclude that the President committed a crime," but "it also does not exonerate him." The report summarized ten damning incidences in which Trump may have obstructed justice, but the report left it to Congress to determine whether the episodes constituted grounds for presidential impeachment.[56]

Before the redacted report appeared in public, Attorney General Barr, a fierce, unapologetic Trump loyalist, sent a four-page letter to Congress. It was a mere two days after Barr had received the Mueller report. Instead of communicating Mueller's ambivalence about the possibility of collusion between the Trump campaign and Russian agents, the attorney general provided his own interpretation. He said that, although the report had not reached legal conclusions about obstruction of justice, he and Deputy Attorney General Rosenstein "have concluded that the evidence developed during the Special Counsel's investigation is not sufficient to establish that the President committed an obstruction-of-justice offense." He promised to release the report on a later date.[57]

Trump wasted no time in claiming complete vindication, even though the Mueller report did not exonerate the president. Speaking to reporters at Palm Beach International Airport on March 24, 2019, he slipped into the victim role he had pioneered throughout his business and political careers: "So, after a long look, after a long investigation, after so many people have been so badly hurt, after not looking at the other side where a lot of bad things happened, a lot of horrible things happened for our country—it was just announced that there was no collusion with Russia." He added a postscript that was not factually accurate, but it became the enduring summary of the Mueller investigation. "It's complete exoneration," he said.[58]

Newspaper headlines the following day made it clear that the cloud hanging over Trump's head was gone. It was a new day for his presidency. Although the Mueller report painted a devastating portrait of an immoral, ignorant, petty president, Trump no longer needed to fear impeachment owing to his ties to the Russian Federation or his campaign's efforts to steal the election from Hillary Clinton. Further recriminations followed, and investigations into Russian interference in the 2016 election continued, but Donald Trump was free and clear of the special prosecutor.[59]

When the heavily redacted Mueller report appeared in April 2019, a pattern of Russian interference in the 2016 election was clear to anyone who sifted through the two volumes. Subsequent congressional hearings explored possible changes to thwart future interference, and members of Congress debated potential sanctions against the Russian Federation. The seriousness with which a member of Congress treated the offenses depended on party affiliation. Democrats expressed concern about the integrity of American elections, citing the Russian campaign against the nation's democracy as one of the biggest threats in the nation's history. Republicans—possibly concerned that an emphasis on Russian election interference would undermine the legitimacy of the Trump victory, and fearful that the president might post nasty remarks about defectors on Twitter—shrugged off the Democrats' concerns. Everyone agreed that future elections must be secured and free from outside interference, but their concern for Russian interference in 2016 remained a hotly debated partisan political issue.[60]

Unencumbered by a special counsel's investigation, and free to pursue a new agenda, most politicians in Trump's position would have allowed the public brouhaha to subside, perhaps quietly exacting revenge against their opponents at some future date. As he demonstrated repeatedly throughout his public career, however, Trump was not like most politicians. His ability and willingness to nurse grievances were legendary. He was not prepared to put the Mueller report behind him. In numerous speeches and social media postings, he referred to the unfairness of the investigation, constantly touting his innocence and complaining that he had been treated worse than any president in American history.[61]

Aside from his public complaints, Trump urged his advisers to "investigate the investigators." By 2019, the Trump administration was staffed with sycophants who had abandoned any pretense at professional objectivity or concern for the public interest. If their president wanted them to inquire into the origins of the Russian election interference probe, the administration supplicants would do exactly that. The same month that the Mueller report appeared in public, Attorney General Barr announced that he had initiated a review of the original FBI investigation into Russian election interference. United States Attorney John Durham would lead the investigation of the investigators.

The inquiry continued into 2020. Attorney General Barr remained integrally involved in the investigation, going so far as to contact foreign intelligence officials to learn about FBI activities. As the 2020 election drew closer, President Trump pressed Barr and Durham to issue a report so that he could

**President Donald J. Trump shakes hands with Russian president Vladimir Putin in Helsinki, Finland, on July 16, 2018. (*Russian Federation*)**

use the results to aid his reelection campaign. When a report was not forthcoming, Director of National Intelligence John Ratcliffe, another shameless Trump ally, approved the release of a large volume of previously classified documents to the DOJ about the Obama administration's handling of the Trump-Russia investigation. Trump hoped that Ratcliffe or Durham would provide him with information leading to indictments of top Obama officials to support the president's repeated assertions that the Russia investigation was the biggest criminal conspiracy in American history.[62]

Despite the multiple investigations and inquiries, the American public never learned everything about the nature and extent of Russian interference in the 2016 election. The evidence overwhelmingly indicated that the Russians interfered, but their coordination with Donald Trump and his agents was unclear. Moreover, Trump's strange affinity for Vladimir Putin remained puzzling. As numerous sources suggested, Trump greatly admired immoral authoritarian strongmen who could exercise power with little or no institutional constraints. Perhaps he envied their lack of accountability. Whatever the case, Trump's willingness to believe Putin's assertions that Russia did not interfere in American elections while discounting information and data from his own intelligence agencies deeply troubled many Americans.[63]

Even the most biased, pro-Trump supporter must admit that the complete story of Russian interference in American elections, which started before 2016 and continued long past that time, was never fully revealed. Too many questions remained unanswered. Trump's involvement with Russia in general, and Putin in particular, was confusing. Trump's associates were not forthcoming with information. Perhaps all that could be said was that foreign interference in American elections, from whatever source, fundamentally threatened (and continues to threaten) the integrity and health of the American republic.[64]

# Afterword

Scandals are a feature of political life across the expanse of American history, as this book illustrates. This observation, while unfortunate, is hardly surprising. Human nature dictates that some individuals presented with an opportunity to acquire a valuable thing—money, property, power, or fame—will take advantage of the opportunity even if acting violates a custom, norm, policy, or law.

Some instances of political corruption are straightforward and easily understood. Bribery is the quintessential example. When Georgia state legislators accepted bribes to sell large tracts of land to speculators in the 1790s, incensed citizens recognized the venality and voted the offenders out of office. Bribery in the Grant administration's many scandals of the 1870s was easily understood as well: government officials accepted payments to manipulate laws and policies and thereby assist private parties in earning a large monetary profit. In the Teapot Dome case, Interior Secretary Albert Fall agreed to lease oil fields to private companies in exchange for financial inducements. "Wild Bill" Langer pressured government employees to contribute funds to a political party and a newspaper that were loyal to him. Spiro Agnew accepted bribes from Maryland contractors and resigned the vice presidency to avoid prosecution. In Abscam, elected officials accepted cash payments to sponsor private legislation for supposed Arab sheiks. Congressman John Jenrette's remark—"I've got larceny in my blood. I'd take it in a goddamn minute"—was unambiguous.[1]

The difficulty in evaluating other political corruption cases is that the facts can be complex and murky. Take, for example, the Aaron Burr conspiracy. To this day, Burr's intentions and actions are unclear. He may have been conspiring with the Spanish empire, but perhaps he sought to carve out an independent nation and install himself as an emperor. He may have been speculating in land for monetary profit or some other inscrutable purpose. Owing to the difficulty in pinning down his aims, judging the level of Burr's corruption is almost impossible. Most historians conclude that he was up to no good, but the nature and extent of his shenanigans are lost to us.

Subsequent scandals such as the savings and loan crises of the 1970s and 1980s as well as the Iran-Contra affair and Russian interference in the 2016 American elections involved convoluted fact patterns and complicated legal standards. Moreover, because few individuals were clearly and unequivocally corrupt (Charles H. Keating Jr. notwithstanding), sustaining public interest in the narratives was difficult. Political scandals require clarity. In cases where the action is clear, and the culprit is identified—Preston Brooks caning Charles Sumner in 1856, William Langer and Spiro Agnew accepting kickbacks, and Jack Abramoff bribing members of Congress—the public can understand the chain of events and support the resultant opprobrium. (In some instances, such as the Brooks-Sumner encounter and "Wild Bill" Langer's bribery charges, partisans are divided about whether the action was corrupt or desirable, but the facts of the case are clear even if the interpretation is not.)

Navigating through the cast of characters as well as the permutations and combinations of the events in the savings and loan scandal, for example, taxes even experts well versed in financial affairs. Charles H. Keating Jr., the Keating Five senators, and House Speaker Jim Wright became the faces of the crises at various times, but they were only a few of the numerous participants. The S&L scandal was in reality a series of scandals that unfolded over many months and years, which meant that the narrative structure was convoluted and lacking a central focus.

In a similar vein, understanding Iran-Contra, with its many moving parts and large number of actors, is challenging. The popular Reagan administration came to power promising to combat left-wing governments that contravened and possibly threatened American interests. Accordingly, the affable president greenlit his administration officials' schemes to fight the Marxist Sandinistas in Nicaragua. When Congress attempted to check his use of power, Reagan tacitly granted discretion to underlings to circumvent the will of Congress.

After the scandal came to light, Reagan expressed befuddlement, which may or may not have been an act. (Reagan was, after all, a former movie actor.) He explained that he sought to halt the global spread of Communism and protect the American people. Yes, his administration violated American policy by trading arms for hostages, but Reagan cared for these captives, and he did not wish to see them tortured or killed. Who could fault him for such noble purposes? Perhaps the ends *should* justify the means.

A new face emerged from the Iran-Contra affair: Lieutenant Colonel Oliver North. The Marine Corps officer was convicted of multiple felonies, but the convictions were vacated, and he emerged as a hero to many politically conservative Americans. North later enjoyed a successful career as a political commentator, author, and president of a powerful interest group—the National Rifle Association. In the meantime, Ronald Reagan retired after his second term as president, widely hailed as one of the most effective communicators ever to occupy the Oval Office. To his legion of fans, he was the president who ended the Cold War. If Iran-Contra was such a terrible scandal, why did these figures emerge as strong American characters? Even lesser-known participants, such as Robert "Bud" McFarlane and Admiral John Poindexter, received presidential pardons or had their convictions reversed on appeal. These results were hardly the comeuppance that scoundrels should receive.

The most recent tale of political corruption in this book—the story of Russian interference in the 2016 American elections—remains muddled, despite multiple investigations. That the Russians sought to interfere (and, in fact, did interfere) in American elections is well established. Unlike some previous political corruption scandals, numerous figures in the Trump administration were convicted of crimes based on a multiyear investigation by a special prosecutor, but key figures such as the president himself escaped legal consequences. Special prosecutor Robert Mueller waffled in his final conclusions, finding no direct evidence of Trump conspiring with Russia to secure his 2016 victory in the presidential election but also refusing to exonerate the president. Trump falsely hailed the findings as total vindication. Even after the release of (a heavily redacted version of) the special counsel's report, a significant percentage of Americans remained unconvinced of Russian election interference.

These cases suggest that political corruption can be difficult to demonstrate to the satisfaction of a large percentage of the American public. The most egregious examples of political corruption that live in public memory are those instances—think of the Grant administration's scandals, Teapot Dome, and Watergate—in which evidence of malfeasance is clear and incontrovertible. The Watergate scandal, for example, featured televised public hearings and tape recordings of the president of the United States condoning bribery, a clearly impeachable offense. All but the most myopic, deluded partisans understood that Richard M. Nixon was a corrupt president.

Scandals always have been (and always will be) a feature of American political life. Although the causes of scandals remain the same—the acquisitive characteristics of human nature—the facts of each scandal vary. These insights may do little to comfort the American people, but they suggest that scandals can be understood as an outgrowth of human nature.

Despite the ubiquity of political scandals, citizens should not despair. Scandals thus far have not imperiled the American system of government. When the Founders convened in Philadelphia in 1787, they recognized the likelihood that political leaders would misbehave from time to time. If the defects of human nature could not be corrected—and the Founders did not count on the perfectibility of human character—institutions of government would have to be constructed to prevent malfeasance from endangering the health of the republic.

Publius referred to this problem in "Federalist 51" when he argued in favor of the separation of powers and checks and balances built into the United States Constitution. He observed that "the great security against a gradual concentration of the several powers in the same department, consists in giving to those who administer each department, the necessary constitutional means, and personal motives, to resist encroachments of the others." In short, government officials could not be counted on to behave, so their institutional powers would have to be divided and limited.

In one of the most famous passages in *The Federalist Papers*, Publius observed the following:

> Ambition must be made to counteract ambition. The interest of the man must be connected with the constitutional rights of the place. It may be a reflection on human nature, that such devices should be necessary to controul the abuses of government. But what is government itself but the greatest of all reflections on human nature? If men were angels, no government would be necessary. If angels were to govern men, neither external nor internal controuls on government would be necessary. In framing a government which is to be administered by men over men, the great difficulty lies in this: You must first enable the government to controul the governed; and in the next place, oblige it to controul itself. A dependence on the people is no doubt the primary controul on the government; but experience has taught mankind the necessity of auxiliary precautions.[2]

In the absence of angels at the helm, auxiliary precautions included the separation of powers into three distinct departments: legislative, executive, and judicial. Checks and balances meant that the departments would share power and require cooperation among the branches. These constitutional safeguards ensured that no one person or faction could eclipse the others.

"This policy of supplying by opposite and rival interests, the defect of better motives, might be traced through the whole system of human affairs, private as well as public," Publius argued. "We see it particularly displayed in all the subordinate distributions of power; where the constant aim is to divide and arrange the several offices in such a manner as that each may be a check on the other; that the private interest of every individual, may be a sentinel over the public rights."[3]

With a government established to restrain the dark impulses of the human character—"But what is government itself but the greatest of all reflections on human nature?"—scoundrels will come and go, engaging in scandalous behavior and exciting the passions of the day, but the republic will endure. Americans will always struggle to form a more perfect Union, but the goal of perfection, in government and in human nature, will never be achieved. The Declaration of Independence famously set aspirational goals—"We hold these truths to be self-evident, that all men are created equal, that they are endowed by their Creator with certain unalienable Rights, that among these are Life, Liberty and the pursuit of Happiness"—and the United States Constitution established limits on government to restrain those government officials who fall short of supporting or achieving the goals.

If the causes of scandals, which reside in human nature, can never be eradicated, at least the effects can be mitigated. The institutions of government created by the United States Constitution ensure that "the private interest of every individual, may be a sentinel over the public rights." Eternal vigilance is required—as are good faith and a commitment to uphold republican principles—but the blessings of a perpetual Union are worth the price.

# Notes

## Introduction

1. Ed Wright, *History's Greatest Scandals: Shocking Stories of Powerful People* (San Diego, CA: Thunder Bay Press, 2013; originally published in 2006), 34.

## Chapter 1

1. Charles F. Hobson, "The Yazoo Lands Sale Case: *Fletcher v. Peck* (1810)," *Journal of Supreme Court History* 42, no. 3 (November 2017): 239–40. See also *Fletcher v. Peck*, 10 U.S. 87 (1810).

2. William Estill Heath, "The Yazoo Land Fraud," *Georgia Historical Quarterly* 16, no. 4 (December 1932): 275–79; Hobson, "The Yazoo Lands Sale Case," 240–41; M. C. Klingelsmith, "James Wilson and the So-Called Yazoo Frauds," *University of Pennsylvania Law Review and American Law Register* 56, no. 1 Volume 47 Series (January 1908): 7–10.

3. Charles F. Hobson, *The Great Yazoo Lands Sale: The Case of Fletcher v. Peck* (Lawrence: University Press of Kansas, 2016), 24.

4. Hobson, *The Great Yazoo Lands Sale*, 24–25. See also Allen Pusey, "The Yazoo Land Fraud Becomes Law," *ABA Journal* 104, no. 1 (January 2018): 72.

5. Hobson, *The Great Yazoo Lands Sale*, 25–28.

6. Heath, "The Yazoo Land Fraud," 280; Hobson, *The Great Yazoo Lands Sale*, 27.

7. Jane Elsmere, "The Notorious Yazoo Land Fraud Case," *Georgia Historical Quarterly* 51, no. 4 (December 1967): 425; Hobson, *The Great Yazoo Lands Sale*, 27–28; Klingelsmith, "James Wilson and the So-Called Yazoo Frauds," 11.

8. Hobson, *The Great Yazoo Lands Sale*, 28.

9. Hobson, *The Great Yazoo Lands Sale*, 28–29.

10. Hobson, *The Great Yazoo Lands Sale*, 29.

11. Hobson, *The Great Yazoo Lands Sale*, 29. See also Elsmere, "The Notorious Yazoo Land Fraud Case," 427.

12. Hobson, *The Great Yazoo Lands Sale*, 29–30.

13. Elsmere, "The Notorious Yazoo Land Fraud Case," 426; Hobson, "The Yazoo Lands Sale Case," 241; George R. Lamplugh, "James Gunn: Georgia Federalist, 1789–1801," *Georgia Historical Quarterly* 94, no. 3 (Fall 2010): 314.

14. Lamplugh, "James Gunn," 325; Pusey, "The Yazoo Land Fraud Becomes Law," 72.

15. Hobson, *The Great Yazoo Lands Sale*, 32.

16. Hobson, *The Great Yazoo Lands Sale*, 32–33.

17. The quote and information are found in Hobson, *The Great Yazoo Lands Sale*, 33.

18. Elsmere, "The Notorious Yazoo Land Fraud Case," 426; Heath, "The Yazoo Land Fraud," 280–81; Klingelsmith, "James Wilson and the So-Called Yazoo Frauds," 12; Pusey, "The Yazoo Land Fraud Becomes Law," 72.

19. Hobson, *The Great Yazoo Lands Sale*, 34–35.

20. Hobson, *The Great Yazoo Lands Sale*, 38–39.

21. Hobson, *The Great Yazoo Lands Sale*, 39.

22. Jackson is quoted in George R. Lamplugh, *Politics on the Periphery: Factions and Politics in Georgia, 1783–1806* (Cranbury, NJ: Associated University Presses, 1986), 122.

23. The quotes from "Letters of Sicilius" and the information are found in Hobson, *The Great Yazoo Lands Sale*, 43–45.

24. The quotes are from Hobson, *The Great Yazoo Lands Sale*, 46. See also Heath, "The Yazoo Land Fraud," 281–82; Lamplugh, "James Gunn," 340–41.

25. Governor Mathews is quoted in Hobson, *The Great Yazoo Lands Sale*, 49. See also Elsmere, "The Notorious Yazoo Land Fraud Case," 426.

26. Hobson, *The Great Yazoo Lands Sale*, 50–53.

27. The committee report is quoted in Hobson, *The Great Yazoo Lands Sale*, 50.

28. The quote is found in Hobson, *The Great Yazoo Lands Sale*, 53. See also Pusey, "The Yazoo Land Fraud Becomes Law," 72.

29. The quote is found in Hobson, *The Great Yazoo Lands Sale*, 54. See also Heath, "The Yazoo Land Fraud," 282; Hobson, "The Yazoo Lands Sale Case," 242; Klingelsmith, "James Wilson and the So-Called Yazoo Frauds," 14; Pusey, "The Yazoo Land Fraud Becomes Law," 72.

30. Hobson, *The Great Yazoo Lands Sale*, 54–55.

31. Hobson, *The Great Yazoo Lands Sale*, 56–58.

32. 10 U.S. 87 at 88. Hobson, "The Yazoo Lands Sale Case," 243–44, 247; Klingelsmith, "James Wilson and the So-Called Yazoo Frauds," 22, 24.

33. Hobson, *The Great Yazoo Lands Sale*, 59–61.

34. 10 U.S. 87. See also Pusey, "The Yazoo Land Fraud Becomes Law," 72.

35. 10 U.S. 87 at 87–88. See also Hobson, "The Yazoo Lands Sale Case," 245–46; Klingelsmith, "James Wilson and the So-Called Yazoo Frauds," 24.

36. Hobson, *The Great Yazoo Lands Sale*, 140–41.

37. Elsmere, "The Notorious Yazoo Land Fraud Case," 428.

38. Hobson, *The Great Yazoo Lands Sale*, 92; Hobson, "The Yazoo Lands Sale Case," 246.

39. Hobson, "The Yazoo Lands Sale Case," 244–45.

40. Elsmere, "The Notorious Yazoo Land Fraud Case," 430; Hobson, "The Yazoo Lands Sale Case," 247.

41. United States Constitution, Article I, Section 10, Clause 1. See also Heath, "The Yazoo Land Fraud," 287; Hobson, "The Yazoo Lands Sale Case," 250.

42. 10 U.S. 87 at 130. See also Elsmere, "The Notorious Yazoo Land Fraud Case," 431.

43. 10 U.S. 87 at 133–34. Marshall wrote for five members of the court. Justice William Johnson filed a separate opinion agreeing that the state could not repeal the original conveyance, but he did not think it was a matter of constitutional law. 10 U.S. 87 at 143–48. See, for example, Elsmere, "The Notorious Yazoo Land Fraud Case," 431–32; Hobson, "The Yazoo Lands Sale Case," 250–51.

44. Hobson, *The Great Yazoo Lands Sale*, 114–17, 133–34, 142.

45. Heath, "The Yazoo Land Fraud," 290–91; Hobson, "The Yazoo Lands Sale Case," 253–54; Klingelsmith, "James Wilson and the So-Called Yazoo Frauds," 23.

46. Elsmere, "The Notorious Yazoo Land Fraud Case," 439–40; Hobson, "The Yazoo Lands Sale Case," 254.

# Chapter 2

1. The term "fallen founder" is from Nancy Isenberg, *Fallen Founder: The Life of Aaron Burr* (New York: Viking, 2007).

2. Stephen G. Christianson, "Aaron Burr Trials: 1807," in *Great American Trials: From Salem Witchcraft to Rodney King*, ed. Edward W. Knappman (Detroit, MI: Visible Ink Press, 2003), 79; Isenberg, *Fallen Founder*, vii–ix, 202–20; Jon Meacham, *Thomas Jefferson: The Art of Power* (New York: Random House, 2012), 327, 330–33, 336, 337, 339; Gordon S. Wood, "The Real Treason of Aaron Burr," *Proceedings of the American Philosophical Society* 143, no. 2 (June 1999): 285–86, 291–93.

3. Christianson, "Aaron Burr Trials," 79; Peter Charles Hoffer, *The Treason Trials of Aaron Burr* (Lawrence: University Press of Kansas, 2008), 35–36, 37; Isenberg, *Fallen Founder*, 256–69.

4. Christianson, "Aaron Burr Trials," 79–80; Hoffer, *The Treason Trials of Aaron Burr*, 3, 190–94; R. Kent Newmyer, "Burr versus Jefferson versus Marshall," *Humanities* 34, no. 3 (May/June 2013): 26.

5. Hoffer, *The Treason Trials of Aaron Burr*, 1–5; Isenberg, *Fallen Founder*, 271–73; Meacham, *Thomas Jefferson*, 419–20; Newmyer, "Burr versus Jefferson versus Marshall," 26; David O. Stewart, *American Emperor: Aaron Burr's Challenge to Jefferson's America* (New York: Simon & Schuster, 2011), 5–6.

6. The description is found in J. J. Coombs, *The Trial of Aaron Burr for High Treason* (New York: Notable Trials Library, 1992; originally published in 1864), viii. See also

Newmyer, "Burr versus Jefferson versus Marshall," 26; Wood, "The Real Treason of Aaron Burr," 280.

7. Isenberg, *Fallen Founder*, 286; Roger G. Kennedy, *Burr, Hamilton, and Jefferson: A Study in Character* (Oxford and New York: Oxford University Press, 1999), 231, 269–70.

8. Isenberg, *Fallen Founder*, 286–87; Stewart, *American Emperor*, 52–53.

9. Coombs, *The Trial of Aaron Burr*, x; Hoffer, *The Treason Trials of Aaron Burr*, 41; Isenberg, *Fallen Founder*, 287.

10. Merry is quoted in Henry Adams, *History of the United States of America: The First Administration of Thomas Jefferson, 1801–1805* (New York: Scribner, 1909), 395. See also Christianson, "Aaron Burr Trials," 80; Hoffer, *The Treason Trials of Aaron Burr*, 40; Isenberg, *Fallen Founder*, 290–92.

11. Richard Cavendish, "Aaron Burr Arrested for Treason, February 19th, 1807," *History Today* 57, no. 2 (February 2007): 58; Isenberg, *Fallen Founder*, 287–90.

12. Coombs, *The Trial of Aaron Burr*, ix–x; Hoffer, *The Treason Trials of Aaron Burr*, 42–43; Isenberg, *Fallen Founder*, 293.

13. Isenberg, *Fallen Founder*, 294, 296.

14. Coombs, *The Trial of Aaron Burr*, viii.

15. The quotes are found in Isenberg, *Fallen Founder*, 297.

16. Stewart, *American Emperor*, 90–91.

17. Isenberg, *Fallen Founder*, 302–3.

18. Burr is quoted in Stewart, *American Emperor*, 311.

19. Hoffer, *The Treason Trials of Aaron Burr*, 50; Isenberg, *Fallen Founder*, 307–8.

20. The quotes are found in Isenberg, *Fallen Founder*, 308. See also Kennedy, *Burr, Hamilton, and Jefferson*, 4; Meacham, *Thomas Jefferson*, 421.

21. Isenberg, *Fallen Founder*, 308–9; Kennedy, *Burr, Hamilton, and Jefferson*, 4; Newmyer, "Burr versus Jefferson versus Marshall," 26; Wood, "The Real Treason of Aaron Burr," 288.

22. Coombs, *The Trial of Aaron Burr*, xxi; Hoffer, *The Treason Trials of Aaron Burr*, 49; Isenberg, *Fallen Founder*, 308–11; Stewart, *American Emperor*, xviii, 146, 172, 298.

23. Isenberg, *Fallen Founder*, 311–12.

24. Wilkinson is quoted in Isenberg, *Fallen Founder*, 313. See also Hoffer, *The Treason Trials of Aaron Burr*, 39–40.

25. Isenberg, *Fallen Founder*, 312–14.

26. Hoffer, *The Treason Trials of Aaron Burr*, 96; Newmyer, "Burr versus Jefferson versus Marshall," 26.

27. Isenberg, *Fallen Founder*, 315–16, 325; Stewart, *American Emperor*, 180.

28. Isenberg, *Fallen Founder*, 316; Newmyer, "Burr versus Jefferson versus Marshall," 26.

29. Isenberg, *Fallen Founder*, 319–20, 325; Stewart, *American Emperor*, xvii, 193, 194, 195.

30. Coombs, *The Trial of Aaron Burr*, xxxvi–xxxviii; Hoffer, *The Treason Trials of Aaron Burr*, 56; Isenberg, *Fallen Founder*, 321–22.

31. Christianson, "Aaron Burr Trials," 80; Hoffer, *The Treason Trials of Aaron Burr*, 7–9; Meacham, *Thomas Jefferson*, 421–22.

32. Cavendish, "Aaron Burr Arrested for Treason," 59; Christianson, "Aaron Burr Trials," 80; Hoffer, *The Treason Trials of Aaron Burr*, 129; Isenberg, *Fallen Founder*, 329.

33. Hoffer, *The Treason Trials of Aaron Burr*, 48; Isenberg, *Fallen Founder*, 330–45; Stewart, *American Emperor*, 141–42.

34. Isenberg, *Fallen Founder*, 334; Stewart, *American Emperor*, 236, 265.

35. Isenberg, *Fallen Founder*, 335–37.

36. Marshall is quoted in Isenberg, *Fallen Founder*, 336. See also Christianson, "Aaron Burr Trials," 80–81.

37. The indictment is quoted in Stewart, *American Emperor*, 313. See also Newmyer, "Burr versus Jefferson versus Marshall," 27.

38. Christianson, "Aaron Burr Trials," 81; Isenberg, *Fallen Founder*, 351–62.

39. Martin is quoted in Isenberg, *Fallen Founder*, 362. See also Hoffer, *The Treason Trials of Aaron Burr*, 156–59; Kennedy, *Burr, Hamilton, and Jefferson*, 349.

40. Cavendish, "Aaron Burr Arrested for Treason," 59; Christianson, "Aaron Burr Trials," 81–82; Coombs, *The Trial of Aaron Burr*, 352–54; Isenberg, *Fallen Founder*, 362–63; Newmyer, "Burr versus Jefferson versus Marshall," 26–27, 53.

41. Cavendish, "Aaron Burr Arrested for Treason," 59; Christianson, "Aaron Burr Trials," 81–82; Isenberg, *Fallen Founder*, 367–69.

42. Christianson, "Aaron Burr Trials," 82; Hoffer, *The Treason Trials of Aaron Burr*, 3, 190–94.

# Chapter 3

1. "Charles Sumner," *New York Times*, March 12, 1874, 4; "Death of Senator Sumner: Last Hours of the Great Statesman, Charles Sumner," *New York Times*, March 12, 1874, 1; Hans L. Trefousse, *The Radical Republicans: Lincoln's Vanguard for Racial Justice* (New York: Knopf, 1969), 5–6.

2. "Charles Sumner," 4; David Herbert Donald, *Charles Sumner and the Coming of the Civil War* (New York: Knopf, 1960), 1–2.

3. Donald, *Charles Sumner and the Coming of the Civil War*, 5–18; Barry M. Goldenberg, *The Unknown Architects of Civil Rights: Thaddeus Stevens, Ulysses S. Grant, and Charles Sumner* (Los Angeles, CA: Critical Minds Press, 2011), 76.

4. For a detailed discussion of Sumner's time in Europe, see especially David McCullough, *The Greater Journey: Americans in Paris* (New York: Simon & Schuster, 2011), 4, 131–32, 223–29, 232, 235. See also Donald, *Charles Sumner and the Coming of the Civil War*, 34–58.

5. Donald, *Charles Sumner and the Coming of the Civil War*, 62–141; Goldenberg, *The Unknown Architects of Civil Rights*, 78–79.

6. "Charles Sumner," 4; Donald, *Charles Sumner and the Coming of the Civil War*, 1, 160; Goldenberg, *The Unknown Architects of Civil Rights*, 79–80; George Henry Haynes, *Charles Sumner* (Philadelphia, PA: George W. Jacobs, 1909), 124–37.

7. Sumner is quoted in Edward Lillie Pierce, ed., *Memoir and Letters of Charles Sumner* (London: Sampson Low, Marston, 1893), 3:298–99. See also Haynes, *Charles Sumner*, 138–43, 155–56, 148–58.

8. Goldenberg, *The Unknown Architects of Civil Rights*, 78; Haynes, *Charles Sumner*, 143, 148–58.

9. "Death of Senator Sumner," 1; Pierce, *Memoir and Letters of Charles Sumner*, 3:18.

10. Sumner's speech is quoted in Pierce, *Memoir and Letters of Charles Sumner*, 3:446. See also Haynes, *Charles Sumner*, 194–95.

11. Sumner is quoted in Donald, *Charles Sumner and the Coming of the Civil War*, 239. See also Haynes, *Charles Sumner*, 197.

12. Brooks is quoted in Michael S. Green, *Politics and America in Crisis: The Coming of the Civil War* (Santa Barbara, CA: Praeger, 2010), 94.

13. Brooks is quoted in Williamjames Hull Hoffer, *The Caning of Charles Sumner: Honor, Idealism, and the Origins of the Civil War* (Baltimore, MD: Johns Hopkins University Press, 2010), 8. Keitt's role is discussed on pages 8–9. See also David Miller DeWitt, *The Impeachment and Trial of Andrew Johnson, Seventeenth President of the United States: A History* (New York: Macmillan, 1903), 32–37; Donald, *Charles Sumner and the Coming of the Civil War*, 278–347; David Herbert Donald, *Lincoln Reconsidered: Essays on the Civil War Era*, 3rd ed. (New York: Vintage, 2001), 112–13; David Herbert Donald, *The Politics of Reconstruction, 1863–1867* (Baton Rouge: Louisiana State University Press, 1965), 7–8; Michael S. Green, *Freedom, Union, and Power: Lincoln and His Party during the Civil War* (New York: Fordham University Press, 2004), 11–12; Robert Selph Henry, *The Story of Reconstruction* (New York: Konecky & Konecky, 1999), 48; Eric L. McKitrick, *Andrew Johnson and Reconstruction* (New York and Oxford: Oxford University Press, 1988; originally published in 1960), 268; Manisha Sinha, "The Caning of Charles Sumner: Slavery, Race, and Ideology in the Age of the Civil War," *Journal of the Early Republic* 23, no. 2 (Summer 2003): 233–62; Kenneth M. Stampp, *America in 1857: A Nation on the Brink* (New York and Oxford: Oxford University Press, 1990), 11; Eric H. Walther, *The Shattering of the Union: America in the 1850s* (Wilmington, DE: SR Books, 2004), 96–100.

14. For more on the Lyon-Griswold incident, see, for example, J. Michael Martinez, *The Safety of the Kingdom: Government Responses to Subversive Threats* (New York: Carrel Books, 2015), 9–11. Benton is quoted in William M. Meigs, *The Life of Thomas Hart Benton* (Philadelphia and London: J. B. Lippincott, 1904), 398.

15. For more on the differing reactions in the North and South, see, for example, Donald, *Charles Sumner and the Coming of the Civil War*, 278–347.

16. DeWitt, *The Impeachment and Trial of Andrew Johnson*, 32–37; Donald, *Charles Sumner and the Coming of the Civil War*, 278–347, especially 286; Donald, *The Politics of Reconstruction*, 7–8; Eric Foner, *Reconstruction: America's Unfinished Revolution: 1863–1877*, Francis Parkman Prize Edition (New York: History Book Club, 2005; originally published in 1988), 239–40; Doris Kearns Goodwin, *Team of Rivals: The Political Genius of Abraham Lincoln* (New York: Simon & Schuster, 2005), 184–85; Henry, *The Story of Reconstruction*, 48; McKitrick, *Andrew Johnson and Reconstruction*, 268; Sinha,

"The Caning of Charles Sumner," 233–62; Stampp, *America in 1857*, 11; Walther, *The Shattering of the Union*, 96–100.

17. Sumner is quoted in Charles Sumner, *Charles Sumner: His Complete Works* (Boston: Lee and Shepard, 1900; originally published in 1872), 127, 132. See also Haynes, *Charles Sumner*, 231–46.

18. William C. Davis, *Look Away! A History of the Confederate States of America* (New York: Free Press, 2002), 30–48, 113–24; James M. McPherson, *Battle Cry of Freedom: The Civil War Era* (New York: Ballantine Books, 1988), 234–37, 246–50.

19. Donald, *Charles Sumner and the Coming of the Civil War*, 305–6; Trefousse, *The Radical Republicans*, 163–67.

20. Philip Dray, *Capitol Men: The Epic Story of Reconstruction through the Eyes of the First Black Congressmen* (Boston and New York: Houghton Mifflin, 2008), 326–32; Haynes, *Charles Sumner*, 428–29; Michael J. Klarman, *From Jim Crow to Civil Rights: The Supreme Court and the Struggle for Equality* (New York and Oxford: Oxford University Press, 2004), 19–20, 49–50; Leon F. Litwack, *Trouble in Mind: Black Southerners in the Age of Jim Crow* (New York: Knopf, 1998), 392.

21. "Charles Sumner," 4; "Charles Sumner: Some Reminiscences of the Deceased Statesman," *New York Times*, March 18, 1873, 5; "Death of Senator Sumner," 1; Haynes, *Charles Sumner*, 432–34.

# Chapter 4

1. Ron Chernow, *Grant* (New York: Penguin, 2017), 624–37.

2. Steven G. Calabresi and Christopher S. Yoo, "The Unitary Executive during the Second Half-Century," *Harvard Journal of Law & Public Policy* 26, no. 3 (Summer 2003): 763–64; Robert Selph Henry, *The Story of Reconstruction* (New York: Konecky & Konecky, 1999), 500; J. Michael Martinez, *Carpetbaggers, Cavalry, and the Ku Klux Klan: Exposing the Invisible Empire during Reconstruction* (Lanham, MD: Rowman & Littlefield, 2007), 63; Jean Edward Smith, *Grant* (New York: Simon & Schuster, 2001), 496–98.

3. Eric Foner, *Reconstruction: America's Unfinished Revolution: 1863–1877*, Francis Parkman Prize Edition (New York: History Book Club, 2005; originally published in 1988), 512–13; Henry, *The Story of Reconstruction*, 500; John M. Lubetkin, *Jay Cooke's Gamble: The Northern Pacific Railroad, the Sioux, and the Panic of 1873* (Norman: University of Oklahoma Press, 2006), xv–xvi; Richard W. Murphy, *The Nation Reunited: War's Aftermath* (Alexandria, VA: Time-Life Books, 1987), 125; Smith, *Grant*, 583.

4. Chernow, *Grant*, 735–37.

5. J. Martin Klotsche, "The Star Route Cases," *Mississippi Valley Historical Review* 22, no. 3 (December 1935): 407–18.

6. Stephen E. Ambrose, *Nothing Like It in the World: The Men Who Built the Transcontinental Railroad, 1863–1869* (New York: Simon & Schuster, 2000), 92–93, 320–21, 373–75; Chernow, *Grant*, 743, 752–53, 754.

7. Lee J. Alston, Jeffrey A. Jenkins, and Tomas Nonnenmacher, "Who Should Govern Congress? Access to Power and the Salary Grab of 1873," *Journal of Economic History* 66, no. 3 (September 2006): 674–75; Foner, *Reconstruction*, 523; Lewis L. Gould, *Grand Old Party: A History of the Republicans* (New York: Random House, 2003), 68; Smith, *Grant*, 561; Hans L. Trefousse, *The Radical Republicans: Lincoln's Vanguard for Racial Justice* (New York: Knopf, 1969), 463; Jules Witcover, *Party of the People: A History of the Democrats* (New York: Random House, 2003), 244.

8. Murphy, *The Nation Reunited*, 112, 114; Smith, *Grant*, 586; Trefousse, *The Radical Republicans*, 463.

9. See, for example, Chernow, *Grant*, 796–809; Jennifer Rose Hopper, "Reexamining the Nineteenth-Century Presidency and Partisan Press: The Case of President Grant and the Whiskey Ring Scandal," *Social Science History* 42, no. 1 (January 2018): 109–33.

10. The story of Babcock's possible participation in the burglary conspiracy and his fall from grace are recounted in many sources. See, for example, Walter Coffey, *The Reconstruction Years* (Bloomington, IN: AuthorHouse, 2014), 282; "Orville Babcock's Diaries Online," *America's Civil War* 30, no. 2 (May 2017): 10.

11. Calabresi and Yoo, "The Unitary Executive during the Second Half-Century," 767–68; Foner, *Reconstruction*, 565–66; Murphy, *The Nation Reunited*, 112, 114–17; Smith, *Grant*, 484, 562, 592–95.

12. Grant is quoted in Zachariah Chandler, *Zachariah Chandler: An Outline Sketch of His Life and Public Services* (Detroit, MI: *Detroit Post and Tribune*, 1880), 345.

13. Chernow, *Grant*, 787.

14. Foner, *Reconstruction*, 461–62; John Hope Franklin, *Reconstruction after the Civil War* (Chicago and London: University of Chicago Press, 1961), 176–77; Henry, *The Story of Reconstruction*, 367–68; Murphy, *The Nation Reunited*, 83–86.

15. Foner, *Reconstruction*, 512–13; Murphy, *The Nation Reunited*, 86; Francis Butler Simkins and Charles Pierce Roland, *A History of the South*, 4th ed. (New York: Knopf, 1972), 321.

16. Foner, *Reconstruction*, 512–17; Heather Cox Richardson, "A Marshall Plan for the South? The Failure of Republican and Democratic Ideology during Reconstruction," *Civil War History* 51, no. 4 (December 2005): 378–87; Simkins and Roland, *A History of the South*, 320–21.

17. Franklin, *Reconstruction after the Civil War*, 185–86; Henry, *The Story of Reconstruction*, 499–500; Murphy, *The Nation Reunited*, 124–25.

18. Milton Friedman, "The Crime of 1873," *Journal of Political Economy* 98, no. 6 (December 1990): 1159–94; Murphy, *The Nation Reunited*, 124–25; Smith, *Grant*, 480, 590.

19. Foner, *Reconstruction*, 512–13; Lubetkin, *Jay Cooke's Gamble*, 280–82, 288–91; Murphy, *The Nation Reunited*, 125–26; Smith, *Grant*, 583.

20. Michael W. Fitzgerald, *Splendid Failure: Postwar Reconstruction in the American South* (Chicago: Ivan R. Dee, 2008), 174; Franklin, *Reconstruction after the Civil War*, 185–86; Murphy, *The Nation Reunited*, 125–27; Brooks D. Simpson, *The Reconstruction Presidents* (Lawrence: University Press of Kansas, 1998), 165.

21. Gould, *Grand Old Party*, 98–99.

22. Foner, *Reconstruction*, 549–50; Gould, *Grand Old Party*, 70; Simpson, *The Reconstruction Presidents*, 173–74; Witcover, *Party of the People*, 244.

# Chapter 5

1. Nancy E. Marion, *The Politics of Disgrace: The Role of Political Scandal in American Politics* (Durham, NC: Carolina Academic Press, 2010), 66–67; David H. Stratton, "Behind Teapot Dome: Some Personal Insights," *Business History Review* 31, no. 4 (Winter 1957): 385–86.

2. Jared Cohen, *Accidental Presidents: Eight Men Who Changed America* (New York and London: Simon & Schuster, 2019), 249; Kim Long, *The Almanac of Political Corruption, Scandals & Dirty Politics* (New York: Delta Paperbacks, 2007), 146; Marion, *The Politics of Disgrace*, 67; Burl Noogle, "The Origins of the Teapot Dome Investigation," *Mississippi Valley Historical Review* 44, no. 2 (September 1957): 237, 244; Bernard Ryan Jr., "The Teapot Dome Trials: 1926–30," in *Great American Trials: From Salem Witchcraft to Rodney King*, ed. Edward W. Knappman (Detroit, MI: Visible Ink Press, 2003), 332–33.

3. M. R. Werner and John Starr, *Teapot Dome* (New York: Viking Press, 1959), 41.

4. Daniels is quoted in Werner and Starr, *Teapot Dome*, 41. See also Noogle, "The Origins of the Teapot Dome Investigation," 244–45; Robert A. Waller, "Business and the Initiation of the Teapot Dome Investigation," *Business History Review* (Autumn 1962): 335–36.

5. Cohen, *Accidental Presidents*, 231–32; Phillip G. Payne, *Dead Last: The Public Memory of Warren G. Harding* (Athens: Ohio University Press, 2009), 192–220; Werner and Starr, *Teapot Dome*, 18–27.

6. Waller, "Business and the Initiation of the Teapot Dome Investigation," 336–38; Werner and Starr, *Teapot Dome*, 39–40.

7. Ryan, "The Teapot Dome Trials," 333; David H. Stratton, "New Mexican Machiavellian? The Story of Albert B. Fall," *Montana: The Magazine of Western History* 7, no. 4 (October 1957): 2–7; Werner and Starr, *Teapot Dome*, 4–5; Earl F. Woodward, "Hon. Albert B. Fall of New Mexico: The Frontier's Fallen Star of Teapot Dome," *Montana: The Magazine of Western History* 23, no. 1 (Winter 1973): 14.

8. Werner and Starr, *Teapot Dome*, 4–5.

9. Stratton, "New Mexican Machiavellian," 8–10; Werner and Starr, *Teapot Dome*, 4–6.

10. Werner and Starr, *Teapot Dome*, 5–6; Woodward, "Hon. Albert B. Fall of New Mexico," 16–17.

11. Stratton, "New Mexican Machiavellian," 10; Werner and Starr, *Teapot Dome*, 6.

12. Stratton, "New Mexican Machiavellian," 11–12; Woodward, "Hon. Albert B. Fall of New Mexico," 20–21.

13. The quote is found in Werner and Starr, *Teapot Dome*, 6. See also Stratton, "Behind Teapot Dome," 386.

14. Stratton, "New Mexican Machiavellian," 10–11; Werner and Starr, *Teapot Dome*, 6–7.

15. Werner and Starr, *Teapot Dome*, 6–7, 55, 56.

16. Marion, *The Politics of Disgrace*, 67–68; Noogle, "The Origins of the Teapot Dome Investigation," 241–42; Stratton, "New Mexican Machiavellian," 12; Woodward, "Hon. Albert B. Fall of New Mexico," 22.

17. Cohen, *Accidental Presidents*, 250; Long, *The Almanac of Political Corruption*, 146–47; Waller, "Business and the Initiation of the Teapot Dome Investigation," 340–41.

18. Lewis L. Gould, *Grand Old Party: A History of the Republicans* (New York: Random House, 2003), 236; Marion, *The Politics of Disgrace*, 67; Ryan, "The Teapot Dome Trials," 333, 335; Stratton, "New Mexican Machiavellian," 14.

19. Werner and Starr, *Teapot Dome*, 61–64.

20. Ryan, "The Teapot Dome Trials," 333–34; Waller, "Business and the Initiation of the Teapot Dome Investigation," 339–40.

21. Werner and Starr, *Teapot Dome*, 64–66.

22. The quotes are found in Werner and Starr, *Teapot Dome*, 65. See also Ryan, "The Teapot Dome Trials," 334.

23. Cohen, *Accidental Presidents*, 250–51; Gould, *Grand Old Party*, 236; Woodward, "Hon. Albert B. Fall of New Mexico," 22.

24. La Follette is quoted in Werner and Starr, *Teapot Dome*, 69. See also David H. Stratton, "Two Western Senators and Teapot Dome: Thomas J. Walsh and Albert B. Fall," *Pacific Northwest Quarterly* 65, no. 2 (April 1974): 88; Waller, "Business and the Initiation of the Teapot Dome Investigation," 341–42; Werner and Starr, *Teapot Dome*, 68–69.

25. Marion, *The Politics of Disgrace*, 69; Ryan, "The Teapot Dome Trials," 334; Stratton, "Two Western Senators and Teapot Dome," 61–62; Waller, "Business and the Initiation of the Teapot Dome Investigation," 344.

26. Stratton, "Two Western Senators and Teapot Dome," 57–58, 59; Werner and Starr, *Teapot Dome*, 108–9.

27. Stratton, "Two Western Senators and Teapot Dome," 62–64.

28. Cohen, *Accidental Presidents*, 251; Werner and Starr, *Teapot Dome*, 107.

29. Stratton, "Two Western Senators and Teapot Dome," 61.

30. Fall is quoted in Werner and Starr, *Teapot Dome*, 111.

31. Werner and Starr, *Teapot Dome*, 111. See also Stratton, "Two Western Senators and Teapot Dome," 61.

32. Werner and Starr, *Teapot Dome*, 113–14.

33. Werner and Starr, *Teapot Dome*, 114–15.

34. Werner and Starr, *Teapot Dome*, 114–15.

35. Doheny is quoted in Werner and Starr, *Teapot Dome*, 116.

36. Doheny is quoted in Werner and Starr, *Teapot Dome*, 117.

37. Doheny is quoted in Werner and Starr, *Teapot Dome*, 136. See also Ryan, "The Teapot Dome Trials," 334; Stratton, "Behind Teapot Dome," 391; Woodward, "Hon. Albert B. Fall of New Mexico," 22–23.

38. Werner and Starr, *Teapot Dome*, 143–45.

39. Fall is quoted in Werner and Starr, *Teapot Dome*, 147.

40. Werner and Starr, *Teapot Dome*, 148. See also Long, *The Almanac of Political Corruption*, 147.

41. Cohen, *Accidental Presidents*, 251; Ryan, "The Teapot Dome Trials," 335.

42. Werner and Starr, *Teapot Dome*, 158–224.

43. Ryan, "The Teapot Dome Trials," 335.

44. Hogan is quoted in "Rich Man's Lawyer," *Life*, August 8, 1938, 16.

45. Hogan is quoted in Werner and Starr, *Teapot Dome*, 219.

46. Hogan is quoted in Werner and Starr, *Teapot Dome*, 220.

47. Hogan is quoted in Werner and Starr, *Teapot Dome*, 220. See also Ryan, "The Teapot Dome Trials," 335.

48. Thompson is quoted in Werner and Starr, *Teapot Dome*, 220–21.

49. Thompson is quoted in Werner and Starr, *Teapot Dome*, 220–21.

50. Ryan, "The Teapot Dome Trials," 335; Werner and Starr, *Teapot Dome*, 225–26.

51. Werner and Starr, *Teapot Dome*, 278–79, 280.

52. Werner and Starr, *Teapot Dome*, 279.

53. Sinclair is quoted in Werner and Starr, *Teapot Dome*, 280.

54. Norris is quoted in Werner and Starr, *Teapot Dome*, 267. See also Ryan, "The Teapot Dome Trials," 335.

55. Ryan, "The Teapot Dome Trials," 335.

56. Werner and Starr, *Teapot Dome*, 280–81.

57. Hogan is quoted in Ryan, "The Teapot Dome Trials," 336.

58. Roberts is quoted in Werner and Starr, *Teapot Dome*, 283. See also Cohen, *Accidental Presidents*, 251; Ryan, "The Teapot Dome Trials," 335.

59. Thompson is quoted in Werner and Starr, *Teapot Dome*, 284.

60. Doheny is quoted in Werner and Starr, *Teapot Dome*, 284. See also Stratton, "Behind Teapot Dome," 394.

61. Marion, *The Politics of Disgrace*, 70; Werner and Starr, *Teapot Dome*, 285.

62. Fall is quoted in Werner and Starr, *Teapot Dome*, 285.

63. Werner and Starr, *Teapot Dome*, 286–89.

64. Werner and Starr, *Teapot Dome*, 286–87.

65. Roberts is quoted in Werner and Starr, *Teapot Dome*, 287. See also Stratton, "Behind Teapot Dome," 387.

66. Hogan is quoted in Werner and Starr, *Teapot Dome*, 287.

67. Doheny is quoted in Werner and Starr, *Teapot Dome*, 288. See also Stratton, "Two Western Senators and Teapot Dome," 65; Woodward, "Hon. Albert B. Fall of New Mexico," 23.

68. Ryan, "The Teapot Dome Trials," 336; Stratton, "New Mexican Machiavellian," 14; Werner and Starr, *Teapot Dome*, 291; Woodward, "Hon. Albert B. Fall of New Mexico," 23.

69. Ryan, "The Teapot Dome Trials," 336; Werner and Starr, *Teapot Dome*, 291–92.

70. See, for example, "Wyoming: U.S. Government Sells Teapot Dome Fields," *New York Times*, January 31, 2015, A15.

71. *McGrain v. Daugherty*, 273 U.S. 135 (1927).

72. Harding is quoted in Ed Wright, *History's Greatest Scandals: Shocking Stories of Powerful People* (San Diego, CA: Thunder Bay Press, 2013; originally published in 2006), 34. See also Cohen, *Accidental Presidents*, 233–43.

# Chapter 6

1. D. Jerome Tweton, "The Politics of Chaos: North Dakota in the 1930s," *Journal of the West* 41, no. 4 (Fall 2002): 32–35.

2. Agnes Geelan, *The Dakota Maverick: The Political Life of William Langer, Also Known as "Wild Bill" Langer* (Fargo, ND: Kaye's Printing, 1975), 8–11; Daniel Rylance, "William Langer and the Themes of North Dakota History," *South Dakota History* 3, no. 1 (Winter 1972): 41, 43.

3. For more details on Langer's early life, see, for example, Geelan, *The Dakota Maverick*, 11–17; Rylance, "William Langer and the Themes of North Dakota History," 45; Tweton, "The Politics of Chaos," 31.

4. Langer is quoted in Geelan, *The Dakota Maverick*, 17.

5. Geelan, *The Dakota Maverick*, 20–21.

6. Geelan, *The Dakota Maverick*, 21–22; Rylance, "William Langer and the Themes of North Dakota History," 47.

7. Geelan, *The Dakota Maverick*, 23.

8. Geelan, *The Dakota Maverick*, 22–24. See also Rylance, "William Langer and the Themes of North Dakota History," 47; Tweton, "The Politics of Chaos," 31.

9. Rylance, "William Langer and the Themes of North Dakota History," 47; Tweton, "The Politics of Chaos," 31.

10. Lawrence H. Larsen, "William Langer: A Maverick in the Senate," *Wisconsin Magazine of History* 44, no. 3 (Spring 1961): 189–90; 189–90; Rylance, "William Langer and the Themes of North Dakota History," 47; Tweton, "The Politics of Chaos," 31.

11. Langer is quoted in Geelan, *The Dakota Maverick*, 34.

12. Geelan, *The Dakota Maverick*, 34–35.

13. Geelan, *The Dakota Maverick*, 35–36.

14. Tweton, "The Politics of Chaos," 32.

15. Langer is quoted in Geelan, *The Dakota Maverick*, 47.

16. Langer is quoted in Geelan, *The Dakota Maverick*, 48.

17. Two sources report the number as 5,414 votes. See Geelan, *The Dakota Maverick*, 49–50; Rylance, "William Langer and the Themes of North Dakota History," 49. Another source reports 5,444 votes. See Tweton, "The Politics of Chaos," 32.

18. Geelan, *The Dakota Maverick*, 51–52.

19. Geelan, *The Dakota Maverick*, 51–57. See also Rylance, "William Langer and the Themes of North Dakota History," 50.

20. Geelan, *The Dakota Maverick*, 56–59; Rylance, "William Langer and the Themes of North Dakota History," 50; Tweton, "The Politics of Chaos," 32.

21. Geelan, *The Dakota Maverick*, 58–60; Tweton, "The Politics of Chaos," 32.

22. Geelan, *The Dakota Maverick*, 61; Rylance, "William Langer and the Themes of North Dakota History," 51–52; Tweton, "The Politics of Chaos," 32–33.

23. Tweton, "The Politics of Chaos," 33.

24. Tweton, "The Politics of Chaos," 33. See also Geelan, *The Dakota Maverick*, 69–70.

25. The quotes are found in Tweton, "The Politics of Chaos," 33. See also Geelan, *The Dakota Maverick*, 69–71; Rylance, "William Langer and the Themes of North Dakota History," 52–53.

26. Geelan, *The Dakota Maverick*, 70; Tweton, "The Politics of Chaos," 33.

27. Langer is quoted in Geelan, *The Dakota Maverick*, 72.

28. Geelan, *The Dakota Maverick*, 72.

29. Geelan, *The Dakota Maverick*, 73; Tweton, "The Politics of Chaos," 33–34.

30. Geelan, *The Dakota Maverick*, 74.

31. Geelan, *The Dakota Maverick*, 74–75; Kim Long, *The Almanac of Political Corruption, Scandals & Dirty Politics* (New York: Delta Paperbacks, 2007), 186; Tweton, "The Politics of Chaos," 34.

32. Geelan, *The Dakota Maverick*, 74–76.

33. Geelan, *The Dakota Maverick*, 75–76. See also Tweton, "The Politics of Chaos," 34.

34. Geelan, *The Dakota Maverick*, 76.

35. Geelan, *The Dakota Maverick*, 74–77. See also Long, *The Almanac of Political Corruption*, 186; Tweton, "The Politics of Chaos," 34.

36. Geelan, *The Dakota Maverick*, 79–80; Tweton, "The Politics of Chaos," 34.

37. Welford is quoted in Geelan, *The Dakota Maverick*, 79.

38. Langer is quoted in Geelan, *The Dakota Maverick*, 79–80.

39. Tweton, "The Politics of Chaos," 34.

40. Geelan, *The Dakota Maverick*, 84; Tweton, "The Politics of Chaos," 34.

41. Tweton, "The Politics of Chaos," 34.

42. Tweton, "The Politics of Chaos," 34–35. See also Geelan, *The Dakota Maverick*, 84–85.

43. Tweton, "The Politics of Chaos," 35.

44. Geelan, *The Dakota Maverick*, 90–91; Long, *The Almanac of Political Corruption*, 186; Rylance, "William Langer and the Themes of North Dakota History," 53; Tweton, "The Politics of Chaos," 35.

45. Geelan, *The Dakota Maverick*, 91; Long, *The Almanac of Political Corruption*, 186–87; Rylance, "William Langer and the Themes of North Dakota History," 53.

46. Geelan, *The Dakota Maverick*, 91–104; Tweton, "The Politics of Chaos," 35.

47. Langer is quoted in Geelan, *The Dakota Maverick*, 92.

48. Geelan, *The Dakota Maverick*, 91–104. See also Rylance, "William Langer and the Themes of North Dakota History," 53, 55; Tweton, "The Politics of Chaos," 35.

49. The report is quoted in Geelan, *The Dakota Maverick*, 103. See also Long, *The Almanac of Political Corruption*, 187.

50. The incident is recounted in Geelan, *The Dakota Maverick*, 93.

51. Geelan, *The Dakota Maverick*, 103. See also Rylance, "William Langer and the Themes of North Dakota History," 55.

52. Geelan, *The Dakota Maverick*, 93–103.
53. Geelan, *The Dakota Maverick*, 104. See also Long, *The Almanac of Political Corruption*, 187; Rylance, "William Langer and the Themes of North Dakota History," 55; United States Senate Historical Office, *United States Senate Election, Expulsion and Censure Cases: 1793–1990* (Washington, DC: Government Printing Office, 1995), 368–70.
54. Larsen, "William Langer," 189–98; Tweton, "The Politics of Chaos," 35.
55. Langer is quoted in Tweton, "The Politics of Chaos," 35.

# Chapter 7

1. Nancy E. Marion, *The Politics of Disgrace: The Role of Political Scandal in American Politics* (Durham, NC: Carolina Academic Press, 2010), 78–79; "Spiro T. Agnew, Ex-Vice President, Dies at 77," *New York Times*, September 18, 1996, A1, D21; "How Agnew Bartered His Office to Keep from Going to Prison," *New York Times*, October 23, 1973, 1, 36.
2. "Spiro T. Agnew, Ex-Vice President, Dies at 77," D1.
3. "Spiro T. Agnew, Ex-Vice President, Dies at 77," A1, D1. See also Francis X. Clines, "Spiro T. Agnew, Point Man for Nixon Who Resigned Vice Presidency, Dies at 77," *New York Times*, September 19, 1996, B15.
4. Clines, "Spiro T. Agnew," B15; "Spiro T. Agnew, Ex-Vice President, Dies at 77," A1; Jules Witcover, *White Knight: The Rise of Spiro Agnew* (New York: Random House, 1972), 37–41.
5. Matthew Arnold, "A Vice President Who Extolled the Old Virtues," *New York Times*, October 11, 1973, 33; "Spiro T. Agnew, Ex-Vice President, Dies at 77," A1, D21.
6. Mrs. Agnew is quoted in "Spiro T. Agnew, Ex-Vice President, Dies at 77," D21.
7. Arnold, "A Vice President Who Extolled the Old Virtues," 33.
8. "Spiro T. Agnew, Ex-Vice President, Dies at 77," D21.
9. Arnold, "A Vice President Who Extolled the Old Virtues," 33; Witcover, *White Knight*, 63.
10. "Spiro T. Agnew, Ex-Vice President, Dies at 77," D21.
11. Arnold, "A Vice President Who Extolled the Old Virtues," 33; "Spiro T. Agnew, Ex-Vice President, Dies at 77," D21.
12. "Spiro T. Agnew, Ex-Vice President, Dies at 77," D21.
13. Arnold, "A Vice President Who Extolled the Old Virtues," 33.
14. Lewis L. Gould, *Grand Old Party: A History of the Republicans* (New York: Random House, 2003), 378; Marion, *The Politics of Disgrace*, 78; "Spiro T. Agnew, Ex-Vice President, Dies at 77," D21; Witcover, *White Knight*, 139–50.
15. Agnew is quoted in Richard M. Cohen and Jules Witcover, *A Heartbeat Away: The Investigation and Resignation of Spiro Agnew* (New York: Viking, 1974), 26.
16. Arnold, "A Vice President Who Extolled the Old Virtues," 33; Peter B. Levy, "Spiro Agnew, the Forgotten Americans, and the Rise of the New Right," *The Historian* 75, no. 4 (Winter 2013): 709; "Spiro T. Agnew, Ex-Vice President, Dies at 77," D21.

17. The quote "lawbreaking has become a socially acceptable and occasionally stylish form of dissent" is found in Levy, "Spiro Agnew, the Forgotten Americans," 713. The quote "not evil conditions that cause riots, but evil men" is found in "Spiro T. Agnew, Ex-Vice President, Dies at 77," D21.

18. Rick Perlstein, *Nixonland: The Rise of a President and the Fracturing of America* (New York: Scribner, 2008), 254–61.

19. Levy, "Spiro Agnew, the Forgotten Americans," 709–11; Perlstein, *Nixonland*, 257–58; Robert B. Semple Jr., "On Tour with Spiro Agnew: Under the Rhetoric, a True Believer," *New York Times*, September 19, 1996, A26; Witcover, *White Knight*, 28.

20. Levy, "Spiro Agnew, the Forgotten Americans," 712; Perlstein, *Nixonland*, 258.

21. Levy, "Spiro Agnew, the Forgotten Americans," 713–14; "Spiro T. Agnew, Ex-Vice President, Dies at 77," D21.

22. "Spiro T. Agnew, Ex-Vice President, Dies at 77," D21.

23. Conrad Black, *Richard M. Nixon: A Life in Full* (New York: Public Affairs, 2007), 535–36; Perlstein, *Nixonland*, 712–19.

24. Agnew is quoted in "Spiro T. Agnew, Ex-Vice President, Dies at 77," D21. See also Black, *Richard M. Nixon*, 536; Witcover, *White Knight*, 275.

25. Perlstein, *Nixonland*, 302–4; "Spiro T. Agnew, Ex-Vice President, Dies at 77," D21; Witcover, *White Knight*, 255–63.

26. Agnew's quotes are found in many sources. See, for example, Perlstein, *Nixonland*, 344; William Safire, "A Heartbeat Away," *New York Times*, September 19, 1996, A27; "Spiro T. Agnew, Ex-Vice President, Dies at 77," D21.

27. The campaign commercial is discussed in Perlstein, *Nixonland*, 344.

28. The information and Nixon's quote are found in Witcover, *White Knight*, 47–49.

29. Joseph Nathan Kane, *Facts about the Presidents* (New York: Ace Books, 1976), 443–44.

30. Justin P. Coffey, *Spiro Agnew and the Rise of the Republican Right* (Santa Barbara, CA: ABC-CLIO, 2015), 93–94.

31. Black, *Richard M. Nixon*, 664–65.

32. Coffey, *Spiro Agnew*, 94.

33. The quotes and information can be found in many sources. See, for example, Perlstein, *Nixonland*, 524–27. See also Semple, "On Tour with Spiro Agnew," A26; Witcover, *White Knight*, 362–63.

34. Coffey, *Spiro Agnew*, 82; Safire, "A Heartbeat Away," A27.

35. Levy, "Spiro Agnew, the Forgotten Americans," 731.

36. Perlstein, *Nixonland*, 432, 446, 472.

37. Black, *Richard M. Nixon*, 765.

38. Spiro Agnew, *Go Quietly . . . or Else* (New York: William Morrow, 1980), 65–69.

39. On the Beall investigation, see Agnew, *Go Quietly*, 50. On the election results, see, for example, Kane, *Facts about the Presidents*, 446–47.

40. Cohen and Witcover, *A Heartbeat Away*, 15; Anthony Ripley, "Evidence Shows Gifts to Agnew; Cites Requests and Receipt of over $100,000—Denial Also Entered in Record," *New York Times*, October 11, 1973, 93, 38.

41. "The Agnew Tragedy . . . and Opportunity," *New York Times*, October 11, 1973, 44; "How Agnew Bartered His Office to Keep from Going to Prison," 1, 36; Marion, *The Politics of Disgrace*, 79; Ripley, "Evidence Shows Gifts to Agnew," 38.

42. Agnew, *Go Quietly*, 191; "How Agnew Bartered His Office to Keep from Going to Prison," 36; James M. Naughton, "President Reportedly Took Initiative on Agnew Talks," *New York Times*, October 12, 1973, 89, 27.

43. Agnew is quoted in Clines, "Spiro T. Agnew," B15. See also Levy, "Spiro Agnew, the Forgotten Americans," 734.

44. "How Agnew Bartered His Office to Keep from Going to Prison," 36.

45. Cohen and Witcover, *A Heartbeat Away*, 305–6, 343; Gould, *Grand Old Party*, 391; Marion, *The Politics of Disgrace*, 79; "Mr. Agnew's Farewell," *New York Times*, October 17, 1973, 46.

46. Agnew, *Go Quietly*, 154–59; Cohen and Witcover, *A Heartbeat Away*, 346; "How Agnew Bartered His Office to Keep from Going to Prison," 1, 36; Marion, *The Politics of Disgrace*, 79; Ripley, "Evidence Shows Gifts to Agnew," 93, 38.

47. James M. Naughton, "Agnew Says He Quit to Aid Nixon in Restoring Trust," *New York Times*, October 16, 1973, 89, 34; "Spiro T. Agnew, Ex-Vice President, Dies at 77," D21.

48. Clines, "Spiro T. Agnew," B15; "Spiro T. Agnew, Ex-Vice President, Dies at 77," A1, D21.

# Chapter 8

1. Matthew Hoag and Maya Salam, "Man Gets 4 Years in Prison for 'Pizzagate' Shooting," *New York Times*, June 23, 2017, A14; Nancy E. Marion, *The Politics of Disgrace: The Role of Political Scandal in American Politics* (Durham, NC: Carolina Academic Press, 2010), 79–80, 107, 150; "Obama Wore a Tan Suit (and Spoke about World Crises)," *New York Times*, August 28, 2014, n.p.

2. Marion, *The Politics of Disgrace*, 79–80, 85–88; Ruth P. Morgan, "Nixon, Watergate, and the Study of the Presidency," *Presidential Studies Quarterly* 26, no. 1 (Winter 1996): 218; Mark Nevin, "Nixon Loyalists, Barry Goldwater, and Republican Support for President Nixon during Watergate," *Journal of Policy History* 29, no. 3 (July 2017): 406–7.

3. John W. Dean, *Blind Ambition* (New York: Simon & Schuster, 1976), 340–43; Marion, *The Politics of Disgrace*, 88–96.

4. Marion, *The Politics of Disgrace*, 95–96; Nevin, "Nixon Loyalists," 418. The case is *United States v. Nixon*, 418 U.S. 683 (1974).

5. Marion, *The Politics of Disgrace*, 98.

6. Marion, *The Politics of Disgrace*, 82–83; See also J. Michael Martinez, *The Safety of the Kingdom: Government Responses to Subversive Threats* (New York: Carrel Books, 2015), 159–68.

7. Marion, *The Politics of Disgrace*, 87; *United States v. New York Times*, 403 U.S. 713 (1971).

8. Ehrlichman is quoted in Rick Perlstein, *Nixonland: The Rise of a President and the Fracturing of America* (New York: Scribner, 2008), 584. See also Carl Bernstein and Bob Woodward, *All the President's Men* (New York: Simon & Schuster, 2014; originally published in 1974), 206, 215, 216; Marion, *The Politics of Disgrace*, 87.

9. Bernstein and Woodward, *All the President's Men*, 307, 312–13; John W. Dean, *The Nixon Defense: What He Knew and When He Knew It* (New York: Penguin, 2014), 4; Marion, *The Politics of Disgrace*, 87.

10. Perlstein, *Nixonland*, 584.

11. Dean is quoted in Dean, *The Nixon Defense*, xvii.

12. Bernstein and Woodward, *All the President's Men*, 216; Dean, *Blind Ambition*, 79–87; Dean, *The Nixon Defense*, 310–12.

13. Dean, *The Nixon Defense*, 12–13.

14. Marion, *The Politics of Disgrace*, 88.

15. Conrad Black, *Richard M. Nixon: A Life in Full* (New York: Public Affairs, 2007), 817–18; Fred Emery, *Watergate: The Corruption of American Politics and the Fall of Richard Nixon* (New York: Touchstone, 1995), 5–6; Marion, *The Politics of Disgrace*, 87–88; Perlstein, *Nixonland*, 666–67.

16. Dean, *The Nixon Defense*, 6; Emery, *Watergate*, 132–33.

17. Emery, *Watergate*, 133–34.

18. Emery, *Watergate*, 134–36.

19. Black, *Richard M. Nixon*, 818; Emery, *Watergate*, 138; Richard Reeves, *President Nixon: Alone in the White House* (New York: Touchstone, 2001), 499–500.

20. Dean, *The Nixon Defense*, 6–10; Reeves, *President Nixon*, 502.

21. Nixon is quoted in Dean, *The Nixon Defense*, 59. See also Marion, *The Politics of Disgrace*, 88; Robert B. Semple Jr., "Rise and Fall: Appraisal of Nixon Career," *New York Times*, August 9, 1974, 1, 11.

22. Nixon is quoted in Dean, *The Nixon Defense*, 146.

23. Bernstein and Woodward, *All the President's Men*, 41–47, 56; Dean, *The Nixon Defense*, 89; Emery, *Watergate*, 188.

24. Dean, *Blind Ambition*, 133; Dean, *The Nixon Defense*, 210.

25. Bernstein and Woodward, *All the President's Men*, 275–77; Emery, *Watergate*, 269–70; Marion, *The Politics of Disgrace*, 91–92; Morgan, "Nixon, Watergate, and the Study of the Presidency," 219.

26. Dean, *The Nixon Defense*, 542.

27. Dean, *Blind Ambition*, 196–274; Bob Woodward, *The Last of the President's Men* (New York: Simon & Schuster, 2015), 148–49.

28. Bernstein and Woodward, *All the President's Men*, 309; Dean, *The Nixon Defense*, 542–43.

29. Emery, *Watergate*, 356–57; Marion, *The Politics of Disgrace*, 92; Bob Woodward and Carl Bernstein, *The Final Days* (New York: Avon Books, 1976), 50, 67.

30. Dean, *The Nixon Defense*, 214; Marion, *The Politics of Disgrace*, 93.

31. Dean, *The Nixon Defense*, 626; Marion, *The Politics of Disgrace*, 93; Woodward, *The Last of the President's Men*, 1, 2–4, 150–56.

32. Emery, *Watergate*, 362, 370, 380.

33. Dean, *Blind Ambition*, 340–42; Emery, *Watergate*, 395–99; Marion, *The Politics of Disgrace*, 94–95.

34. Nixon is quoted in Emery, *Watergate*, 415. See also Bernstein and Woodward, *All the President's Men*, 334; Nevin, "Nixon Loyalists," 413–14.

35. Dean, *Blind Ambition*, 343–48; Emery, *Watergate*, 407, 422, 424–27.

36. Dean, *Blind Ambition*, 348.

37. Black, *Richard M. Nixon*, 955; Dean, *Blind Ambition*, 351; Emery, *Watergate*, 493.

38. Scott is quoted in Emery, *Watergate*, 430. See also Bernstein and Woodward, *All the President's Men*, 79.

39. Emery, *Watergate*, 406–7, 434.

40. Emery, *Watergate*, 434. The vote was 8–0 because Justice Rehnquist recused himself. He had served in the Nixon administration and knew many administration officials well. See also Marion, *The Politics of Disgrace*, 95–96.

41. 418 U.S. 683 at 686–716.

42. Dean is quoted in Dean, *The Nixon Defense*, 317. See also Reeves, *President Nixon*, 577.

43. Emery, *Watergate*, 189–92, 455–56; Marion, *The Politics of Disgrace*, 96–97; Nevin, "Nixon Loyalists," 421.

44. Black, *Richard M. Nixon*, 823; Emery, *Watergate*, 414–18; Marion, *The Politics of Disgrace*, 95.

45. Black, *Richard M. Nixon*, 970–71; Emery, *Watergate*, 443–54; Marion, *The Politics of Disgrace*, 97–98.

46. Nixon is quoted in Dean, *The Nixon Defense*, 60. See also Black, *Richard M. Nixon*, 956–57, 974.

47. Emery, *Watergate*, 380, 381, 409–14.

48. Black, *Richard M. Nixon*, 978–79; Emery, *Watergate*, 472–74; Nevin, "Nixon Loyalists," 419–22; Woodward and Bernstein, *The Final Days*, 459–63.

49. The quote is found in many sources. See, for example, Brian M. Harward, ed., *The Presidency in Times of Crisis and Disaster: Primary Documents in Context* (Santa Barbara, CA: ABC-CLIO, 2019), 193. See also Black, *Richard M. Nixon*, 982; Woodward and Bernstein, *The Final Days*, 497–98.

50. Marion, *The Politics of Disgrace*, 98–99.

51. "The Nixon Resignation," *New York Times*, August 9, 1974, 32.

52. Nixon's remarks have been reprinted in many sources. See, for example, Jeff Wallenfeldt, ed., *The Growth of a Superpower: America from 1945 to Today* (New York: Rosen, 2012), 140. See also Black, *Richard M. Nixon*, 984–85; Woodward and Bernstein, *The Final Days*, 505–8.

53. Black, *Richard M. Nixon*, 985–86; Woodward and Bernstein, *The Final Days*, 508–9.

54. Ford and Nixon are quoted in Barry Werth, *31 Days: Gerald Ford, the Nixon Pardon, and a Government in Crisis* (New York: Anchor Books, 2007), 301. See also Marion, *The Politics of Disgrace*, 98–99.

55. Ford is quoted in Werth, *31 Days*, 12.

56. Morgan, "Nixon, Watergate, and the Study of the Presidency," 317–38; Semple, "Rise and Fall," 1, 11.

# Chapter 9

1. Jenrette is quoted in United States House of Representatives, Committee on the Judiciary, *Report on the Committee on the Judiciary, House of Representatives, Ninety-Eighth Congress, First Session, Identifying Court Proceedings and Actions of Vital Interest to the Congress* (Washington, DC: US Government Printing Office, 1984), 774. See also Bennett L. Gershman, "Abscam, the Judiciary, and the Ethics of Entrapment," *Yale Law Journal* 91, no. 8 (July 1982): 1571–72; Erwin N. Griswold, "*Sed Quis Custodiet Ipsos Custodies?* Some Reflections on ABSCAM," *Proceedings of the American Philosophical Society* 126, no. 6 (December 17, 1982): 452–55; Kim Long, *The Almanac of Political Corruption, Scandals & Dirty Politics* (New York: Delta Paperbacks, 2007), 248–49; Nancy E. Marion, *The Politics of Disgrace: The Role of Political Scandal in American Politics* (Durham, NC: Carolina Academic Press, 2010), 196–202.

2. Weinberg is quoted in Robert W. Greene, *The Sting Man: Inside Abscam* (New York: Penguin, 2013; originally published in 1981), 6. See also Henry Biggs, "Suppuration of Powers: Abscam, Entrapment and the Politics of Expulsion," *Legislation and Policy Brief* 6, no. 2 (2014): 251; Greene, *The Sting Man*, 20–67; Griswold, "*Sed Quis Custodiet Ipsos Custodies*," 452, 454–55, 457; Matthew W. Kinskey, "Note: American Hustle: Reflections on Abscam and the Entrapment Defense," *American Journal of Criminal Law* 41, no. 3 (Summer 2014): 235–36; Marion, *The Politics of Disgrace*, 197–98.

3. Biggs, "Suppuration of Powers," 251–52; Greene, *The Sting Man*, 92–141; Kinskey, "Note," 236; Marion, *The Politics of Disgrace*, 196, 197.

4. Marion, *The Politics of Disgrace*, 197.

5. Greene, *The Sting Man*, 6–14, 92; Marion, *The Politics of Disgrace*, 198.

6. Greene, *The Sting Man*, 13–14.

7. Weinberg is quoted in Greene, *The Sting Man*, 191.

8. Biggs, "Suppuration of Powers," 252; Gershman, "Abscam, the Judiciary, and the Ethics of Entrapment," 1572; Griswold, "*Sed Quis Custodiet Ipsos Custodies*," 452–53; Marion, *The Politics of Disgrace*, 197–98.

9. Gershman, "Abscam, the Judiciary, and the Ethics of Entrapment," 1572.

10. Biggs, "Suppuration of Powers," 259; Gershman, "Abscam, the Judiciary, and the Ethics of Entrapment," 1572; Kinskey, "Note," 236–37; Marion, *The Politics of Disgrace*, 199.

11. Biggs, "Suppuration of Powers," 252–53, 256–58, 267; Gershman, "Abscam, the Judiciary, and the Ethics of Entrapment," 1577; Griswold, "*Sed Quis Custodiet Ipsos Custodies*," 452–54; Kinskey, "Note," 237, 252–54; Long, *The Almanac of Political Corruption*, 248–49; Marion, *The Politics of Disgrace*, 198–201.

12. Gershman, "Abscam, the Judiciary, and the Ethics of Entrapment," 1577; Marion, *The Politics of Disgrace*, 198–201.

13. Long, *The Almanac of Political Corruption*, 249; Marion, *The Politics of Disgrace*, 201.

14. Biggs, "Suppuration of Powers," 255–56; Gershman, "Abscam, the Judiciary, and the Ethics of Entrapment," 1572, 1577–78; Marion, *The Politics of Disgrace*, 200, 201; Kinskey, "Note," 248–50; Bill Winter, "Probing the Probers: Does Abscam Go Too

Far?" *American Bar Association Journal* 68, no. 1 (November 1982): 1348–49; Long, *The Almanac of Political Corruption*, 249.

15. The leading book on Congressman Jenrette is John F. Clark and Cookie Miller VanSice, *Capitol Steps and Missteps: The Wild, Improbable Ride of Congressman John Jenrette* (North Charleston, SC: CreateSpace, 2017), especially pages 241–314. See also Rita Jenrette, *My Capitol Secrets* (New York: Bantam, 1981); Long, *The Almanac of Political Corruption*, 247, 249, 250; Marion, *The Politics of Disgrace*, 200, 201.

16. Marion, *The Politics of Disgrace*, 200.

17. Pressler is quoted in Robert E. Landesman, *Rx America* (Morrisville, NC: Lulu Press, 2011), 41.

18. Kinskey, "Note," 258–60; Winter, "Probing the Probers," 1349–50.

19. Marion, *The Politics of Disgrace*, 201.

20. Biggs, "Suppuration of Powers," 249; Kinskey, "Note," 234–35, 260.

21. Kinskey, "Note," 258–60.

22. Kinskey, "Note," 260.

23. Winter, "Probing the Probers," 1349–50.

# Chapter 10

1. See, for example, Kitty Calavita, Henry N. Pontell, and Robert Tillman, *Big Money Crime: Fraud and Politics in the Savings and Loan Crisis* (Berkeley: University of California Press, 1999), 1–2.

2. Calavita, Pontell, and Tillman, *Big Money Crime*, 9, 42, 43, 97, 169. See also Martin E. Lowry, *High Rollers: Inside the Savings and Loan Debacle* (Westport, CT: Praeger, 1991), 14–17.

3. Lowry, *High Rollers*, 15–17.

4. Lowry, *High Rollers*, 15–26.

5. Calavita, Pontell, and Tillman, *Big Money Crime*, 9, 11, 15, 97–104.

6. The Depository Institutions Deregulation and Monetary Control Act of 1980 is excerpted in Andrew T. Carswell, Katrin B. Anacker, Kenneth B. Tremblay, and Sarah D. Kirby, *Introduction to Housing* (Athens: University of Georgia Press, 2018), 456. See also Calavita, Pontell, and Tillman, *Big Money Crime*, 11–12, 90, 91, 92, 100; Kim Long, *The Almanac of Political Corruption, Scandals & Dirty Politics* (New York: Delta Paperbacks, 2007), 270; Davita Silfen Glasberg and Dan L. Skidmore, "The Role of the State in the Criminogenesis of Corporate Crime: A Case Study of the Savings and Loan Crisis," *Social Science Quarterly* 79, no. 1 (March 1998): 116.

7. Calavita, Pontell, and Tillman, *Big Money Crime*, 11–15, 88–94, 133.

8. Seidman is quoted in Susanne Trimbath, *Lessons Not Learned: 10 Steps to Stable Financial Markets* (London: Spiramus, 2015), 234. See also Long, *The Almanac of Political Corruption*, 270.

9. Lowry, *High Rollers*, 27–33.

10. Lowry, *High Rollers*, 27–33.

11. Resolution Trust Corporation, Office of Investigations, *Massachusetts Office of Dispute Resolution Progress Report, September 30, 1990* (Washington, DC: US Government Printing Office, 1990), 7, 19.

12. Calavita, Pontell, and Tillman, *Big Money Crime*, 110, 188; Lowry, *High Rollers*, 140–43.

13. Nancy E. Marion, *The Politics of Disgrace: The Role of Political Scandal in American Politics* (Durham, NC: Carolina Academic Press, 2010), 213; Dennis F. Thompson, "Mediated Corruption: The Case of the Keating Five," *American Political Science Review* 87, no. 2 (June 1993): 369–70; Rob Wells, *The Enforcers: How Little-Known Trade Reporters Exposed the Keating Five and Advanced Business Journalism* (Urbana, Chicago, and Springfield: University of Illinois Press, 2019), 2–3.

14. Richard W. Stevenson, "California's Daring Thrift Unit," *New York Times*, May 25, 1987, 34; Wells, *The Enforcers*, 113.

15. Marion, *The Politics of Disgrace*, 213; Wells, *The Enforcers*, 113.

16. Calavita, Pontell, and Tillman, *Big Money Crime*, 107; Wells, *The Enforcers*, 112–14.

17. Wells, *The Enforcers*, 114.

18. Jill Abramson and David Rogers, "The Keating 535: Five Are on the Grill, but Other Lawmakers Help Big Donors, Too; Constituent Services Is Pivotal to the Way Congress Works, and Ethical Line Is Fuzzy; There but for the Grace of God," *Wall Street Journal*, January 10, 1991, A1. See also "The Keating Five: A Final Chapter," *New York Times*, November 21, 1991, D21; "The Keating One?" *New York Times*, February 22, 1991, A28; Long, *The Almanac of Political Corruption*, 271; Wells, *The Enforcers*, 76.

19. "The Keating Five: A Final Chapter," D21; Long, *The Almanac of Political Corruption*, 271; Wells, *The Enforcers*, 82.

20. "The Keating Five: A Final Chapter," D21; Wells, *The Enforcers*, 82.

21. Abramson and Rogers, "The Keating 535," A1; "The Keating Five: A Final Chapter," D21; Long, *The Almanac of Political Corruption*, 271; Thompson, "Mediated Corruption," 371; Wells, *The Enforcers*, 71.

22. "The Keating Five: A Final Chapter," D21; "Senator Riegle's Duty," *New York Times*, November 26, 1991, A20; Wells, *The Enforcers*, 71.

23. "The Keating Five: A Final Chapter," D21; Long, *The Almanac of Political Corruption*, 270–71; Thompson, "Mediated Corruption," 370.

24. Keating is quoted in United States Congress, *Preliminary Inquiry into Allegations Regarding Senators Cranston, DeConcini, Glenn, McCain, and Riegle, and Lincoln Savings and Loan: Open Session Hearing before the Select Committee on Ethics, United States Senate, One Hundred First Congress, Second Session, Part 2 of 8, November 15, 1990, through January 16, 1991* (Washington, DC: US Government Printing Office, 1991), 205.

25. The incident is recounted in United States Congress, *Preliminary Inquiry into Allegations*, 101, 127, 728.

26. Abramson and Rogers, "The Keating 535," A1; Thompson, "Mediated Corruption," 370; United States Congress, *Preliminary Inquiry into Allegations*, 107; Wells, *The Enforcers*, 138.

27. DeConcini is quoted in United States Congress, *Preliminary Inquiry into Allegations*, 238, 323.

28. Glenn is quoted in United States Congress, *Preliminary Inquiry into Allegations*, 674.

29. Calavita, Pontell, and Tillman, *Big Money Crime*, 108–11; United States Congress, *Preliminary Inquiry into Allegations*, 138–39.

30. Calavita, Pontell, and Tillman, *Big Money Crime*, 100, 108–11.

31. Richard L. Berke, "Senators Seek Exoneration as Hearings on Ethics End," *New York Times*, January 17, 1991, B6; Thompson, "Mediated Corruption," 370.

32. "An Apology of Sorts, from a Senator," *New York Times*, November 24, 1991, E7; Berke, "Senators Seek Exoneration as Hearings on Ethics End," B6; "Senator Riegle's Duty," A20; "The Keating One?" A28; Thompson, "Mediated Corruption," 370, 374–75.

33. Calavita, Pontell, and Tillman, *Big Money Crime*, 101–5; Lowry, *High Rollers*, 185–86; Wells, *The Enforcers*, 81.

34. The quotes are found in Michael Waldman, *Who Robbed America? A Citizen's Guide to the S&L Scandal* (New York: Random House, 1990), 67. See also Lowry, *High Rollers*, 186.

35. "Transcript of Wright's Address to House of Representatives," *New York Times*, June 1, 1989, D22.

36. William K. Black, *The Best Way to Rob a Bank Is to Own One: How Corporate Executives and Politicians Looted the S&L Industry* (Austin: University of Texas Press, 2014), 83–85; Long, *The Almanac of Political Corruption*, 269; Marion, *The Politics of Disgrace*, 213; Robin Toner, "Wright Confirms Plan to Resign from the House," *New York Times*, June 27, 1989, A14; "Transcript of Wright's Address to House of Representatives," D22; "Wright Returns to Ft. Worth," *New York Times*, July 1, 1989, 1.

37. Lowry, *High Rollers*, 245–86.

38. Thompson, "Mediated Corruption," 372–74.

# Chapter 11

1. Steven J. Maranville, "Teaching Case for the Iran-Contra Affair: 'Will No One Rid Me of This Troublesome Priest?'" *Academy of Management Proceedings & Membership Directory* (2001): 2–3; Richard Reeves, *President Reagan: The Triumph of Imagination* (New York: Simon & Schuster, 2005), 372–97, 429–30.

2. Nancy E. Marion, *The Politics of Disgrace: The Role of Political Scandal in American Politics* (Durham, NC: Carolina Academic Press, 2010), 118; Maranville, "Teaching Case for the Iran-Contra Affair," 8; Richard Secord with Jay Wurts, *Honored and Betrayed: Irangate, Covert Affairs, and the Secret War in Laos* (Hoboken, NJ: Wiley, 1992), 203.

3. Malcolm Byrne, *Iran-Contra: Reagan's Scandal and the Unchecked Abuse of Presidential Power* (Lawrence: University Press of Kansas, 2014), 8–9; Marion, *The Politics of Disgrace*, 118; Maranville, "Teaching Case for the Iran-Contra Affair," 8.

4. Byrne, *Iran-Contra*, 8–10, 21–22, 36, 139, 170, 178.

5. Byrne, *Iran-Contra*, 12, 15, 124; Marion, *The Politics of Disgrace*, 118–19.

6. Marion, *The Politics of Disgrace*, 118–19.

7. Byrne, *Iran-Contra*, 16–19, 22, 127, 132–34, 175; Marion, *The Politics of Disgrace*, 118–19.

8. Maranville, "Teaching Case for the Iran-Contra Affair," 8.

9. The amendment is quoted in Marion, *The Politics of Disgrace*, 119. See also Byrne, *Iran-Contra*, 20, 42–44; Maranville, "Teaching Case for the Iran-Contra Affair," 8.

10. D. Bruce Hicks, "Presidential Foreign Policy Prerogative after the Iran-Contra Affair: A Review Essay," *Presidential Studies Quarterly* 26, no. 4 (Fall 1996): 965; Marion, *The Politics of Disgrace*, 119; Maranville, "Teaching Case for the Iran-Contra Affair," 8; Sean Wilentz, *The Age of Reagan: A History, 1974–2008* (New York: Harper, 2008), 212.

11. Marion, *The Politics of Disgrace*, 119–20.

12. Scott Armstrong, Malcolm Byrne, Tom Blanton, and the National Security Archive, *Secret Military Assistance to Iran and the Contras: A Chronology of Events and Individuals* (New York: Warner Books, 1987), 1:117; Byrne, *Iran-Contra*, 8–9.

13. Byrne, *Iran-Contra*, 9–10.

14. The amendment is quoted in United States Senate, Select Committee to Investigate Covert Arms Transactions with Iran, the United States House of Representatives Select Committee to Investigate Covert Arms Transactions with Iran, and United States Senate Select Committee on Secret Military Assistance to Iran and the Nicaraguan Opposition, *Report of the Congressional Committees Investigating the Iran-Contra Affair, with Supplemental, Minority, and Additional Views* (Washington, DC: US Government Printing Office, 1987), 492.

15. David E. Kyvig, *The Age of Impeachment: American Constitutional Culture since 1960* (Lawrence: University Press of Kansas, 2008), 238–41, 244.

16. Byrne, *Iran-Contra*, 42–44, 291, 295; Marion, *The Politics of Disgrace*, 119–20.

17. Marion, *The Politics of Disgrace*, 120.

18. Wilentz, *The Age of Reagan*, 213–15.

19. Marion, *The Politics of Disgrace*, 120; Secord, *Honored and Betrayed*, 211; Wilentz, *The Age of Reagan*, 213.

20. Marion, *The Politics of Disgrace*, 120; Oliver North, with William Novak, *Under Fire: An American Story* (Grand Rapids, MI: Zondervan, 1991), 287; Secord, *Honored and Betrayed*, 211.

21. Maranville, "Teaching Case for the Iran-Contra Affair," 9; North, *Under Fire*, 322; Wilentz, *The Age of Reagan*, 214–15.

22. Marion, *The Politics of Disgrace*, 121; Secord, *Honored and Betrayed*, 147.

23. Marion, *The Politics of Disgrace*, 121.

24. Weinberger is quoted in William E. Leuchtenburg, *The American President: From Theodore Roosevelt to Bill Clinton* (Oxford and New York: Oxford University Press, 2015), 644. See also Maranville, "Teaching Case for the Iran-Contra Affair," 4–5.

25. Mark Bowden, *Guests of the Ayatollah: The First Battle in America's War with Militant Islam* (New York: Atlantic Monthly Press, 2006), 552–58; Marion, *The Politics of Disgrace*, 121–22.

26. Bowden, *Guests of the Ayatollah*, 557–58, 575–78.

27. Kyvig, *The Age of Impeachment*, 234–36; Marion, *The Politics of Disgrace*, 122.

28. Hicks, "Presidential Foreign Policy Prerogative," 968; Leuchtenburg, *The American President*, 643; Maranville, "Teaching Case for the Iran-Contra Affair," 6; North, *Under Fire*, 29; Wilentz, *The Age of Reagan*, 218.

29. Shultz is quoted in Wilentz, *The Age of Reagan*, 219.

30. United States Senate, Select Committee to Investigate Covert Arms Transactions with Iran, *Report of the Congressional Committees Investigating the Iran-Contra Affair*, 787; Secord, *Honored and Betrayed*, 279.

31. Reeves, *President Reagan*, 362; Wilentz, *The Age of Reagan*, 221–22.

32. Maranville, "Teaching Case for the Iran-Contra Affair," 4; Wilentz, *The Age of Reagan*, 221.

33. Leuchtenburg, *The American President*, 644.

34. Marion, *The Politics of Disgrace*, 124–25.

35. Wilentz, *The Age of Reagan*, 219, 220.

36. McFarlane is quoted in Armstrong et al., *Secret Military Assistance to Iran and the Contras*, 1:546. See also Leuchtenburg, *The American President*, 644–45; Maranville, "Teaching Case for the Iran-Contra Affair," 7; Wilentz, *The Age of Reagan*, 211.

37. Leuchtenburg, *The American President*, 645; Maranville, "Teaching Case for the Iran-Contra Affair," 7.

38. Marion, *The Politics of Disgrace*, 124; Secord, *Honored and Betrayed*, 280.

39. Peter Kornbluh and Malcolm Byrne, eds., *The Iran-Contra Scandal: A Declassified History* (New York: New Press, 1993), 402; North, *Under Fire*, 334.

40. Kornbluh and Byrne, *The Iran-Contra Scandal*, 402–4.

41. Wilentz, *The Age of Reagan*, 225.

42. Hicks, "Presidential Foreign Policy Prerogative," 968.

43. Leuchtenburg, *The American President*, 642–43; North, *Under Fire*, 7.

44. Reagan is quoted in Reeves, *President Reagan*, 364. See also H. W. Brands, *Reagan: The Life* (New York: Doubleday, 2015), 615–17; Ronald Lee and Shawn J. Spano, "Technical Discourse in Defense of Public Virtue: Ronald Reagan's Explanation of the Iran/Contra Affair," *Political Communication* 13, no. 1 (January–March 1996): 115.

45. Reagan is quoted in Brands, *Reagan*, 615–16. See also North, *Under Fire*, 370.

46. Reeves, *President Reagan*, 364–65.

47. Reagan is quoted in Brands, *Reagan*, 620. See also Lee and Spano, "Technical Discourse in Defense of Public Virtue," 115; Reeves, *President Reagan*, 366.

48. Hicks, "Presidential Foreign Policy Prerogative," 970; Reeves, *President Reagan*, 368; Bernard Weintraub, "Iran Payment Found Diverted to Contras; Reagan Security Adviser and Aide Are Out," *New York Times*, November 26, 1986, A1.

49. Leuchtenburg, *The American President*, 647; Reeves, *President Reagan*, 367, 368; Wilentz, *The Age of Reagan*, 227–28.

50. Brands, *Reagan*, 634–35; Byrne, *Iran-Contra*, 2; Leuchtenburg, *The American President*, 647–48; Lee and Spano, "Technical Discourse in Defense of Public Virtue," 115–16; Reeves, *President Reagan*, 368–69; Wilentz, *The Age of Reagan*, 228.

51. Brands, *Reagan*, 634; North, *Under Fire*, 5; Weintraub, "Iran Payment Found Diverted to Contras," A1.

52. The quote is found in John G. Tower, Edmund Muskie, and Brent Scowcroft, *Report of the President's Special Review Board* (Washington, DC: US Government Print-

ing Office, 1987), I-1. See also Reeves, *President Reagan*, 378–85; Lee and Spano, "Technical Discourse in Defense of Public Virtue," 116; Maranville, "Teaching Case for the Iran-Contra Affair," 1, 9–10; Wilentz, *The Age of Reagan*, 229–31.

53. Tower, Muskie, and Scowcroft, *Report of the President's Special Review Board*, IV-10–IV-12. See also Brands, *Reagan*, 645–48; Wilentz, *The Age of Reagan*, 228–29.

54. Leuchtenburg, *The American President*, 648–49; Wilentz, *The Age of Reagan*, 230–31.

55. Brands, *Reagan*, 648–53; Marion, *The Politics of Disgrace*, 128–29.

56. Brands, *Reagan*, 652.

57. Wilentz, *The Age of Reagan*, 228.

58. See, for example, United States Senate, Select Committee to Investigate Covert Arms Transactions with Iran, *Report of the Congressional Committees Investigating the Iran-Contra Affair*.

59. Brands, *Reagan*, 723–27.

60. Leuchtenburg, *The American President*, 654–55; Reeves, *President Reagan*, 404–10; Wilentz, *The Age of Reagan*, 237–38.

61. Wilentz, *The Age of Reagan*, 229.

62. Reagan is quoted in Leuchtenburg, *The American President*, 653. See also Lee and Spano, "Technical Discourse in Defense of Public Virtue," 116, 117–18; Reeves, *President Reagan*, 386–88; Wilentz, *The Age of Reagan*, 232–33.

63. Reagan is quoted in Office of the Federal Register, National Archives & Records Administration, *Public Papers of the Presidents of the United States: Ronald Reagan, 1987*, book 1, *January 1 to July 1, 1987* (Washington, DC: US Government Printing Office, 1989), 209.

64. Office of the Federal Register, *Public Papers of the Presidents of the United States: Ronald Reagan, 1987*, 1:209.

65. Leuchtenburg, *The American President*, 649–50; Reeves, *President Reagan*, 429–30.

66. Leuchtenburg, *The American President*, 654–56; Wilentz, *The Age of Reagan*, 239.

67. Brands, *Reagan*, 726; Wilentz, *The Age of Reagan*, 242.

68. United States Court of Appeals for the District of Columbia Circuit, Division for the Purpose of Appointing Independent Counsel, Division No. 86-6, *Final Report of the Independent Counsel for Iran/Contra Matters*, vol. 1, *Investigations and Prosecutions* (Washington, DC: US Government Printing Office, 1993). See also Kyvig, *The Age of Impeachment*, 262–64; Marion, *The Politics of Disgrace*, 132.

69. Marion, *The Politics of Disgrace*, 132; Wilentz, *The Age of Reagan*, 242.

70. Marion, *The Politics of Disgrace*, 132–33; Reeves, *President Reagan*, 488.

71. Marion, *The Politics of Disgrace*, 135.

72. Marion, *The Politics of Disgrace*, 134–35; North, *Under Fire*, 477–78, 490–91; Reeves, *President Reagan*, 488.

73. Marion, *The Politics of Disgrace*, 136–38.

74. Marion, *The Politics of Disgrace*, 138–39.

# Chapter 12

1. Gary S. Chafetz, *The Perfect Villain: John McCain and the Demonization of Lobbyist Jack Abramoff* (Omaha, NE: Notable Trials Library, 2015; originally published in 2008), xii–xv; Norman J. Ornstein, "The House That Jack Built," *New York Times*, January 14, 2007, C25.

2. Chafetz, *The Perfect Villain*, 3–21; Peter H. Stone, *Heist: Superlobbyist Jack Abramoff, His Republican Allies, and the Buying of Washington* (New York: Farrar, Straus & Giroux, 2006), 13, 41–24; Del Quentin Wilber and Carrie Johnson, "Abramoff Gets Reduced Sentence of Four Years in Prison," *Washington Post*, September 5, 2008, A3.

3. The quote is found in Chafetz, *The Perfect Villain*, 26. See also Sheryl Stolberg, "Lobbyist Accepts Plea Deal and Becomes Star Witness in a Wider Corruption Case," *New York Times*, January 4, 2006, A12.

4. Chafetz, *The Perfect Villain*, 19, 24–32; Citizens for Responsibility and Ethics in Washington, "Caught in Jack's Web: The Abramoff Associates' File," *Multinational Monitor* 27, no. 3 (May/June 2006): 28; Stolberg, "Lobbyist Accepts Plea Deal," A12.

5. Chafetz, *The Perfect Villain*, 25–26.

6. Chafetz, *The Perfect Villain*, 21, 35–36, 38; Stone, *Heist*, 45.

7. Chafetz, *The Perfect Villain*, 58–62, 72–73. The quotes are found on page 59. See also Ornstein, "The House That Jack Built," C25; Stone, *Heist*, 46–47, 142.

8. DeLay is quoted in Stone, *Heist*, 13, 55. See also Chafetz, *The Perfect Villain*, 81, 99, 103, 122; Citizens for Responsibility and Ethics in Washington, "Caught in Jack's Web," 29; Stolberg, "Lobbyist Accepts Plea Deal," A1, A12.

9. Citizens for Responsibility and Ethics in Washington, "Caught in Jack's Web," 24–29.

10. Chafetz, *The Perfect Villain*, 40, 79, 82–90, 93, 94–98, 159, 246, 276; Citizens for Responsibility and Ethics in Washington, "Caught in Jack's Web," 24, 26; Stone, *Heist*, 36, 61–62, 64.

11. Chafetz, *The Perfect Villain*, 132–37. See also Rob Boston, "Wheel of Misfortune: Religious Right Leaders Are Praying that the Jack Abramoff Casino-Lobbying Scandal Won't Make Them Big-Time Losers," *Church & State* 59, no. 3 (March 2006): 8–11.

12. Chafetz, *The Perfect Villain*, 46, 73–74; Stone, *Heist*, 117, 121–22, 132, 133–35.

13. Chafetz, *The Perfect Villain*, 226, 230; Wilber and Johnson, "Abramoff Gets Reduced Sentence of Four Years in Prison," A3.

14. Chafetz, *The Perfect Villain*, 238–39, 245–47, 275; Citizens for Responsibility and Ethics in Washington, "Caught in Jack's Web," 27.

15. Chafetz, *The Perfect Villain*, 231.

16. Chafetz, *The Perfect Villain*, 304–9; Ornstein, "The House That Jack Built," C25; Stone, *Heist*, 158.

17. Chafetz, *The Perfect Villain*, 316; Citizens for Responsibility and Ethics in Washington, "Caught in Jack's Web," 25; Rick Lyman, "Abramoff and 4 Others Sued by Tribe over Casino Closing," *New York Times*, July 13, 2006, A16; Stolberg, "Lobbyist Accepts Plea Deal," A12.

18.  Sprague is quoted in Wilber and Johnson, "Abramoff Gets Reduced Sentence of Four Years in Prison," A3. See also Chafetz, *The Perfect Villain*, 252, 254–55, 257–58.

19.  Chafetz, *The Perfect Villain*, 145–50; Stone, *Heist*, 65–72.

20.  The amounts continually changed and later became a matter of dispute. See, for example, Chafetz, *The Perfect Villain*, 150–66; Citizens for Responsibility and Ethics in Washington, "Caught in Jack's Web," 29; Stone, *Heist*, 72.

21.  Chafetz, *The Perfect Villain*, 174–81; Stone, *Heist*, 26, 85–86, 107–8.

22.  "Florida Jury Convicts 'Big Tony' in 2001 Businessman Murder," *Tampa Bay Times*, July 1, 2015, n.p.; Chafetz, *The Perfect Villain*, 179, 279, 316–17.

23.  "Abramoff Says Top Republicans Were Allies," *New York Times*, March 9, 2006, A21; Chafetz, *The Perfect Villain*, 317–18; Philip Shenon, "Abramoff Set to Start Prison Term," *New York Times*, November 16, 2006, A18; Philip Shenon, "Lobbyist Stripped of Good Name, but Not of Good Vacation," *New York Times*, April 28, 2006, A20; Wilber and Johnson, "Abramoff Gets Reduced Sentence of Four Years in Prison," A3.

24.  Philip Shenon, "Demotion of a Prosecutor Is Investigated; Action Halted Inquiry on Influential Lobbyist, Officials Say," *New York Times*, September 27, 2005, A22; Philip Shenon, "Outside Inquiry Sought on Prosecutor's Demotion," *New York Times*, October 7, 2005, A24.

25.  Ashby Jones, "Guam-O-Rama! Prosecutors Drop Charges against Greenberg Traurig," *Wall Street Journal*, April 15, 2008, n.p.

26.  Neil A. Lewis, "Abramoff Gets 4 Years in Prison for Corruption; Reduced Sentence Reflects His Cooperation," *New York Times*, September 5, 2008, A16.

27.  Abramoff is quoted in Wilber and Johnson, "Abramoff Gets Reduced Sentence of Four Years in Prison," A3.

28.  Chafetz, *The Perfect Villain*, 267–70, 357, 372; Citizens for Responsibility and Ethics in Washington, "Caught in Jack's Web," 26; Stone, *Heist*, 95–97, 99, 101, 154, 190–91; Stolberg, "Lobbyist Accepts Plea Deal," A1; Wilber and Johnson, "Abramoff Gets Reduced Sentence of Four Years in Prison," A3.

29.  Jack Abramoff, *Capitol Punishment: The Hard Truth about Washington Corruption from America's Most Notorious Lobbyist* (New York: WND Books, 2011), 273; Shenon, "Abramoff Set to Start Prison Term," A18.

30.  Mark Leibovich, "Abramoff: From Prison to a Pizzeria Job," *New York Times*, June 24, 2010, A15; Nathaniel Popper, "Lobbyist Faces Prison for Flouting Changed Law," *New York Times*, June 26, 2020, A20.

31.  Byron Tau, "Jack Abramoff Sought Meeting with Trump for Congo's Leader: Details Attempts to Arrange Florida Visit in a Disclosure with Justice Department," *Wall Street Journal*, June 23, 2017, n.p.

32.  "Lobbyist Caught by His Own Law," *Toronto Star*, June 28, 2020, IN.2; Popper, "Lobbyist Faces Prison for Flouting Changed Law," A20.

33.  A. O. Scott, "Want a Deal on a Used Country?" *New York Times*, December 17, 2010, C20.

34.  Abramoff, *Capitol Punishment*, especially pages 265–77. See also Alan Feuer, "For Ex-Lobbyist Abramoff, a Multimedia Effort at Redemption," *New York Times*, November 13, 2011, 16.

# Chapter 13

1. Bob Woodward, *Fear: Trump in the White House* (New York: Simon & Schuster, 2018), 27–29, 45–47, 162–66, 168. See also Robert Dallek, *How Did We Get Here? From Theodore Roosevelt to Donald Trump* (New York: Harper, 2020), 3, 230–31.

2. Derek E. Bambauer, "Information Hacking," *Utah Law Review* 2020, no. 4 (2020): 989; John Bolton, *The Room Where It Happened: A White House Memoir* (New York: Simon & Schuster, 2020), 156; Michael Isikoff and David Corn, *Russian Roulette: The Inside Story of Putin's War on America and the Election of Donald Trump* (New York: Twelve, an Imprint of the Hachette Book Group, 2018), 31–32; Woodward, *Fear*, 60–71, 298; Bob Woodward, *Rage* (New York: Simon & Schuster, 2020), 44.

3. Special Counsel Robert S. Mueller III, *Report on the Investigation into Russian Interference in the 2016 Presidential Election* (New York: Scribner, 2019), 1:4–5, 1:14–15; Isikoff and Corn, *Russian Roulette*, 56–59, 270, 274; Jeffrey Toobin, *True Crimes and Misdemeanors: The Investigation of Donald Trump* (New York: Doubleday, 2020), 151–54.

4. Mueller, *Report on the Investigation*, 1:4, 1:22–29. See also Bambauer, "Information Hacking," 1005; Duchess Harris and Marcia Amidon Lusted, *Russian Hacking in American Elections* (Minneapolis, MN: Essential Library, 2018), 52; Toobin, *True Crimes and Misdemeanors*, 154–59.

5. Mueller, *Report on the Investigation*, 1:4–5.

6. Mueller, *Report on the Investigation*, 1:41–49. See also Harris and Lusted, *Russian Hacking in American Elections*, 10; Isikoff and Corn, *Russian Roulette*, 131–38; Toobin, *True Crimes and Misdemeanors*, 19–22; Philip Rucker and Carol Leonnig, *A Very Stable Genius: Donald J. Trump's Testing of America* (New York: Penguin, 2020), 159–60; Woodward, *Fear*, 28.

7. Mueller, *Report on the Investigation*, 1:36–41. See also Bolton, *The Room Where It Happened*, 151–52.

8. Isikoff and Corn, *Russian Roulette*, 134–35, 168–69, 173–75.

9. Isikoff and Corn, *Russian Roulette*, 241–48; Jonathan Karl, *Front Row at the Trump Show* (New York: Dutton, 2020), 60–62; Toobin, *True Crimes and Misdemeanors*, 22–24; Woodward, *Fear*, 29–37.

10. Toobin, *True Crimes and Misdemeanors*, 19–22.

11. Harris and Lusted, *Russian Hacking in American Elections*, 10, 35; Woodward, *Fear*, 28, 30, 36.

12. Mueller, *Report on the Investigation*, 2:15, 2:17–21.

13. James Comey, *A Higher Loyalty: Truth, Lies, and Leadership* (New York: Flatiron Books, 2018), 2, 161–74, 207–9; Michael Wolff, *Siege: Trump under Fire* (New York: Henry Holt, 2019), 169–70; Woodward, *Fear*, 163, 172–73, 327, 331, 350.

14. Mary L. Trump, *Too Much and Never Enough: How My Family Created the World's Most Dangerous Man* (New York: Simon & Schuster, 2020), 11–13. See also John W. Dean and Bob Altemeyer, *Authoritarian Nightmare: Trump and His Followers* (Brooklyn, NY, and London: Melville House, 2020), 57–77, 119–23.

15. Trump is quoted in Woodward, *Fear*, 173. See also Rucker and Leonnig, *A Very Stable Genius*, 255–56; Toobin, *True Crimes and Misdemeanors*, 19.
16. Rucker and Leonnig, *A Very Stable Genius*, 23–24.
17. Mueller, *Report on the Investigation*, 1:50–51. See also Massimo Calabresi, "Hacking the Voter," *Time* 188, no. 14 (October 10, 2016): 33.
18. Rucker and Leonnig, *A Very Stable Genius*, 21–23; Woodward, *Fear*, 62–65.
19. Isikoff and Corn, *Russian Roulette*, 177–78, 181–84, 195–96; Woodward, *Fear*, 28.
20. Mark Mazzetti, "Candidates Set to Get Intelligence Briefings as Each Questions the Other's Trustworthiness," *New York Times*, July 29, 2016, A14; David E. Sanger, "FBI Examining If Hackers Gained Access to Clinton Aides' Emails," *New York Times*, July 26, 2016, A14; Woodward, *Fear*, 29.
21. Michael J. Pomante II and Scot Schaufnagel, *Historical Dictionary of Barack Obama Administration* (Lanham, MD: Rowman & Littlefield, 2018), 326; Elizabeth Van Wie Davis, *Shadow Warfare: Cyberwar Policy in the United States, Russia, and China* (Lanham, MD: Rowman & Littlefield, 2021), 130.
22. Woodward, *Fear*, 62.
23. Mueller, *Report on the Investigation*, 1:7, 1:168–73; Mueller, *Report on the Investigation*, 2:22–23. See also Isikoff and Corn, *Russian Roulette*, 283–84; Rucker and Leonnig, *A Very Stable Genius*, 21–22; Toobin, *True Crimes and Misdemeanors*, 34–36; Woodward, *Fear*, 80.
24. Mueller, *Report on the Investigation*, 1:110–23, 1:185–88. See also Isikoff and Corn, *Russian Roulette*, 121–23, 200–201; Toobin, *True Crimes and Misdemeanors*, 109–13; Michael Wolff, *Fire and Fury: Inside the Trump White House* (New York: Henry Holt, 2018), 254–56; Woodward, *Fear*, 197. The question of whether President Trump attempted to cover up the content of the Trump Tower meeting was a major focus of the special counsel's subsequent investigation. See, for example, Mueller, *Report on the Investigation*, 2:100–107, 2:134–44.
25. Mueller, *Report on the Investigation*, 1:129–44. See also Rucker and Leonnig, *A Very Stable Genius*, 18, 101, 154; Woodward, *Fear*, 20–22, 26.
26. Mueller, *Report on the Investigation*, 1:194–95; Mueller, *Report on the Investigation*, 2:24–26, 2:31–38. See also Anonymous, *A Warning* (New York: Twelve, an Imprint of the Hachette Book Group, 2019), 126–27; Isikoff and Corn, *Russian Roulette*, 112–13, 279, 284, 286–87, 297; Rucker and Leonnig, *A Very Stable Genius*, 11–14; Woodward, *Fear*, 80–82.
27. Mueller, *Report on the Investigation*, 1:107–8, 1:197–98. See also Isikoff and Corn, *Russian Roulette*, 107, 115, 207–11; James B. Stewart, *Deep State: Trump, the FBI, and the Rule of Law* (New York: Penguin, 2019), 178–79.
28. Mueller, *Report on the Investigation*, 1:6, 1:95–103. See also Isikoff and Corn, *Russian Roulette*, 105–6, 158–61, 164–67.
29. Rucker and Leonnig, *A Very Stable Genius*, 201–2, 207–9; Woodward, *Rage*, 144.
30. Mueller, *Report on the Investigation*, 1:69–78, 1:195–96; Mueller, *Report on the Investigation*, 2:144–52. See also Woodward, *Fear*, 199. After he became president, Trump may have violated the Foreign Emoluments Clause of the United States Constitution, Article I, Section 9, Clause 8, which prohibits anyone holding a federal office

from receiving gifts or items of value from a foreign entity. The clause reads, "No Title of Nobility shall be granted by the United States: And no Person holding any Office of Profit or Trust under them, shall, without the Consent of the Congress, accept of any present, Emolument, Office, or Title, of any kind whatever, from any King, Prince, or foreign State." U.S. Const. art. I, § 9, cl. 8.

31. Isikoff and Corn, *Russian Roulette*, 139–53, 287–89; Toobin, *True Crimes and Misdemeanors*, 30–32; Wolff, *Fire and Fury*, 37–39, 92–93, 102, 151, 156; Woodward, *Fear*, 63–64, 327.

32. Karl, *Front Row at the Trump Show*, 135–36; Wolff, *Fire and Fury*, 9–18.

33. Woodward, *Fear*, 30, 36.

34. Mueller, *Report on the Investigation*, 1:5–6, 1:81–95, 1:192–94. See also Isikoff and Corn, *Russian Roulette*, 106–9; Toobin, *True Crimes and Misdemeanors*, 20, 36.

35. Josh Campbell, *Crossfire Hurricane: Inside Donald Trump's War on Justice and the FBI* (Chapel Hill, NC: Algonquin Books, 2019), 253–59; Stewart, *Deep State*, 91–93, 99–100, 109–10. The name came from a Rolling Stones song, "Jumpin' Jack Flash," which begins, "I was born in a crossfire hurricane." Stewart, *Deep State*, 91.

36. Pompeo is quoted in Richard Painter and Leanne Watt, "The Gospel of War Presidency," in *Rocket Man: Nuclear Madness and the Mind of Donald Trump*, ed. John Gartner and Steven Buser (Asheville, NC: Chiron, 2018), 91.

37. Jamieson argues this point, among others, in Kathleen Hall Jamieson, *Cyberwar: How Russian Hackers and Trolls Helped Elect a President; What We Don't, Can't, and Do Know* (New York and Oxford: Oxford University Press, 2020). Clapper is quoted on page 34 of the book.

38. Mueller, *Report on the Investigation*, 2:3. See also Toobin, *True Crimes and Misdemeanors*, 25–28.

39. Trump is quoted in Woodward, *Fear*, 164. See also pages 162–66. Comey recounts the episode, among other encounters with Trump, in his book, *A Higher Loyalty*, 253–56. See also Isikoff and Corn, *Russian Roulette*, 154–57, 257–59, 274–75, 298, 299; Mueller, *Report on the Investigation*, 2:12, 2:38–41; Stewart, *Deep State*, 158–61, 165–68, 172–74.

40. Bannon is quoted in Woodward, *Fear*, 162. See also Isikoff and Corn, *Russian Roulette*, 296–301; Wolff, *Fire and Fury*, 217.

41. Trump is quoted in Woodward, *Fear*, 162. Another source provides a slightly different quote: "Don't talk me out of it. I've made my decision." Rucker and Leonnig, *A Very Stable Genius*, 55.

42. Comey, *A Higher Loyalty*, 263–67; Mueller, *Report on the Investigation*, 1:8; Mueller, *Report on the Investigation*, 2:4, 2:62–71, 2:74–77.

43. The letter is quoted in Heather Kerrigan, ed., *Historic Documents of 2017: Current Events That Chronicle the Year; Introductory Essays That Build Understanding; Primary Sources That Aid Research* (Thousand Oaks, CA: Sage, 2018), 250–51. See also Anonymous, *A Warning*, 137–38; Comey, *A Higher Loyalty*, 263–67; Daniel W. Drezner, *The Toddler in Chief: What Donald Trump Teaches Us about the Modern Presidency* (Chicago and London: University of Chicago Press, 2020), 43; Isikoff and Corn, *Russian Roulette*, 299; Karl, *Front Row at the Trump Show*, 164–68; Rucker and Leonnig, *A Very Stable Genius*, 57–61; Stewart, *Deep State*, 1–10; Woodward, *Rage*, 44–52.

44. Trump is quoted in Kerrigan, *Historic Documents of 2017*, 248. See also Mueller, *Report on the Investigation*, 2:72. See also Woodward, *Fear*, 162–65; Woodward, *Rage*, 56–57.

45. Trump is quoted in Isikoff and Corn, *Russian Roulette*, 299. See also Mueller, *Report on the Investigation*, 2:71; Rucker and Leonnig, *A Very Stable Genius*, 63.

46. Trump is quoted in Stewart, *Deep State*, 213. See also Isikoff and Corn, *Russian Roulette*, 299; Mueller, *Report on the Investigation*, 2:73; Rucker and Leonnig, *A Very Stable Genius*, 63; Woodward, *Fear*, 164; Woodward, *Rage*, 56–57.

47. Mueller, *Report on the Investigation*, 1:8, 1:11–12; Mueller, *Report on the Investigation*, 2:4–5, 2:9–12, 2:78–80. See also Drezner, *The Toddler in Chief*, 50; Stewart, *Deep State*, 19–20; Woodward, *Fear*, 165, 168–69; Wolff, *Fire and Fury*, 220–21; Woodward, *Rage*, 60–61.

48. Trump is quoted in Woodward, *Fear*, 165. See also Woodward, *Fear*, 166; Anonymous, *A Warning*, 139; Comey, *A Higher Loyalty*, 271; Karl, *Front Row at the Trump Show*, 169–70; Mueller, *Report on the Investigation*, 1:8; Mueller, *Report on the Investigation*, 2:80–81; Rucker and Leonnig, *A Very Stable Genius*, 68–71; Stewart, *Deep State*, 232–33; Toobin, *True Crimes and Misdemeanors*, 89–91.

49. Mueller, *Report on the Investigation*, 1:12–13. See also Isikoff and Corn, *Russian Roulette*, 301–2; Toobin, *True Crimes and Misdemeanors*, 87, 132.

50. Isikoff and Corn, *Russian Roulette*, 302; Rucker and Leonnig, *A Very Stable Genius*, 160; Toobin, *True Crimes and Misdemeanors*, 131.

51. Mueller, *Report on the Investigation*, 2:122–28. See also Isikoff and Corn, *Russian Roulette*, 101–2, 201, 302; Rucker and Leonnig, *A Very Stable Genius*, 154.

52. Anonymous, *A Warning*, 137; Toobin, *True Crimes and Misdemeanors*, 233; Wolff, *Siege*, 168, 170–71.

53. Rucker and Leonnig, *A Very Stable Genius*, 77–78, 378–79; Toobin, *True Crimes and Misdemeanors*, 233–34, 262–70.

54. Stewart, *Deep State*, 310–24; Toobin, *True Crimes and Misdemeanors*, 299–305; Wolff, *Siege*, 313–14.

55. Toobin, *True Crimes and Misdemeanors*, 299–300.

56. Toobin, *True Crimes and Misdemeanors*, 300–302. The quotes are found on page 302.

57. Barr's letter is quoted in Woodward, *Rage*, 156. See also Woodward, *Rage*, 155–57; Stewart, *Deep State*, 310–11; Toobin, *True Crimes and Misdemeanors*, 305–7.

58. Trump is quoted in Woodward, *Rage*, 157.

59. Ironically, a reinvigorated Trump felt liberated enough to hold up military assistance to Ukraine in exchange for manufactured dirt on his possible opponent in the 2020 election, Joe Biden. This incident, not Trump's ties to Russia, became the basis for the 2019–2020 impeachment. See, for example, Bolton, *The Room Where It Happened*, 466–68; Toobin, *True Crimes and Misdemeanors*, 311–21.

60. Rucker and Leonnig, *A Very Stable Genius*, 378–79, 380–94; Toobin, *True Crimes and Misdemeanors*, 321–25.

61. Toobin, *True Crimes and Misdemeanors*, 332–25, 443; Wolff, *Siege*, 315.

62. Julian E. Barnes and Adam Goldman, "Trump's Spy Chief Pledged to Stay Out of Politics: He Hasn't," *New York Times*, October 10, 2020, A12.

63. Toobin, *True Crimes and Misdemeanors*, 80.

64. Dean and Altemeyer, *Authoritarian Nightmare*, 119–23; Rucker and Leonnig, *A Very Stable Genius*, 23–34, 52–53, 91–92, 104, 114–15, 116–18; Toobin, *True Crimes and Misdemeanors*, 443–49.

# Afterword

1. John W. Jenrette, quoted in United States House of Representatives, Committee on the Judiciary, *Report on the Committee on the Judiciary, House of Representatives, Ninety-Eighth Congress, First Session, Identifying Court Proceedings and Actions of Vital Interest to the Congress* (Washington, DC: US Government Printing Office, 1984), 774.

2. Publius [James Madison], "Federalist 51," in *The Federalist Papers*, by Alexander Hamilton, James Madison, and John Jay, ed. Clinton Rossiter (New York: New American Library, 1961; originally published in 1788), 322.

3. Publius, "Federalist 51," 322.

# Bibliography

Abramoff, Jack. *Capitol Punishment: The Hard Truth about Washington Corruption from America's Most Notorious Lobbyist.* New York: WND Books, 2011.

"Abramoff Says Top Republicans Were Allies." *New York Times*, March 9, 2006, A21.

Abramson, Jill, and David Rogers. "The Keating 535: Five Are on the Grill, but Other Lawmakers Help Big Donors, Too; Constituent Services Is Pivotal to the Way Congress Works, and Ethical Line Is Fuzzy; There but for the Grace of God." *Wall Street Journal*, January 10, 1991, A1.

Adams, Henry. *History of the United States of America: The First Administration of Thomas Jefferson, 1801–1805.* New York: Scribner, 1909.

Agnew, Spiro. *Go Quietly . . . or Else.* New York: William Morrow, 1980.

"The Agnew Tragedy . . . and Opportunity." *New York Times*, October 11, 1973, 44.

Alston, Lee J., Jeffrey A. Jenkins, and Tomas Nonnenmacher. "Who Should Govern Congress? Access to Power and the Salary Grab of 1873." *Journal of Economic History* 66, no. 3 (September 2006): 674–706.

Ambrose, Stephen E. *Nothing Like It in the World: The Men Who Built the Transcontinental Railroad, 1863–1869.* New York: Simon & Schuster, 2000.

Anonymous. *A Warning.* New York: Twelve, an Imprint of the Hachette Book Group, 2019.

"An Apology of Sorts, from a Senator." *New York Times*, November 24, 1991, E7.

Armstrong, Scott, Malcolm Byrne, Tom Blanton, and the National Security Archive. *Secret Military Assistance to Iran and the Contras: A Chronology of Events and Individuals.* Vol. 1. New York: Warner Books, 1987.

Arnold, Matthew. "A Vice President Who Extolled the Old Virtues." *New York Times*, October 11, 1973, 33.

Bambauer, Derek E. "Information Hacking." *Utah Law Review* 2020, no. 4 (2020): 987–1007.

Barnes, Julian E., and Adam Goldman. "Trump's Spy Chief Pledged to Stay Out of Politics: He Hasn't." *New York Times*, October 10, 2020, A12.

Berke, Richard L. "Senators Seek Exoneration as Hearings on Ethics End." *New York Times*, January 17, 1991, B6.

Bernstein, Carl, and Bob Woodward. *All the President's Men*. New York: Simon & Schuster, 2014. Originally published in 1974.

Biggs, Henry. "Suppuration of Powers: Abscam, Entrapment and the Politics of Expulsion." *Legislation and Policy Brief* 6, no. 2 (2014): 249–69.

Black, Conrad. *Richard M. Nixon: A Life in Full*. New York: Public Affairs, 2007.

Black, William K. *The Best Way to Rob a Bank Is to Own One: How Corporate Executives and Politicians Looted the S&L Industry*. Austin: University of Texas Press, 2014.

Bolton, John. *The Room Where It Happened: A White House Memoir*. New York: Simon & Schuster, 2020.

Boston, Rob. "Wheel of Misfortune: Religious Right Leaders Are Praying that the Jack Abramoff Casino-Lobbying Scandal Won't Make Them Big-Time Losers." *Church & State* 59, no. 3 (March 2006): 8–11.

Bowden, Mark. *Guests of the Ayatollah: The First Battle in America's War with Militant Islam*. New York: Atlantic Monthly Press, 2006.

Brands, H. W. *Reagan: The Life*. New York: Doubleday, 2015.

Byrne, Malcolm. *Iran-Contra: Reagan's Scandal and the Unchecked Abuse of Presidential Power*. Lawrence: University Press of Kansas, 2014.

Calabresi, Massimo. "Hacking the Voter." *Time* 188, no. 14 (October 10, 2016): 30–35.

Calabresi, Steven G., and Christopher S. Yoo. "The Unitary Executive during the Second Half-Century." *Harvard Journal of Law & Public Policy* 26, no. 3 (Summer 2003): 667–801.

Calavita, Kitty, Henry N. Pontell, and Robert Tillman. *Big Money Crime: Fraud and Politics in the Savings and Loan Crisis*. Berkeley: University of California Press, 1999.

Campbell, Josh. *Crossfire Hurricane: Inside Donald Trump's War on Justice and the FBI*. Chapel Hill, NC: Algonquin Books, 2019.

Carswell, Andrew T., Katrin B. Anacker, Kenneth B. Tremblay, and Sarah D. Kirby. *Introduction to Housing*. Athens: University of Georgia Press, 2018.

Cavendish, Richard. "Aaron Burr Arrested for Treason, February 19th, 1807." *History Today* 57, no. 2 (February 2007): 58–59.

Chafetz, Gary S. *The Perfect Villain: John McCain and the Demonization of Lobbyist Jack Abramoff*. Omaha, NE: Notable Trials Library, 2015. Originally published in 2008.

Chandler, Zachariah. *Zachariah Chandler: An Outline Sketch of His Life and Public Services*. Detroit, MI: *Detroit Post and Tribune*, 1880.

"Charles Sumner." *New York Times*, March 12, 1874, 4.

"Charles Sumner: Some Reminiscences of the Deceased Statesman." *New York Times*, March 18, 1873, 5.

Chernow, Ron. *Grant*. New York: Penguin, 2017.

Christianson, Stephen G. "Aaron Burr Trials: 1807." In *Great American Trials: From Salem Witchcraft to Rodney King*, edited by Edward W. Knappman, 78–82. Detroit, MI: Visible Ink Press, 2003.

Citizens for Responsibility and Ethics in Washington. "Caught in Jack's Web: The Abramoff Associates' File." *Multinational Monitor* 27, no. 3 (May/June 2006): 24–29.

Clark, John F., and Cookie Miller VanSice. *Capitol Steps and Missteps: The Wild, Improbable Ride of Congressman John Jenrette*. North Charleston, SC: CreateSpace, 2017.

Clines, Francis X. "Spiro T. Agnew, Point Man for Nixon Who Resigned Vice Presidency, Dies at 77." *New York Times*, September 19, 1996, B15.

Coffey, Justin P. *Spiro Agnew and the Rise of the Republican Right*. Santa Barbara, CA: ABC-CLIO, 2015.

Coffey, Walter. *The Reconstruction Years*. Bloomington, IN: AuthorHouse, 2014.

Cohen, Jared. *Accidental Presidents: Eight Men Who Changed America*. New York and London: Simon & Schuster, 2019.

Cohen, Richard M., and Jules Witcover. *A Heartbeat Away: The Investigation and Resignation of Spiro Agnew*. New York: Viking, 1974.

Comey, James. *A Higher Loyalty: Truth, Lies, and Leadership*. New York: Flatiron Books, 2018.

Coombs, J. J. *The Trial of Aaron Burr for High Treason*. New York: Notable Trials Library, 1992. Originally published in 1864.

*CQ Press Guide to Congress*. 7th ed. Vol. 1. Thousand Oaks, CA: Sage, 2013.

Dallek, Robert. *How Did We Get Here? From Theodore Roosevelt to Donald Trump*. New York: Harper, 2020.

Davis, Elizabeth Van Wie. *Shadow Warfare: Cyberwar Policy in the United States, Russia, and China*. Lanham, MD: Rowman & Littlefield, 2021.

Davis, William C. *Look Away! A History of the Confederate States of America*. New York: Free Press, 2002.

Dean, John W. *Blind Ambition*. New York: Simon & Schuster, 1976.

———. *The Nixon Defense: What He Knew and When He Knew It*. New York: Penguin, 2014.

Dean, John W., and Bob Altemeyer. *Authoritarian Nightmare: Trump and His Followers*. Brooklyn, NY, and London: Melville House, 2020.

"Death of Senator Sumner: Last Hours of the Great Statesman, Charles Sumner." *New York Times*, March 12, 1874, 1.

Dee, Jim. "Pushing Our Politicians." *Belfast Telegraph*, November 1, 2014, 7.

DeWitt, David Miller. *The Impeachment and Trial of Andrew Johnson, Seventeenth President of the United States: A History*. New York: Macmillan, 1903.

Donald, David Herbert. *Charles Sumner and the Coming of the Civil War*. New York: Knopf, 1960.

———. *Lincoln Reconsidered: Essays on the Civil War Era*. 3rd ed. New York: Vintage, 2001.

———. *The Politics of Reconstruction, 1863–1867*. Baton Rouge: Louisiana State University Press, 1965.

Dray, Philip. *Capitol Men: The Epic Story of Reconstruction through the Eyes of the First Black Congressmen*. Boston and New York: Houghton Mifflin, 2008.

Drezner, Daniel W. *The Toddler in Chief: What Donald Trump Teaches Us about the Modern Presidency*. Chicago and London: University of Chicago Press, 2020.

Elsmere, Jane. "The Notorious Yazoo Land Fraud Case." *Georgia Historical Quarterly* 51, no. 4 (December 1967): 425–42.

Emery, Fred. *Watergate: The Corruption of American Politics and the Fall of Richard Nixon*. New York: Touchstone, 1995.

Feuer, Alan. "For Ex-Lobbyist Abramoff, a Multimedia Effort at Redemption." *New York Times*, November 13, 2011, 16.

Fitzgerald, Michael W. *Splendid Failure: Postwar Reconstruction in the American South*. Chicago: Ivan R. Dee, 2008.

*Fletcher v. Peck*, 10 U.S. 87 (1810).

"Florida Jury Convicts 'Big Tony' in 2001 Businessman Murder." *Tampa Bay Times*, July 1, 2015, n.p.

Foner, Eric. *Reconstruction: America's Unfinished Revolution: 1863–1877*. Francis Parkman Prize Edition. New York: History Book Club, 2005. Originally published in 1988.

Franklin, John Hope. *Reconstruction after the Civil War*. Chicago and London: University of Chicago Press, 1961.

Friedman, Milton. "The Crime of 1873." *Journal of Political Economy* 98, no. 6 (December 1990): 1159–94.

Geelan, Agnes. *The Dakota Maverick: The Political Life of William Langer, Also Known as "Wild Bill" Langer*. Fargo, ND: Kaye's Printing, 1975.

Gershman, Bennett L. "Abscam, the Judiciary, and the Ethics of Entrapment." *Yale Law Journal* 91, no. 8 (July 1982): 1565–91.

Glasberg, Davita Silfen, and Dan L. Skidmore. "The Role of the State in the Criminogenesis of Corporate Crime: A Case Study of the Savings and Loan Crisis." *Social Science Quarterly* 79, no. 1 (March 1998): 110–28.

Goldenberg, Barry M. *The Unknown Architects of Civil Rights: Thaddeus Stevens, Ulysses S. Grant, and Charles Sumner*. Los Angeles, CA: Critical Minds Press, 2011.

Goodwin, Doris Kearns. *Team of Rivals: The Political Genius of Abraham Lincoln*. New York: Simon & Schuster, 2005.

Gould, Lewis L. *Grand Old Party: A History of the Republicans*. New York: Random House, 2003.

Green, Michael S. *Freedom, Union, and Power: Lincoln and His Party during the Civil War*. New York: Fordham University Press, 2004.

———. *Politics and America in Crisis: The Coming of the Civil War*. Santa Barbara, CA: Praeger, 2010.

Greene, Robert W. *The Sting Man: Inside Abscam*. New York: Penguin, 2013. Originally published in 1981.

Griswold, Erwin N. "*Sed Quis Custodiet Ipsos Custodies?* Some Reflections on ABSCAM." *Proceedings of the American Philosophical Society* 126, no. 6 (December 17, 1982): 452–60.

Hamilton, Alexander, James Madison, and John Jay. *The Federalist Papers*. Edited by Clinton Rossiter. New York: New American Library, 1961. Originally published in 1788.

Harris, Duchess, and Marcia Amidon Lusted. *Russian Hacking in American Elections*. Minneapolis, MN: Essential Library, 2018.

Harward, Brian M., ed. *The Presidency in Times of Crisis and Disaster: Primary Documents in Context*. Santa Barbara, CA: ABC-CLIO, 2019.

Haynes, George Henry. *Charles Sumner.* Philadelphia, PA: George W. Jacobs, 1909.

Heath, William Estill. "The Yazoo Land Fraud." *Georgia Historical Quarterly* 16, no. 4 (December 1932): 274–91.

Henry, Robert Selph. *The Story of Reconstruction.* New York: Konecky & Konecky, 1999.

Hicks, D. Bruce. "Presidential Foreign Policy Prerogative after the Iran-Contra Affair: A Review Essay." *Presidential Studies Quarterly* 26, no. 4 (Fall 1996): 962–77.

Hoag, Matthew, and Maya Salam. "Man Gets 4 Years in Prison for 'Pizzagate' Shooting." *New York Times,* June 23, 2017, A14.

Hobson, Charles F. *The Great Yazoo Lands Sale: The Case of* Fletcher v. Peck. Lawrence: University Press of Kansas, 2016.

———. "The Yazoo Lands Sale Case: *Fletcher v. Peck* (1810)." *Journal of Supreme Court History* 42, no. 3 (November 2017): 239–55.

Hoffer, Peter Charles. *The Treason Trials of Aaron Burr.* Lawrence: University Press of Kansas, 2008.

Hoffer, Williamjames Hull. *The Caning of Charles Sumner: Honor, Idealism, and the Origins of the Civil War.* Baltimore, MD: Johns Hopkins University Press, 2010.

Hopper, Jennifer Rose. "Reexamining the Nineteenth-Century Presidency and Partisan Press: The Case of President Grant and the Whiskey Ring Scandal." *Social Science History* 42, no. 1 (January 2018): 109–33.

"How Agnew Bartered His Office to Keep from Going to Prison." *New York Times,* October 23, 1973, 1, 36.

Isenberg, Nancy. *Fallen Founder: The Life of Aaron Burr.* New York: Viking, 2007.

Isikoff, Michael, and David Corn. *Russian Roulette: The Inside Story of Putin's War on America and the Election of Donald Trump.* New York: Twelve, an Imprint of the Hachette Book Group, 2018.

Jamieson, Kathleen Hall. *Cyberwar: How Russian Hackers and Trolls Helped Elect a President; What We Don't, Can't, and Do Know.* New York and Oxford: Oxford University Press, 2020.

Jenrette, Rita. *My Capitol Secrets.* New York: Bantam, 1981.

Jones, Ashby. "Guam-O-Rama! Prosecutors Drop Charges against Greenberg Traurig." *Wall Street Journal,* April 15, 2008, n.p.

Kane, Joseph Nathan. *Facts about the Presidents.* New York: Ace Books, 1976.

Karl, Jonathan. *Front Row at the Trump Show.* New York: Dutton, 2020.

"The Keating Five: A Final Chapter." *New York Times,* November 21, 1991, D21.

"The Keating One?" *New York Times,* February 22, 1991, A28.

Kennedy, Roger G. *Burr, Hamilton, and Jefferson: A Study in Character.* Oxford and New York: Oxford University Press, 1999.

Kerrigan, Heather, ed. *Historic Documents of 2017: Current Events That Chronicle the Year; Introductory Essays That Build Understanding; Primary Sources That Aid Research.* Thousand Oaks, CA: Sage, 2018.

Kinskey, Matthew W. "Note: American Hustle: Reflections on Abscam and the Entrapment Defense." *American Journal of Criminal Law* 41, no. 3 (Summer 2014): 233–61.

Klarman, Michael J. *From Jim Crow to Civil Rights: The Supreme Court and the Struggle for Equality.* New York and Oxford: Oxford University Press, 2004.

Klingelsmith, M. C. "James Wilson and the So-Called Yazoo Frauds." *University of Pennsylvania Law Review and American Law Register* 56, no. 1 Volume 47 Series (January 1908): 1–27.

Klotsche, J. Martin. "The Star Route Cases." *Mississippi Valley Historical Review* 22, no. 3 (December 1935): 407–18.

Kornbluh, Peter, and Malcolm Byrne, eds. *The Iran-Contra Scandal: A Declassified History*. New York: New Press, 1993.

Kyvig, David E. *The Age of Impeachment: American Constitutional Culture since 1960*. Lawrence: University Press of Kansas, 2008.

Lamplugh, George R. "James Gunn: Georgia Federalist, 1789–1801." *Georgia Historical Quarterly* 94, no. 3 (Fall 2010): 313–41.

———. *Politics on the Periphery: Factions and Politics in Georgia, 1783–1806*. Cranbury, NJ: Associated University Presses, 1986.

Landesman, Robert E. *Rx America*. Morrisville, NC: Lulu Press, 2011.

Larsen, Lawrence H. "William Langer: A Maverick in the Senate." *Wisconsin Magazine of History* 44, no. 3 (Spring 1961): 189–98.

Lee, Ronald, and Shawn J. Spano. "Technical Discourse in Defense of Public Virtue: Ronald Reagan's Explanation of the Iran/Contra Affair." *Political Communication* 13, no. 1 (January–March 1996): 115–29.

Leibovich, Mark. "Abramoff: From Prison to a Pizzeria Job." *New York Times*, June 24, 2010, A15.

Leuchtenburg, William E. *The American President: From Theodore Roosevelt to Bill Clinton*. Oxford and New York: Oxford University Press, 2015.

Levy, Peter B. "Spiro Agnew, the Forgotten Americans, and the Rise of the New Right." *The Historian* 75, no. 4 (Winter 2013): 707–39.

Lewis, Neil A. "Abramoff Gets 4 Years in Prison for Corruption; Reduced Sentence Reflects His Cooperation." *New York Times*, September 5, 2008, A16.

Litwack, Leon F. *Trouble in Mind: Black Southerners in the Age of Jim Crow*. New York: Knopf, 1998.

"Lobbyist Caught by His Own Law." *Toronto Star*, June 28, 2020, IN.2.

Long, Kim. *The Almanac of Political Corruption, Scandals & Dirty Politics*. New York: Delta Paperbacks, 2007.

Lowry, Martin E. *High Rollers: Inside the Savings and Loan Debacle*. Westport, CT: Praeger, 1991.

Lubetkin, M. John. *Jay Cooke's Gamble: The Northern Pacific Railroad, the Sioux, and the Panic of 1873*. Norman: University of Oklahoma Press, 2006.

Lyman, Rick. "Abramoff and 4 Others Sued by Tribe over Casino Closing." *New York Times*, July 13, 2006, A16.

Maranville, Steven J. "Teaching Case for the Iran-Contra Affair: 'Will No One Rid Me of This Troublesome Priest?'" *Academy of Management Proceedings & Membership Directory* (2001): 1–14.

Marion, Nancy E. *The Politics of Disgrace: The Role of Political Scandal in American Politics*. Durham, NC: Carolina Academic Press, 2010.

Martinez, J. Michael. *Carpetbaggers, Cavalry, and the Ku Klux Klan: Exposing the Invisible Empire during Reconstruction*. Lanham, MD: Rowman & Littlefield, 2007.

————. *The Safety of the Kingdom: Government Responses to Subversive Threats.* New York: Carrel Books, 2015.

Mazzetti, Mark. "Candidates Set to Get Intelligence Briefings as Each Questions the Other's Trustworthiness." *New York Times,* July 29, 2016, A14.

McCullough, David. *The Greater Journey: Americans in Paris.* New York: Simon & Schuster, 2011.

*McGrain v. Daugherty,* 273 U.S. 135 (1927).

McKitrick, Eric L. *Andrew Johnson and Reconstruction.* New York and Oxford: Oxford University Press, 1988. Originally published in 1960.

McPherson, James M. *Battle Cry of Freedom: The Civil War Era.* New York: Ballantine Books, 1988.

Meacham, Jon. *Thomas Jefferson: The Art of Power.* New York: Random House, 2012.

Meigs, William M. *The Life of Thomas Hart Benton.* Philadelphia and London: J. B. Lippincott, 1904.

Morgan, Ruth P. "Nixon, Watergate, and the Study of the Presidency." *Presidential Studies Quarterly* 26, no. 1 (Winter 1996): 217–38.

"Mr. Agnew's Farewell." *New York Times,* October 17, 1973, 46.

Mueller, Robert S., III, Special Counsel. *Report on the Investigation into Russian Interference in the 2016 Presidential Election.* Vols. 1 and 2. New York: Scribner, 2019.

Murphy, Larry F. *Trump and Congressional Republicans Must Go!* Bloomington, IN: AuthorHouse, 2019.

Murphy, Richard W. *The Nation Reunited: War's Aftermath.* Alexandria, VA: Time-Life Books, 1987.

Naughton, James M. "Agnew Says He Quit to Aid Nixon in Restoring Trust." *New York Times,* October 16, 1973, 89, 34.

————. "President Reportedly Took Initiative on Agnew Talks." *New York Times,* October 12, 1973, 89, 27.

Nevin, Mark. "Nixon Loyalists, Barry Goldwater, and Republican Support for President Nixon during Watergate." *Journal of Policy History* 29, no. 3 (July 2017): 403–30.

Newmyer, R. Kent. "Burr versus Jefferson versus Marshall." *Humanities* 34, no. 3 (May/June 2013): 24–27, 52–53.

"The Nixon Resignation." *New York Times,* August 9, 1974, 32.

Noogle, Burl. "The Origins of the Teapot Dome Investigation." *Mississippi Valley Historical Review* 44, no. 2 (September 1957): 237–66.

North, Oliver, with William Novak. *Under Fire: An American Story.* Grand Rapids, MI: Zondervan, 1991.

"Obama Wore a Tan Suit (and Spoke about World Crises)." *New York Times,* August 28, 2014, n.p.

Office of the Federal Register, National Archives & Records Administration. *Public Papers of the Presidents of the United States: Ronald Reagan, 1987.* Book 1, *January 1 to July 1, 1987.* Washington, DC: US Government Printing Office, 1989.

Ornstein, Norman J. "The House That Jack Built." *New York Times,* January 14, 2007, C25.

"Orville Babcock's Diaries Online." *America's Civil War* 30, no. 2 (May 2017): 10.

Painter, Richard, and Leanne Watt. "The Gospel of War Presidency." In *Rocket Man: Nuclear Madness and the Mind of Donald Trump*, edited by John Gartner and Steven Buser, 81–106. Asheville, NC: Chiron, 2018.

Payne, Phillip G. *Dead Last: The Public Memory of Warren G. Harding*. Athens: Ohio University Press, 2009.

Perlstein, Rick. *Nixonland: The Rise of a President and the Fracturing of America*. New York: Scribner, 2008.

———. *Reaganland: America's Right Turn, 1976–1980*. New York: Simon & Schuster, 2020.

Pierce, Edward Lillie, ed. *Memoir and Letters of Charles Sumner*. Vol. 3. London: Sampson Low, Marston, 1893.

Pomante, Michael J., II, and Scot Schaufnagel. *Historical Dictionary of the Barack Obama Administration*. Lanham, MD: Rowman & Littlefield, 2018.

Popper, Nathaniel. "Lobbyist Faces Prison for Flouting Changed Law." *New York Times*, June 26, 2020, A20.

Pusey, Allen. "The Yazoo Land Fraud Becomes Law." *ABA Journal* 104, no. 1 (January 2018): 72.

Reeves, Richard. *President Nixon: Alone in the White House*. New York: Touchstone, 2001.

———. *President Reagan: The Triumph of Imagination*. New York: Simon & Schuster, 2005.

Resolution Trust Corporation, Office of Investigations. *Massachusetts Office of Dispute Resolution Progress Report, September 30, 1990*. Washington, DC: US Government Printing Office, 1990.

"Rich Man's Lawyer." *Life*, August 8, 1938, 16.

Richardson, Heather Cox. "A Marshall Plan for the South? The Failure of Republican and Democratic Ideology during Reconstruction." *Civil War History* 51, no. 4 (December 2005): 378–87.

Ripley, Anthony. "Evidence Shows Gifts to Agnew; Cites Requests and Receipt of over $100,000—Denial Also Entered in Record." *New York Times*, October 11, 1973, 93, 38.

Rucker, Philip, and Carol Leonnig. *A Very Stable Genius: Donald J. Trump's Testing of America*. New York: Penguin, 2020.

Ryan, Bernard, Jr. "The Teapot Dome Trials: 1926–30." In *Great American Trials: From Salem Witchcraft to Rodney King*, edited by Edward W. Knappman, 332–37. Detroit, MI: Visible Ink Press, 2003.

Rylance, Daniel. "William Langer and the Themes of North Dakota History." *South Dakota History* 3, no. 1 (Winter 1972): 41–62.

Safire, William. "A Heartbeat Away." *New York Times*, September 19, 1996, A27.

Sanger, David E. "FBI Examining If Hackers Gained Access to Clinton Aides' Emails." *New York Times*, July 26, 2016, A14.

Scott, A. O. "Want a Deal on a Used Country?" *New York Times*, December 17, 2010, C20.

Secord, Richard, with Jay Wurts. *Honored and Betrayed: Irangate, Covert Affairs, and the Secret War in Laos*. Hoboken, NJ: Wiley, 1992.

Semple, Robert B., Jr. "On Tour with Spiro Agnew: Under the Rhetoric, a True Believer." *New York Times*, September 19, 1996, A26.

———. "Rise and Fall: Appraisal of Nixon Career." *New York Times*, August 9, 1974, 1, 11.

"Senator Riegle's Duty." *New York Times*, November 26, 1991, A20.

Shenon, Philip. "Abramoff Set to Start Prison Term." *New York Times*, November 16, 2006, A18.

———. "Demotion of a Prosecutor Is Investigated; Action Halted Inquiry on Influential Lobbyist, Officials Say." *New York Times*, September 27, 2005, A22.

———. "Lobbyist Stripped of Good Name, but Not of Good Vacation." *New York Times*, April 28, 2006, A20.

———. "Outside Inquiry Sought on Prosecutor's Demotion." *New York Times*, October 7, 2005, A24.

Simkins, Francis Butler, and Charles Pierce Roland. *A History of the South.* 4th ed. New York: Knopf, 1972.

Simpson, Brooks D. *The Reconstruction Presidents.* Lawrence: University Press of Kansas, 1998.

Sinha, Manisha. "The Caning of Charles Sumner: Slavery, Race, and Ideology in the Age of the Civil War." *Journal of the Early Republic* 23, no. 2 (Summer 2003): 233–62.

Smith, Jean Edward. *Grant.* New York: Simon & Schuster, 2001.

Spencer, Suzette. "Historical Memory, Romantic Narrative, and Sally Hemings." *African American Review* 40, no. 3 (Fall 2006): 507–31.

"Spiro T. Agnew, Ex-Vice President, Dies at 77." *New York Times*, September 18, 1996, A1, D21.

Stampp, Kenneth M. *America in 1857: A Nation on the Brink.* New York and Oxford: Oxford University Press, 1990.

Stevenson, Richard W. "California's Daring Thrift Unit." *New York Times*, May 25, 1987, 33, 34.

Stewart, David O. *American Emperor: Aaron Burr's Challenge to Jefferson's America.* New York: Simon & Schuster, 2011.

Stewart, James B. *Deep State: Trump, the FBI, and the Rule of Law.* New York: Penguin, 2019.

Stolberg, Sheryl. "Lobbyist Accepts Plea Deal and Becomes Star Witness in a Wider Corruption Case." *New York Times*, January 4, 2006, A1, A12.

Stone, Peter H. *Heist: Superlobbyist Jack Abramoff, His Republican Allies, and the Buying of Washington.* New York: Farrar, Straus & Giroux, 2006.

Stratton, David H. "Behind Teapot Dome: Some Personal Insights." *Business History Review* 31, no. 4 (Winter 1957): 385–402.

———. "New Mexican Machiavellian? The Story of Albert B. Fall." *Montana: The Magazine of Western History* 7, no. 4 (October 1957): 2–14.

———. "Two Western Senators and Teapot Dome: Thomas J. Walsh and Albert B. Fall." *Pacific Northwest Quarterly* 65, no. 2 (April 1974): 57–65.

Sumner, Charles. *Charles Sumner: His Complete Works.* Boston: Lee and Shepard, 1900. Originally published in 1872.

Tau, Byron. "Jack Abramoff Sought Meeting with Trump for Congo's Leader: Details Attempts to Arrange Florida Visit in a Disclosure with Justice Department." *Wall Street Journal*, June 23, 2017, n.p.

Thompson, Dennis F. "Mediated Corruption: The Case of the Keating Five." *American Political Science Review* 87, no. 2 (June 1993): 369–81.

Toner, Robin. "Wright Confirms Plan to Resign from the House." *New York Times*, June 27, 1989, A14.

Toobin, Jeffrey. *True Crimes and Misdemeanors: The Investigation of Donald Trump*. New York: Doubleday, 2020.

Tower, John G., Edmund Muskie, and Brent Scowcroft. *Report of the President's Special Review Board*. Washington, DC: US Government Printing Office, 1987.

"Transcript of Wright's Address to House of Representatives." *New York Times*, June 1, 1989, D22.

Trefousse, Hans L. *The Radical Republicans: Lincoln's Vanguard for Racial Justice*. New York: Knopf, 1969.

Trimbath, Susanne. *Lessons Not Learned: 10 Steps to Stable Financial Markets*. London: Spiramus, 2015.

Trump, Mary L. *Too Much and Never Enough: How My Family Created the World's Most Dangerous Man*. New York: Simon & Schuster, 2020.

Tweton, D. Jerome. "The Politics of Chaos: North Dakota in the 1930s." *Journal of the West* 41, no. 4 (Fall 2002): 30–35.

United States Congress. *Preliminary Inquiry into Allegations Regarding Senators Cranston, DeConcini, Glenn, McCain, and Riegle, and Lincoln Savings and Loan: Open Session Hearing before the Select Committee on Ethics, United States Senate, One Hundred First Congress, Second Session, Part 2 of 8, November 15, 1990, through January 16, 1991*. Washington, DC: US Government Printing Office, 1991.

United States Court of Appeals for the District of Columbia Circuit, Division for the Purpose of Appointing Independent Counsel, Division No. 86-6. *Final Report of the Independent Counsel for Iran/Contra Matters*. Vol. 1, *Investigations and Prosecutions*. Washington, DC: US Government Printing Office, 1993.

United States House of Representatives, Committee on the Judiciary. *Report on the Committee on the Judiciary, House of Representatives, Ninety-Eighth Congress, First Session, Identifying Court Proceedings and Actions of Vital Interest to the Congress*. Washington, DC: US Government Printing Office, 1984.

United States Senate, Select Committee to Investigate Covert Arms Transactions with Iran, the United States House of Representatives Select Committee to Investigate Covert Arms Transactions with Iran, and United States Senate Select Committee on Secret Military Assistance to Iran and the Nicaraguan Opposition. *Report of the Congressional Committees Investigating the Iran-Contra Affair, with Supplemental, Minority, and Additional Views*. Washington, DC: US Government Printing Office, 1987.

United States Senate Historical Office. *United States Senate Election, Expulsion and Censure Cases: 1793–1990*. Washington, DC: Government Printing Office, 1995.

*United States v. New York Times*, 403 U.S. 713 (1971).

*United States v. Nixon*, 418 U.S. 683 (1974).

Waldman, Michael. *Who Robbed America? A Citizen's Guide to the S&L Scandal*. New York: Random House, 1990.

Wallenfeldt, Jeff, ed. *The Growth of a Superpower: America from 1945 to Today*. New York: Rosen, 2012.

Waller, Robert A. "Business and the Initiation of the Teapot Dome Investigation." *Business History Review* (Autumn 1962): 334–53.

Walther, Eric H. *The Shattering of the Union: America in the 1850s*. Wilmington, DE: SR Books, 2004.

Weintraub, Bernard. "Iran Payment Found Diverted to Contras; Reagan Security Adviser and Aide Are Out." *New York Times*, November 26, 1986, A1.

Wells, Rob. *The Enforcers: How Little-Known Trade Reporters Exposed the Keating Five and Advanced Business Journalism*. Urbana, Chicago, and Springfield: University of Illinois Press, 2019.

Werner, M. R., and John Starr. *Teapot Dome*. New York: Viking, 1959.

Werth, Barry. *31 Days: Gerald Ford, the Nixon Pardon, and a Government in Crisis*. New York: Anchor Books, 2007.

Wilber, Del Quentin, and Carrie Johnson. "Abramoff Gets Reduced Sentence of Four Years in Prison." *Washington Post*, September 5, 2008, A3.

Wilentz, Sean. *The Age of Reagan: A History, 1974–2008*. New York: Harper, 2008.

Winter, Bill. "Probing the Probers: Does Abscam Go Too Far?" *American Bar Association Journal* 68, no. 1 (November 1982): 1347–50.

Witcover, Jules. *Party of the People: A History of the Democrats*. New York: Random House, 2003.

———. *White Knight: The Rise of Spiro Agnew*. New York: Random House, 1972.

Wolff, Michael. *Fire and Fury: Inside the Trump White House*. New York: Henry Holt, 2018.

———. *Siege: Trump under Fire*. New York: Henry Holt, 2019.

Wood, Gordon S. "The Real Treason of Aaron Burr." *Proceedings of the American Philosophical Society* 143, no. 2 (June 1999): 280–95.

Woodward, Bob. *Fear: Trump in the White House*. New York: Simon & Schuster, 2018.

———. *The Last of the President's Men*. New York: Simon & Schuster, 2015.

———. *Rage*. New York: Simon & Schuster, 2020.

Woodward, Bob, and Carl Bernstein. *The Final Days*. New York: Avon Books, 1976.

Woodward, Earl F. "Hon. Albert B. Fall of New Mexico: The Frontier's Fallen Star of Teapot Dome." *Montana: The Magazine of Western History* 23, no. 1 (Winter 1973): 14–23.

Wright, Ed. *History's Greatest Scandals: Shocking Stories of Powerful People*. San Diego, CA: Thunder Bay Press, 2013. Originally published in 2006.

"Wright Returns to Ft. Worth." *New York Times*, July 1, 1989, 1.

"Wyoming: U.S. Government Sells Teapot Dome Fields." *New York Times*, January 31, 2015, A15.

# Index

South Carolina Yazoo Company, 15, 16, 17
South Dakota, 80
Soviet Union, 138, 162
Spacey, Kevin, 158
Spain, 14, 15, 28, 29, 30, 31, 33
Spanish-American War, 59
stagflation, 124
State Department, 60, 136, 140, 165
St. Clair, James, 111
Steele, Christopher, 169–70
Stewart, Robert W., 60, 66, 69
Stillwell, Roger, 153
Stone, Roger, 169
Story, Joseph, 40
Strachan, Gordon C., 108
Stuart, H. A., 58
Sturgis, Frank, 105
Sugerman, Danny, 149
Sumner, Charles, *43*; attack on, 5, 39, 43–45, 182; background of, 40–41; and Civil War, 45–46; speeches by, 39, 40–42, 45
SunCruz Casinos, 155, 156, 157
Supreme Court, 34, 50; and Teapot Dome scandal, 68, 72–73; and Watergate scandal, 102, 110, 111; and Yazoo land fraud, 4, 13, 23–25
Symington, J. Fife, 91

Taft, William Howard, 57–58
Taylor, Elizabeth, 96
Teapot Dome, Wyoming, 57, 58, 60, 61, 63, 72
Teapot Dome scandal, 2, 3, 6, 57–73, 181, 183
Tehran, Iran, 138, 141, 142
Tennessee Yazoo Company, 15, 17, 19
Thompson, Frank, 119, 120
Thompson, Mark P., 67–68, 69, *70*, 70–71
Tower, John, 133, 144
Tower Commission, 133, 144–45, 146, 148
Trading Post Ring, 53

Treasury Department, 5, 48, 52
Trump, Donald J., *178*; campaign of, 162, 165–66, 171; and impeachment, 3, 173, 175, 176, 177, 217n59; and Jack Abramoff, 158; and January 6, 2021, insurrection, 3; and Russian election interference, 10, 161–79, 183; and Spiro Agnew, 96
Trump, Donald, Jr., 168
Trump, Mary L., 165
Trump Tower, 168, 169
Twenty-Fifth Amendment, 89
Twitter, 162, 177

Ukraine, 217n59
Union of Soviet Socialist Republics. *See* Soviet Union
Union Pacific Railroad, 5, 49
United States District Court for the District of Columbia, 168
United States Foreign Intelligence Surveillance (FISA) Court, 169, 170
United States Navy, 6, 57–58, 63, 71, 72
*United States v. Aaron Burr* (court case), 4, 34–37
*United States v. Richard M. Nixon* (court case), 102, 110, 111
Upper Mississippi Company, 19

Veselnitskaya, Natalia, 168
Vietnam War, 92, 102
Virginia Yazoo Company, 15, 17, 19

Wallace, George, 93, 94, 95
Wall, M. Danny, 129
Walton, George, 15
Walsh, Lawrence, 133–34, 145, 146, 149
Walsh, Thomas. *See* Washington, Thomas
Walsh, Thomas J., 62, 63, 64, 65
Ward, Samuel, Jr., 22
Warren, C. H., 22
Washington, George, 16, 27, 29, 41

# About the Author

**J. Michael Martinez** is the author of more than a dozen books, including *The Greatest Criminal Cases: Changing the Course of American Law* (2015) and *Political Assassinations and Attempts in U.S. History* (2017). He resides in Monroe, Georgia, and teaches political science and public administration courses at Kennesaw State University in Kennesaw, Georgia. Visit him online at www .jmichaelmartinez.com.